AMERICAN PATRIOTS

American Patriots

A Short History of Dissent

Ralph Young

NEW YORK UNIVERSITY PRESS

New York

NEW YORK UNIVERSITY PRESS
New York
www.nyupress.org

© 2024 by New York University
All rights reserved
This book is based on *Dissent: The History of an American Idea*, which was published in 2015.

Please contact the Library of Congress for Cataloging-in-Publication data.
ISBN: 9781479826520 (hardback)
ISBN: 9781479826506 (library ebook)
ISBN: 9781479826513 (consumer ebook)

This book is printed on acid-free paper, and its binding materials are chosen for strength and durability. We strive to use environmentally responsible suppliers and materials to the greatest extent possible in publishing our books.

Manufactured in the United States of America

10 9 8 7 6 5 4 3 2 1

Also available as an ebook

In memory of my sister Mildred Isaksen

And for my wife Pat

and our grandchildren

Finn, Amelia, Josephine, and Sullivan

for proving that love and magic are alive

and well in the twenty-first century

CONTENTS

American Patriots: A Short History of Dissent is a concise overview of the vital role that dissent has played in American history. The United States is a product of dissent, and dissenters have been the catalyst for change from the first days of the republic. Slavery was ended, women got the vote, unions won the right to organize, minority groups gained their civil rights because American patriots protested and forced the United States to live up to what it had put down on paper.

My previous book, *Dissent: The History of an American Idea* (a comprehensive narrative of 400 years of American history viewed through the lens of dissent), was published in 2015. In the past eight years dissent has exploded at an exponential pace and in unexpected directions. Black Lives Matter, #MeToo, March for Our Lives, and climate activism are all responses to the real problems of racism, sexism, gun violence, and the threat that climate change poses to all of us living on this planet. These are significant issues that need to be addressed. There has also been considerable faux dissent that has not targeted actual injustices, but is grounded in an upsurge of lies, conspiracy theories, and disinformation spread by web-based propagandists, disaffected reactionaries, and even the president of the United States.

The events of the Trump years, the election of 2020, and the January 6, 2021 storming of the Capitol captured the headlines and compelled me to reexamine the definition, scope, and future of American dissent. Dissenters have always challenged existing reality, the way things are, and pushed those in power to make changes. Historically, such dissent against the status quo was in essence apolitical in that it has come from both the right and the left. Actual grievances were actual grievances, not political spin. Dissent was not the property of a political party; it transcended politics, even though politics was often the means that was used to redress those grievances.

So, is it dissent if one is protesting against an injustice that does not exist? If one is motivated by lies, disinformation, and conspiracy theories? If one is fighting a delusion? No. Perhaps a psychologist would have a term for it, but some of what has transpired over the past few years is certainly not dissent. It can be more accurately categorized as synthetic dissent. What does this mean for the future of dissent in America?

My goal with *American Patriots* is to provide an accessible overview for both the historian and the general reader of how dissent has been a key factor in shaping the United States, especially after the advent of such technological advances in the twentieth century as the phonograph, radio, TV, the Internet, and social media that has made it possible and certainly easier for dissenters to disseminate their message and win converts to their cause. So this book concentrates on the last hundred-plus years of American history when the U.S. emerged as the preeminent and most culturally relevant and influential power on the world's stage. *Time/Life* publisher Henry Luce famously called the twentieth century "America's Century" and certainly, for better or worse, the U.S. has had an extraordinary impact on world affairs, even as it is in decline.

The first chapter of *American Patriots* highlights the historical context and some of the most influential individuals who advanced the philosophy of dissent from the colonial period to the Gilded Age. Then, starting with the twentieth century, I explore the details of the struggles for workers' rights, women's rights, civil rights, and indeed, all the minority rights movements as well as the antiwar movements that have dominated public discourse for more than a century. These chapters are updated and thoroughly revised versions of material that appeared in *Dissent: The History of an American Idea*. Chapter 11 and the Conclusion focus on the enormous number of protests that have taken place since 2015.

* * *

Despite the fact that the United States considers itself the most influential, inclusive democracy in the world, the early years of the twenty-first century have seen massive protests that challenge that perception. Millions of Americans took to the streets protesting the police killing of unarmed African Americans, sexism, unchecked environmental destruction, gun violence, white supremacy, critical race theory, censorship in public education, and the controversial decisions of a politicized Supreme Court. Meanwhile, other protests, based on disinformation, fabrications, and conspiracy theories, have deliberately added a fog of bewilderment to an already volatile atmosphere. And all of this, in the Internet age, has been amplified by an unregulated social media that publicizes causes (both real and imagined), recruits adherents, develops strategies, and organizes demonstrations, protests, insurrections.

It is imperative for concerned citizens to closely analyze how dissent is practiced in this country as we go forward into the rest of the twenty-first century. We have to continue to scrutinize dissent movements in order to understand if they express legitimate grievances or act as a smokescreen for those who are more interested in undermining democracy and thwarting its extension to the disempowered in order to bolster their own self-centered interests. The right to dissent is central to democracy, but we must protect that right and ensure it as the means of our salvation, and not our ruin.

Introduction

Dissent and America

If a man does not keep pace with his companions, perhaps it is because he hears a different drummer. Let him step to the music which he hears, however measured or far away.
—Henry David Thoreau, Walden Pond, 1854

All we say to America is to be true to what you said on paper. . . . Somewhere I read [*pause*] of the freedom of speech. Somewhere I read [*pause*] of the freedom of press. Somewhere I read [*pause*] that the greatness of America is the right to protest for right.
—Martin Luther King, Jr., Memphis, April 3, 1968

There are many ways to tell the story of the United States, many possible perspectives. This is the story of the U.S. told through a somewhat unlikely assortment of voices. It is the story of a countless number of Americans who prodded, provoked, and pushed the United States to actually be the nation it imagined itself to be. Throughout these stories runs the thread of dissent, protest, conflict, and change.

American Patriots is the personal reflection of a historian on the centrality of dissent in American history. Of course dissent is not specific to America, but Americans have instinctively understood, even if mostly unconsciously, the interrelatedness of dissent and what it means to be an American. Dissent created this nation, and it played, indeed still plays, a fundamental role in fomenting change and pushing the nation in sometimes-unexpected directions. My goal has been to write the story

1

of the United States from the standpoint of those who did not see eye-to-eye with the powers that be, from the standpoint of those who marched to the beat of a different drummer, constantly challenging the government to fulfill the promise laid down in the nation's founding documents. There has not been a time in American history when dissenters have not spoken out against the powerful and entrenched interests. At the same time, there were many occasions when dissenters against the dissenters fought ever harder to maintain, or restore, a social order that they feared would vanish if dissenters had their way. And so dissent did not propel the United States on a steady path toward the progress that dissenters sought. It was a rocky road.

* * *

Dissent is one of this nation's defining characteristics. Every decade since the earliest days of colonization, Americans have protested for just about every cause imaginable, and every time they did, defenders of the status quo denounced the protesters as unpatriotic and in more recent times as un-American. But protest is one of the consummate expressions of "Americanness." It *is* patriotic in the deepest sense.

Even before the United States was conceived, there was dissent. During the seventeenth century religious dissent played a significant role in the planting and development of the English colonies. In the eighteenth century political dissent led to the open rebellion that resulted in the birth of the United States. In the nineteenth century dissenters demanded the abolition of slavery, suffrage for women, fair treatment of Native Americans, and the banning of immigrants. And they protested against the War of 1812, the Mexican War, the Civil War (on both sides), and the Spanish-American War. In the twentieth century dissenters organized to prohibit alcohol but also demanded workers' rights, women's rights, African American rights, Chicano rights, reproductive rights, and LGBTQ+ rights. They also protested against every war (declared and undeclared) fought by the United States. In the twenty-first century dissenters have protested against abortion, NAFTA, globalization, the

Iraq War, the PATRIOT Act, the National Security Agency, bank bail-outs, and out-of-control deficits. Most recently dissenters have mobilized to protest against systemic racism, sexual harassment and assault, and Congress's inability (or refusal) to enact meaningful legislation to address climate change and gun violence. And then there are those who, despite their real grievances, having fallen for the widespread disinformation circulating on untrustworthy Internet sites, raise their voices in protest on the basis of conspiracy theories, lies, and a distorted view of American history. Clearly, dissent has many faces.

On the broadest level, dissent is going against the grain. It is speaking out and protesting against what *is* (whatever that *is* is), most often by a minority group unhappy with majority opinion and rule. However, history has shown that dissent is far more complex, that it comes from all political perspectives and in a variety of categories: mostly religious, political, economic, and cultural/social. Religious dissent is the insistence that everyone be allowed to worship according to the dictates of conscience and not according to the rules of an established religion. Although most religious dissent occurred during the colonial period, when individuals insisted on religious liberty, and during the early national period, when the new nation endorsed the principle of separation of church and state, the demand for religious autonomy persists to this day. Religious dissent was expressed when new sects such as the Shakers, the Mormons, or the Branch Davidians were formed, and it is still being expressed on a different level in the debates over school prayer, intelligent design versus evolution, abortion, capital punishment, and the right to die.

Political dissent is a critique of governance. As the United States grew from a fledgling nation into a world power, political dissenters expressed dissatisfaction about the way those who were in charge governed, and usually (but not always) they provided a plan or recipe for redressing what they perceived as wrong. Most often they used the nation's founding documents as the authority to legitimize their protest. Antebellum abolitionists demanded the end of slavery, declaring that holding persons in bondage was contrary to the principle that "all men are created equal." In recent years hundreds of thousands of Americans protested the decision to invade Iraq, proclaiming that doing so transforms the United States into an aggressive imperial power and that by embracing imperialism the United States is renouncing its democratic birthright.

When the economy crashes, economic dissent comes to the fore. People take to the streets protesting economic injustice and inequality. And as distress and suffering expands from the lower classes to the middle class, so too does protest. One thinks of the Richmond bread riots during the Civil War, the violent labor disputes of the nineteenth century, the Bonus Army's encampment at the Capitol in 1932, the militant labor activism during Franklin Delano Roosevelt's liberal presidency, the tax revolts of the 1970s, the occupation of Zuccotti Park in 2011.

Cultural and social dissent is a rejection of the predominant attitudes, beliefs, and behavior of mainstream society. Utopian groups in the nineteenth century defied the conventional values of their time and established communities where all men and women would be treated equally. "Beatniks" and "hippies" in the mid-twentieth century rejected the conventional middle-class morality of their time, urged their fellow Americans to "do their own thing," and influenced millions to reevaluate their views of race, gender, and sexuality.

But this is only part of the story. There is significant and frequent overlapping of religious, political, and cultural/social dissent. For example, many dissenters, such as temperance activists in the early twentieth century and the Christian right today, can be labeled as political, religious, *and* social dissenters. The 1960s counterculture's challenge to American values was also intricately tied up in the political protests against the Vietnam War and the struggle for racial equality. Furthermore, there are economic and psychological factors that often play roles in dissent movements.

There are some decades that are relatively quiet dissentwise and others when significant problems intensify so rapidly that tens of millions of people get involved in the discussion to find solutions. During these periods we see a sharp rise in dissent, and that dissent can take many forms as different groups propose different solutions. Some dissenters are *reformers* who wish to fix the problems through a process of reform. Some are *reactionaries* who seek to address the problems by returning to the policies that existed before the problems arose. Some are *radicals* or even *revolutionaries* who propose to solve the problems by smashing the system and starting over. The debate over slavery and the events leading to the Civil War, the Progressive era, and the 1960s, and the present day are periods when dissent, in all its diverse forms, exploded.

There are several levels or stages of dissent. At the beginning individuals might simply disagree with a policy or a law or an issue. Perhaps they are willing to tolerate a wrong or an injustice for a while, but when it becomes less tolerable, the next step is to become active. Individuals might write a letter or an article, give a speech, lead a protest march, or conduct a demonstration. Dissent and protest carried to a higher level entails resistance, civil disobedience, breaking laws, or even participating in a riot or insurrection.

The methods and forms of dissent are wide-ranging. Many protesters express dissent through petitions and protest marches. Some use music or art or theater or comedy to articulate their message. Some engage in acts of civil disobedience, willfully breaking laws to put pressure on the system to force those who have political and economic power to acknowledge and address the issues. They are often marginalized individuals and groups that lack power but have a legitimate grievance against the way things are. Most times these types of dissenters have criticized the United States from the left. They have sought more equality, more moral rectitude, more freedom. They have demanded that America live up to what it had committed itself to on paper at the Constitutional Convention. Many of these dissenters have viewed the Constitution and the Declaration of Independence as binding contracts between the people and the government and protested when they believed the government was not fulfilling its part of the contract.

Dissenters often have a keen sense of history and build on the experiences and methods of earlier dissenters. It is not unusual to see dissenters quote those who have gone before as well as draw on the successful tactics and strategies of earlier dissent movements. The Civil Rights Movement of the 1950s and 1960s employed many of the tactics of the labor movement of the 1930s, while antiwar activists adopted the tactics of the Civil Rights Movement in their protests against the war in Vietnam and later the Iraq War. Dissenters with a vision for the future look to the past for inspiration.

But there are some dissenters who have a sketchy understanding of American history who want to return to an imagined past that never existed. For example, those who protest against immigration in order to keep America white, not realizing that the country has always been a nation of diversity, peopled by immigrants of all ethnic, racial, and religious backgrounds. The Ku Klux Klan in the 1920s opposing anyone who was not "One Hundred Percent American" and the Unite the Right protesters in Charlottesville, Virginia in 2017 chanting "You will not replace us!" are examples of this.

Individuals and groups that protest against the protesters are also expressing dissent. Reactionaries have frequently resisted change and fought to maintain the special privileges and supremacy of their class or race or gender. Some have wanted to maintain the status quo and prevent change, while others have sought to turn back the clock to a "simpler," more "trouble-free" time. When abolitionists denounced slavery, antiabolitionists argued just as passionately to preserve the institution. When women demanded equality, millions of Americans reacted with hostility and formed antisuffrage associations.

Although most dissent springs from those who lack political power, there are instances when a dissent movement is part of the power structure—the temperance movement and the Know-Nothings of the nineteenth century; the anti-tax ideologues of the twentieth and twenty-first centuries. There are also notable individuals who fought entrenched interests from a position of political power—Senators Robert M. La

Follette and Margaret Chase Smith, for example, spoke out against what they believed was a usurpation or misuse of power on the part of the federal government.

Over the years dissenters achieved varying levels of success. Some got in trouble. Some were arrested. Many were beaten. Some were killed. But they kept hammering away at the powers that be until those powers began to listen. As a result, public opinion was swayed, laws were enacted or repealed, slavery was abolished, unions were organized, women got the right to vote, the Jim Crow laws were invalidated. In fact, many dissenters who were maligned, vilified, and even demonized as unpatriotic and anti-American by their contemporaries are now considered heroes. Some dissenters never achieved the change they were seeking, but though their goals were dismissed, they raised new questions and had an influence on the political discussion.

For the most part dissenters have embraced lofty ideals and have a moral purpose. And most of them believe they are acting to ensure that the United States lives up to its promise to secure Americans' natural rights. But there are dissenters whose goals are not well-intended or virtuous and who use questionable means to attain their goals—they are not in it to grant equal rights to a downtrodden minority but to restrict rights or to promote their own narrow interests at the expense of others.

During times of heightened passions—the Antebellum period, the Progressive era, the Great Depression, the Vietnam War—dissenters have protested from liberal, conservative, *and* radical standpoints. In the debates about the war in Vietnam, for example, there were those who believed that America was acting as an imperial power and that the capitalist system should be toppled. There were those who opposed the war primarily on ethical grounds because the United States was acting immorally. And there were those who opposed the war simply because the United States was losing it and thus argued that if the government was not going to go all-out in its effort to destroy communism in Vietnam, then there was no point in being there. In the end, for completely different reasons, radicals, doves, and hawks all came to protest the war in Vietnam.

Obviously not all dissenters are created equal. Nor are the consequences of their efforts necessarily positive or socially useful. There is a difference between dissenters whose goal is to create a more just society by expanding the rights of the disempowered, and those who are self-aggrandizing troublemakers interested only in disrupting society or denying rights to others. Historian Eric Foner, in *The Story of American Freedom*, points out that "freedom" is a "contested concept."[1] So too is "dissent."

1

Dissent and the Shaping of a Nation

As I stood considering the walls of solid stone, two or three feet thick, the door of wood and iron, a foot thick, and the iron grating which strained the light, I could not help being struck with the foolishness of that institution which treated me as if I were mere flesh and blood and bones, to be locked up. . . . I saw that, if there was a wall of stone between me and my townsmen, there was a still more difficult one to climb or break through before they could get to be as free as I was. I did not for a moment feel confined, and the walls seemed a great waste of stone and mortar. . . . I saw that the State was half-witted . . . and that it did not know its friends from its foes, and I lost all my remaining respect for it, and pitied it.
—Henry David Thoreau, "Resistance to Civil Government," 1847

After more than a century of conflict with and exploitation of the First Nations of the New World, Spain had successfully established scores of missions and permanent colonies from Florida to California, while French explorers and missionaries were setting up outposts along the St. Lawrence River. Into this volatile mix of cultures, thousands of English colonists began in the early seventeenth century to establish permanent settlements along the east coast of North America. Most were seeking economic opportunity, but many, especially those settling in New England, were religious dissenters. Almost as soon as these religious dissenters arrived in New England, dissidents rose up to challenge them.

Although the Puritans were religious dissenters, they did not come to the New World for the noble cause of "religious freedom." What the

Puritans of Massachusetts Bay Colony were seeking was to practice what *they* regarded as the one true faith, not freedom for all religions. They did not favor religious toleration, as anyone entering the colony wishing to worship according to a "false" belief system quickly discovered. Those who did not see eye to eye with the colony's authorities found themselves ostracized and banished. It was Roger Williams, arriving in Massachusetts Bay in 1631, who pushed for religious freedom. Williams, one of the first dissenters in the English colonies, took exception to several tenets of the Puritan oligarchy. He called for the complete separation of church and state and for religious toleration. Williams argued that to compel people to conform to a specific, authorized religious belief was counterproductive because it simply convinced them that a belief that had to be imposed must be false. If governing officials seek to enforce one religion in a society, then they obviously have to punish those who refuse to accept the authorized religion. "A *civill sword*," meaning the punishment that civil authorities must use to enforce conformity of religion, Williams argued with impeccable logic, "is so far from bringing or helping forward an *opposite* in *Religion* to *repentance* that *Magistrates* sin grievously against the *worke* of God and *blood* of Soules by such proceedings. . . . *Violence* and a *sword* of *steele* begets such an *impression* in the sufferers that certainly they conclude . . . that *Religion* cannot be true which needs such *instruments* of *violence* to uphold it so." Regarding separation of church and state, Williams maintained that it is imperative to keep a well-defined distinction between the two to protect freedom of religion. If there were too much blurring of the lines between church and state, both institutions would be endangered, but worst of all it would mean religion would have to be sanctioned by the state. And as far as Williams was concerned, he did not want the colony to have, like the nations of Europe, an established religion. Religious belief should not be dependent on the whim of a monarch. "Magistrates," he insisted, "have no power of setting up the Forme of Church Government, electing church officers, [or] punishing with church censures." Likewise, "the Churches as Churches, have no power . . . of erecting or altering forms of Civill Government, electing of Civill officers, inflicting Civill punishments . . ."[1]

In the end, Williams's dissension led to his banishment. He established a new colony—Providence—that became a haven for those who held unpopular views. Over the next century and a half, as the colonial settlements grew increasingly diverse and multicultural, Williams's advocacy of toleration and the separation of church and state became a fundamental part of eighteenth-century political discourse. By the time of the Constitutional Convention, these principles were regarded as natural rights and were included in the Bill of Rights.

* * *

Another significant act of dissent during the colonial period that had long-lasting repercussions was newspaper publisher John Peter Zenger's protest against political corruption in New York. In November 1733, Zenger's paper, the *New York Weekly Journal*, began running a series of articles scathingly denouncing Governor William Cosby for his corrupt administration of the colony. It was public knowledge that Cosby was bribing legislators and judges, embezzling funds from the colony's treasury, and falsifying election results. The *Journal* argued that freedom of the press was necessary because the press was the only institution that could serve as a watchdog against political corruption and the misuse of power. Zenger maintained that if the magistrates and rulers were not held accountable to the law and for their actions, then Britain and its colonies had not progressed at all from the absolutism of the Tudors. "If men in power were always men of integrity," he wrote, "we might venture to trust them with the direction of the press, and there would be no occasion to plead against the restraint of it."[2] But men are corruptible, and therefore a free press is essential to keep them in check. If freedom of the press and freedom of speech were restricted, liberty itself would be snuffed out.

Governor Cosby ordered the publisher's arrest on charges of seditious libel and had the newspaper shut down. According to eighteenth-century

British law, it was only necessary to prove that Zenger had published the articles in order to obtain a conviction. The question of whether Zenger's allegations against Cosby's administration were true or false was irrelevant, because "truth" was not deemed a valid defense against libel. Zenger's lawyer, Andrew Hamilton, however, argued that truth *was* a defense: "If Libel is understood in the unlimited Sense urged by [the attorney general], there is scarce a Writing I know that may not be called a Libel or scarce a Person safe from being called to Account as a Libeller: For *Moses*, meek as he was, Libelled *Cain*—and who is it that has not libeled the Devil?"[3] When the court acquitted Zenger, it was a momentous victory for the principle of freedom of press. The acquittal also was pivotal in establishing the precedent that no political official was exempt from public censure.

Of course, the most momentous dissent movement in the colonies during the eighteenth century was the protest against Parliament's taxation policies that led to the American Revolution and the founding of the United States. Not only did the revolution lead to independence, the ideological rhetoric of the struggle had an inspiring effect on two groups that were not even considered participants: African Americans and women. The notions of freedom and equality that had been unloosed by the revolutionary fervor motivated enslaved African Americans to petition for their emancipation, and, in a few states, slavery was indeed abolished. And many women insisted that they too should enjoy political equality in the new republic. For example, in 1776 Abigail Adams counseled her husband, John Adams, not to leave women out of the new system of government that the delegates to the Continental Congress in Philadelphia were establishing. "By the way," she wrote,

> in the new Code of Laws which I suppose it will be necessary for you to make, I desire you would Remember the Ladies, and be more generous and favorable to them than your ancestors. Do not put such unlimited power into the hands of the Husbands. Remember, all Men would be tyrants if they could. If particular care and attention is not paid to the

Ladies we are determined to foment a Rebellion, and will not hold ourselves bound by any Laws in which we have no voice, or Representation.[4]

Abigail Adams's entreaty went unheeded. It took more than 140 years of
continued protest and activism on the part of women before they gained
the right to vote or hold political office in the United States. Clearly,
though, her views reveal that the concepts of liberty and equality were
contagious and were being taken seriously even by those for whom they
were not intended.

It is important to keep in mind that three of the core principles of the
American canon—Roger Williams' religious liberty and separation of
church and state, and John Peter Zenger's freedom of the press—were
all products of the colonial era. They helped give birth to the United
States. By the time of the Constitutional Convention these principles
were regarded as so essential for a democratic republic that they were
enshrined in the First Amendment of the Bill of Rights. Additionally, the
experience of the revolution underscored the importance of the right to
dissent and so the framers of the Constitution also placed that right in
the First Amendment. And Americans, ever since, have taken that right
seriously.

* * *

Once the United States was established, dissent became part of the natural order of things. Farmers in western Pennsylvania rose up against
excise taxes on whiskey; the Shawnee leader Tecumseh forged a short-
lived Indigenous confederacy to fight American expansion into the
Ohio River valley; Federalists protested vigorously against the War of
1812; the Cherokee resisted their forced removal west of the Mississippi;
the "Lowell Mill Girls" and other factory workers attempted to organize
for better wages and working conditions. And by the 1830s, hundreds
of thousands of Americans, troubled by the discrepancy between the
nation's democratic/republican principles and the existence of slavery,
joined the abolitionist crusade. In 1831 William Lloyd Garrison began

publication of a weekly antislavery newspaper, the *Liberator*, in which he unconditionally condemned slavery and demanded immediate emancipation and the granting of full citizenship to all enslaved people. Frederick Douglass, after he escaped from bondage, traveled from town to town speaking out against slavery. Harriet Tubman played a central role escorting runaway slaves to freedom on the Underground Railroad. Slaves themselves acted to destroy the "peculiar institution" through sabotage, shirking, disruption, and rebellion.

As the antislavery movement grew, a philosophical movement emerged in Concord, Massachusetts, that had a major impact on fortifying abolitionism and the legitimacy of dissent. Ralph Waldo Emerson, Henry David Thoreau, and Margaret Fuller, influenced by Platonism, the Romantic movement, and German philosopher Immanuel Kant, developed a new way of looking at the individual's place in the world—transcendentalism. And the writings of Emerson, Thoreau, and Fuller have inspired dissenters ever since. According to Emerson, there are two forms of knowledge: understanding and reason. Understanding is externally imposed knowledge—the knowledge we get through formal education and books—whereas reason is the innate, intuitive capacity that each individual has for recognizing truth and beauty. To Emerson, reason is the highest human faculty. It is an intuitive awareness of where our wisdom lies. He argues that in order to live a meaningful life each individual must strive to transcend the narrow confines of externally imposed knowledge and cultivate this intuitive wisdom. Learning a discipline, such as biology or mathematics, is important, but such knowledge is limited. Deeper insight, higher wisdom comes through an intimate and direct relationship with the universe. No one needs to read a book to know what truth is. No one needs to be told what beauty is. We recognize truth and beauty the moment we see it, because, in essence, at that moment we are connecting to the creative force of the universe. Emerson calls this creative force the "oversoul," and our individual souls are all part of the oversoul. We are all part of the godhead. We all have a spark of divinity within us. When we see this, we achieve self-realization; we recognize our interconnectedness with nature, with the universe, with all living creatures. In this way we see that there is no difference between humans, no difference on the soul level between races or the genders. Therefore self-realization leads us to a deeper engagement with the world.

"To believe your own thought," Emerson writes in his essay "Self-Reliance," "to believe that what is true for you in your private heart is true for all men,—that is genius." In order to live an authentic life each individual must resist the impulse to conform. Each individual must become self-reliant, must think for themselves and not be concerned about what everyone else thinks or expects. Have the courage to think broadly; have the courage to expand the mind, even when you have to change your mind. "Trust thyself," Emerson counsels: "every heart vibrates to that iron string. Accept the place the divine Providence has found for you; the society of your contemporaries, the connexion of events." But even though you are part of a society, a time, and a place, and even though it is your duty to respond to the events and issues surrounding you, you must be cognizant of the pressures that society constantly exerts to destroy individuality. "Society everywhere is in conspiracy against the manhood of every one of its members. Society is a joint-stock company, in which the members agree, for the better securing of his bread to each shareholder, to surrender the liberty and culture of the eater. The virtue in most request is conformity. Self-reliance is its aversion. It loves not realities and creators, but names and customs."[5]

The self-reliant individual should strive always for honesty and integrity and not be stubbornly wedded to a particular viewpoint. A person should be ready to abandon a dearly held belief and acknowledge the truth of a contrary position even if it means appearing inconsistent.

A foolish consistency is the hobgoblin of little minds, adored by little statesmen and philosophers and divines. With consistency a great soul has simply nothing to do. He may as well concern himself with his shadow on the wall. . . . Speak what you think to-day in words as hard as cannon-balls, and to-morrow speak what to-morrow thinks in hard words again, though it contradict every thing you said to-day. Ah, then, exclaim the aged ladies, you shall be sure to be misunderstood. . . . Is it so bad then to be misunderstood? Pythagoras was misunderstood, and Socrates, and Jesus, and Luther, and Copernicus, and Galileo, and New-ton, and every pure and wise spirit that ever took flesh. To be great is to be misunderstood.[6]

Emerson's friend Henry David Thoreau went even further in his ad-vocacy of nonconformity. The individual, according to Thoreau, *must* resist the pressures to conform, *must* resist the pressures to do what soci-ety expects and instead follow his or her own instincts. Most people fail to see this and as a result are living "lives of quiet desperation." Thoreau conducted his two-year experiment at Walden Pond so that, as he put it, when it came time for him to die, he would know that he had lived. Re-jecting the party politics and materialism of a nation whose prosperity was based on slavery, he wanted to simplify his life and experience the basics. He chided those who were so busy chasing after material goods that they failed to see what is essential. We need to simplify our lives and recognize that most of what we own we do not need. We spend our whole lives striving to accumulate things without ever noticing what is meaningful. If we learned to see what really *is*, if we examined our hearts and followed in the direction of our own dreams, we would no longer be content with the false values of society.

I learned this, at least, by my experiment: that if one advances confi-dently in the direction of his dreams, and endeavors to live the life which he has imagined, he will meet with a success unexpected in common hours. . . .

Why should we be in such desperate haste to succeed and in such desperate enterprises? If a man does not keep pace with his companions, perhaps it is because he hears a different drummer. Let him step to the music which he hears, however measured or far away.[7]

Like Emerson and Thoreau, Margaret Fuller believed that inwardly, on the soul level, all human beings are equal. There is no fundamental difference between races; there is no fundamental difference between man and woman. "Male and female represent the two sides of the great radical dualism. But, in fact, they are perpetually passing into one another. Fluid hardens to solid, solid rushes to fluid. There is no wholly masculine man, no purely feminine woman." Each man, according to Fuller, possesses the feminine principle just as each woman the masculine. It is through the union of the feminine and the masculine that human beings find fulfillment. Because the sexes *are* equal, women should no longer submit to being shunted aside as somehow less than a man; they should have faith in their own innate abilities and intellect and strive for self-realization. "It is therefore that I would have Woman lay aside all thought, such as she habitually cherishes, of being taught and led by men. I would have her, like the Indian girl, dedicate herself to the Sun, the Sun of Truth, and go nowhere if his beams did not make clear the path. I would have her free from compromise, from complaisance, from helplessness, because I would have her good enough and strong enough to love one and all beings, from the fulness, not the poverty of being."[8]

If the central premise of transcendentalism is true—that the human soul is part of the oversoul, that all humans are part of the godhead—than the only reasonable conclusion that can be drawn is that all people are truly equal. So, to the transcendentalist, slavery is not only wrong, not only immoral; it is also illogical. After all, how can one individual own another when they are both divine? How can God own God? In this way transcendentalism helped shape the philosophical foundations and increase the credibility of abolitionism and feminism. Not only in the nineteenth century but today, their writings still have relevance and are part of the core texts—the Bible as it were—for dissenters.

When the United States invaded Mexico in 1846, abolitionists were almost unanimously opposed to the war because it was clear that the war was being waged in order to seize more territory into which cotton, and therefore slavery, could be extended. When war was declared,

FIGURE 1.1. Henry David Thoreau, 1856. "Unjust laws exist: shall we be content to obey them, or shall we endeavor to amend them, and obey them until we have succeeded, or shall we transgress them at once?" Daguerreotype by Benjamin D. Maxham.
Credit: Public domain; courtesy of National Portrait Gallery, Smithsonian Institution.

Thoreau in a small gesture of protest famously refused to pay his poll tax because he could not in good conscience support a government that was initiating an unjust war to spread the unjust institution of slavery. In July 1846 he was arrested and jailed. The incident inspired him to write "Resistance to Civil Government."

In the essay Thoreau wrote that it is the individual's duty to oppose injustice. He argued that laws supporting the institution of slavery are unjust; therefore, anyone who values justice must do all they can to overturn such laws. If this means breaking the law, then break the law. What is necessary is to put enough pressure on the government so that lawmakers would have no recourse but to change the law. When the United States is pursuing a war against a neighbor solely to acquire land to expand slavery and increase the nation's wealth, it compels the individual to examine his or her conscience. "How does it become a man to behave toward this American government to-day? I answer, that he cannot without disgrace be associated with it. I cannot for an instant recognize that political organization as *my* government which is the *slave's* government also. . . ."[9]

To those who argue that we must obey the law, Thoreau drew a distinction between just and unjust laws. Unjust laws attempt to withdraw natural rights from individuals; just laws protect those natural rights. "Unjust laws exist: shall we be content to obey them, or shall we endeavor to amend them, and obey them until we have succeeded, or shall we transgress them at once?" But we must pick our fights carefully. "If the injustice is part of the necessary friction of the machine of government, let it go, let it go"; we should not engage in civil disobedience frivolously. But if the injustice "is of such a nature that it requires you to be the agent of injustice to another, then I say, break the law. Let your life be a counter-friction to stop the machine. What I have to do is to see, at any rate, that I do not lend myself to the wrong which I condemn."[10]

But civil disobedience means that when you break an unjust law, when you refuse to be part of the injustice, you must be ready to pay the consequences. And by paying the consequences, by going to prison, you force the system to change. "Under a government which imprisons unjustly, the true place for a just man is also a prison. . . . If any think that their influence would be lost there, and their voices no longer afflict the ear of the State, that they would not be as an enemy within its walls, they do not know by how much truth is stronger than error, nor how much more eloquently and effectively he can combat injustice who has experienced a little in his own person. . . ."[11]

Although Thoreau's essay had no impact on the outcome of the Mexican War, "Resistance to Civil Government" became one of the foundation stones of American dissent. In subsequent decades the essay inspired millions of dissenters, not only in the United States but around the world—Gandhi in India, King in the USA, Havel in Czechoslovakia, Mandela in South Africa.

* * *

By the middle of the nineteenth century, dissent was pervasive. Women led by Elizabeth Cady Stanton and Lucretia Mott met at Seneca Falls, New York, and issued a "Declaration of Sentiments" in which they demanded their equal rights as citizens. Anti-Catholic nativists had formed the American Party (aka the Know-Nothings) in a determined effort to prevent immigrants from non-Protestant countries from entering the United States. And by 1850 controversy over the extension of slavery into the territories acquired from Mexico raised passions so high that the issue dominated discourse for the rest of the decade. From the publication of Harriet Beecher Stowe's *Uncle Tom's Cabin* to John Brown's raid at Harpers Ferry, dissent was clearly leading the nation into a conflict that threatened the continued existence of the United States.

During the Civil War thousands of Americans on *both* sides protested against the war, against the suspension of habeas corpus, against the infringement of civil liberties, and against conscription (most notoriously the violent draft riots in New York City). When the war ended, the backlash was immediate when groups of southerners formed terrorist organizations such as the Ku Klux Klan and the Knights of the White Camellia to protest the new social order.

The KKK was founded in 1865 for the explicit purpose of preventing former slaves from gaining political and economic power. In a campaign of terror and violence, Klansmen rode through the South intimidating and murdering freedpeople and creating a climate of subjugation and suppression that lasted for more than a century. The Klan was not interested in constitutional rights; its goal was to make sure that African Americans were denied those rights. The KKK illustrates one of the paradoxes of dissent. If dissent is defined merely as opposing the status quo, challenging the way things are without regard to moral considerations, then the Klan is a dissent organization. Certainly, the Klan is an example of reactionary dissent. The post–Civil War status quo was that former slaves were legally free and equal. The Klan opposed African Americans' new status and sought to restore white supremacy. But since white supremacy was always at the heart of social relations in the South (and in the North), the Klan's dissent was simply an effort to maintain the old status quo.

The Klan dwindled away in the 1880s when "Redemptionists" (former Confederates) resumed power and devised literacy tests and poll taxes to prevent freedmen from registering to vote, and Jim Crow laws to create a rigid system of apartheid. These laws were more than enough to keep African Americans from exercising political power. But southern whites, seeking to accentuate the imperative that white supremacy should never be challenged, made sure that no one ever misunderstood their intentions. African Americans were reminded daily that they were not fit for white society, through systematic and constant denigration, humiliation, and condescension. They were expected to be obsequious and deferential to whites, to step off the sidewalk if they encountered a white person, to show respect by lowering their heads, and never to make eye contact with a white woman. They were barred from industry and the skilled trades. The only option open to those who were not chained to a life of sharecropping was the low-paying, low-status jobs no one else wanted. Those who ran afoul of the law were subject to chain gangs and the convict lease system that put Black prisoners to work (most of whom had been convicted for petty crimes or simply vagrancy) in hazardous, grueling, and often brutal jobs such as mining, clearing land, and constructing roads. These jobs were so hazardous that the mortality rate reached 25 percent.[12]

And then there was the continued prevalence of lynching. In the 1890s alone there was an average of 187 lynchings per year. Lynchings were so common, so widespread, that they became public spectacles conducted in a festive atmosphere. It was not uncommon for a lynching to become a social event, with scores of jubilant whites eagerly and cheerfully crowding around the victim's corpse to pose for the camera.

Black men, no matter how serious or trivial the crime for which they had been arrested, could be dragged out of jail and lynched. In 1891, Ed Coy, who had been arrested and charged with raping a white woman, was seized by a mob and tied to a stake. While his tormentors poured oil over his body and the woman he was accused of raping set fire to him, the terrified man continued to cry out that he was innocent. In March 1899, nine African Americans in Palmetto, Georgia, had been arrested on suspicion of arson. A mob of over one hundred white men dragged them out of jail, tied them together and, while they begged and pleaded for mercy, the mob coolly and carefully took aim with their pistols and Winchesters and fired volley after volley until the moans and sobs of the victims ceased.

While such atrocities were spreading throughout the South, Ida B. Wells-Barnett, a courageous young editor of the *Memphis Free Speech*, began an antilynching campaign after three of her friends who were partners in a small grocery store were lynched. She published articles, pamphlets, and books detailing the lynchings and went on lectures tours demanding that the federal government enact strong, enforceable laws against the practice. She denounced the racist tropes that whites employed to justify murder. It was a boldfaced lie, she insisted, that Black men were sexually obsessed with white women and were chomping at the bit to rape them. White reliance on this myth was merely a ploy to justify murdering African Americans whose real crime was that they were economic competitors for whites.

In 1899 Wells-Barnett published *Lynch Law in Georgia*, describing the lynchings she had researched. One case was the lynching of Samuel

Hose "by the Christian white people of Georgia." Hose had murdered a white man, and while he was still at large, the *Atlanta Constitution* published several editorials inciting citizens to take the law into their own hands. On April 23 Hose was caught by a mob of about two thousand people. They stripped him of his clothing and then tied him to a sapling. Wood was piled up around him, but before it was ignited, his ears, toes, fingers, and genitals were cut off. Though he remained conscious while being mutilated, he never groaned or begged for mercy. "He writhed in agony," Wells-Barnett wrote,

> and his sufferings can be imagined when it is said that several blood vessels burst during the contortions of his body. When he fell from the stake he was kicked back and the flames renewed. Then it was that the flames consumed his body and in a few minutes only a few bones and a small part of the body was all that was left of Sam Hose.
>
> One of the most sickening sights of the day was the eagerness with which the people grabbed after souvenirs, and they almost fought over the ashes of the dead criminal. Large pieces of his flesh were carried away, and persons were seen walking through the streets carrying bones in their hands.[13]

Body parts and bones were auctioned off for twenty-five cents each. His "crisply cooked" liver sold for ten cents. Even the remnants of the sapling were sold as a souvenir.[14]

In 1900 Representative George Henry White of North Carolina introduced a bill in the House of Representatives to make lynching a federal hate crime. This was the first of more than 200 antilynching bills that were introduced only to be tabled, voted down, or filibustered for more than a century. The cause that Ida B. Wells-Barnett devoted herself to invariably faced the insurmountable obstacle of powerful southern Democrats (later Republicans) in the Senate for more than 120 years. In March 2022 the Senate finally passed H.R.55, and President Joseph

MISS GARRITY.
PHOTOGRAPHER.

CHICAGO.

FIGURE 1.2. Ida B. Wells-Barnett, c. 1893. The outspoken journalist and civil rights activist led the fight for federal antilynching legislation.
Credit: Photograph by Mary Garrity. Public domain.

Biden signed, the "Emmett Till Antilynching Act" making lynching a federal crime.[15]

* * *

During the Gilded Age, other marginalized Americans fought to expand their rights as citizens. Women stepped up their campaign for voting rights, while workers struggled mightily for the right to unionize.

In 1872, Susan B. Anthony, as a protest against the exclusion of women from the suffrage, voted in the presidential election. She was arrested and brought to trial in June 1873. When she challenged the guilty verdict, the judge told her she could not argue the question for she had been tried "under the forms of law." "Yes," she replied, "but laws made by men, under a government of men, interpreted by men and for the benefit of men. The only chance women have for justice in this country is to violate the law, as I have done, and as I shall *continue* to do."[16] Newspaper coverage of her trial, as well as a speech she delivered around the nation titled "Is It a Crime for a U.S. Citizen to Vote?," brought considerable attention to women's suffrage. "It was *we the people*," she insisted—"not we, *white male citizens*—nor yet we male citizens—but we the *whole people*, who formed this Union; and we formed it, not to *give* the blessings of liberty, but to *secure* them—not to the *half* of ourselves and the half of our posterity, but to the whole people, *women* as well as men. And it is downright *mockery* to talk to women of their enjoyment of the *blessings* of liberty while they are *denied the use of the only means of securing them* provided by this democratic-republican government [the ballot]."[17] She tirelessly campaigned for women's suffrage well into her eighties, but she never saw the passage of the woman's suffrage amendment that she had introduced to Congress in 1878.

In response to the rapid rise of industrialization and the accumulation of great wealth by the "Robber Barons," workers strove to establish unions to fight for collective bargaining rights, better wages, and safer working conditions. There were hundreds of clashes between labor and corporations during the Gilded Age: Molly Maguires sabotaging and resorting to physical violence in the coal mines of northeastern Pennsylvania, the Great Railway Strike of 1877, the Homestead Strike, and perhaps most notoriously the Haymarket Affair.

On May 1, 1886, 350,000 American workers, protesting the sixty-hour week and demanding an eight-hour workday, participated in a nationwide general strike. In Chicago, when striking workers at the McCormick Harvester Works were picketing in front of the plant, a skirmish broke out between strikers and scabs. The police fired into the crowd, killing three strikers. Outraged at the killings, August Spies and Albert Parsons, leaders of an anarchist organization, the International Working People's Association, called for a mass protest rally at Haymarket Square on May 4.

Nearly three thousand protesters attended the rally. For several hours they listened to union leaders and anarchists exhorting them to fight for their rights, but when policemen moved in to break up the rally someone threw a bomb. The police opened fire. When the smoke cleared, four protesters and seven police officers were mortally wounded, and more than two hundred people were injured. Eight anarchists were arrested and charged with murder.

There was no evidence against any of the eight men arrested, but they were tried and convicted. Most observers maintained that the accused were put on trial because of their political beliefs, not for murder. Five of the eight were sentenced to death, and during the months before their execution there were major protest demonstrations in the United States and Europe. In November 1887 Albert Parsons, August Spies, Adolph Fischer, and George Engel were hanged. The day of the funerals twenty-five thousand people marched in Chicago and in other cities around the nation. Still, despite the protests, what happened at Haymarket set back the union movement for decades. The affair convinced middle-class Americans that industrial workers were violent anarchists and that unions were un-American.

* * *

Just as the nineteenth century was drawing to a close, the United States went to war against Spain. Within four months the war was over and Spain ceded to the United States its colonies of Puerto Rico, Guam, and the Philippines as part of the peace settlement. Many Americans were proud that the United States had acquired colonies, but many others found it alarming, as well as ironic, that the United States, after defeating imperial Spain, had become an imperial power. What most irked anti-imperialists was that the occupation of Spain's former colonies went against the core American principle of consent of the governed. The United States, after all, was the result of a revolution against an imperial power. By annexing these colonies, the United States was undermining its own principles. Hundreds of well-known Americans, from all political persuasions, joined the chorus of dissenting voices against imperialism. Republican Carl Schurz, for example, emphatically condemned the annexation of the Philippines. If we become an imperial power, Schurz declared in an 1899 speech, "we shall transform the government of the people, for the people, and by the people . . . into a government of one part of the people, the strong, over another part, the weak." Such a policy was just as hurtful to the United States as it was to a subjugated population, for "such an abandonment of a fundamental principle as a permanent policy . . . can hardly fail in its ultimate effects to disturb the rule of the same principle in the conduct of democratic government at home. And I warn the American people that a democracy cannot so deny its faith as to the vital conditions of its being—it cannot long play the king over subject populations without creating within itself ways of thinking and habits of action most dangerous to its own vitality."[18]

Democrat William Jennings Bryan also denounced America's imperialist course. "Those who would have this nation enter upon a career of empire must consider not only the effect of imperialism on the Filipinos but they must also calculate its effects upon our own nation. We cannot repudiate the principle of self-government in the Philippines without weakening that principle here." Presciently, Bryan warned that if the United States became an imperialist power, it would create a dangerously powerful military. "If we have an imperial policy," he predicted, "we must have a great standing army as its natural and necessary complement. The spirit which will justify the forcible annexation of the Philippine Islands will justify the seizure of other islands and the domination of other people, and with wars of conquest we can expect a certain, if not rapid, growth of our military establishment."[19]

Despite these protests, the United States turned its back on its isolationist past and looked forward, optimistically, to the twentieth century.

2

Progressives, Reformers, Radicals

I have never had a vote, and I have raised hell all over this
country. You don't need a vote to raise hell! You need convictions and a voice!
—Mother Jones

Despite the glittering wealth of the nation at the turn of the century
and the rise of a middle class, millions of Americans lived in abject
poverty. While rich industrialists and investors lived lives of opulent
splendor, the people who worked for them barely eked out a living.
Whether they were newly arrived immigrants or long-established citizens, unskilled workers toiled intolerably long hours for intolerably low
wages, they were crammed into squalid urban slums, and there was little
opportunity to improve their lot. Industrialists resisted every attempt by
workers to organize, and they did whatever it took, including bribery, to
make sure lawmakers did nothing to regulate the consolidation of their
businesses into vast monopolies.

The complexity of the political, economic, and social problems
caused by rapid industrialization, urbanization, and mechanization
spawned a range of responses: middle-class reformers, appalled about
unsafe working conditions, child labor, rampant political corruption,
and the indifference of the public; leftist radicals determined to sweep
away the negative features of capitalism; and even a number of wealthy
philanthropists, fearing that excessive privation could lead to a violent
uprising. As historian Richard Hofstadter has pointed out, some middle-
class Americans—educators, clergymen, lawyers, small shop owners—
became reformers because they felt they were losing status in direct
proportion to the rising power and dominance of the superrich.[1] Thus

the impulse for their dissent was partly an attempt to return to the time when they enjoyed a prominent place in society.

Philosophically speaking, reformers were influenced by such progressive thinkers as Edward Bellamy, Henry George, and John Dewey, who offered recipes for enriching life and creating a better future. Charles Darwin's theory of evolution also influenced many reformers. Just as Social Darwinists used evolutionary theory to justify inequality and the exploitive practices of big business as an example of natural selection at work, intellectuals such as Lester Frank Ward also adapted the theory, but for more progressive purposes. The technological inventions of the nineteenth century seemed proof that the world was a constantly progressing, constantly evolving place. Just as humans harnessed science and technology to bring about progress, so too could human intelligence be used to create a more equitable, more just society. In "Mind as a Social Factor" Ward argued that it was intelligence and self-reflection that set *homo sapiens* apart from animals. Because of this, humans have the ability to guide the course of evolution. Ward's Reform Darwinism called for a system of planned government intervention in the economy and in social relations, replacing "survival of the fittest" with the survival of as many as possible. Through laws regulating industry, establishing a minimum wage, improving safety conditions, permitting workers to organize unions, and providing aid to education, the government could improve the lives of the poor and make them more fit for survival. The human species will evolve, Ward believed, more effectively through co-operation than through competition.[2] Ward's belief that humanity was moving ever upward, that society was ever progressing, and that human beings can expedite the process influenced and inspired many reformers, among them Jane Addams, Walter Rauschenbusch, and Frances E. Willard.

* * *

One area that was of particular concern was unbridled political corruption. Alarmed that government was not responsive to the people and that politicians were increasingly in the pocket of corporations, reformers targeted corruption at the municipal, state, and federal levels and simultaneously sought to open up democracy so that more Americans could participate in the political process.

The complexity and anonymity of city life, along with the long-established reign of political bosses in urban centers, was a recipe for fraud and dishonesty. Politicians routinely accepted, indeed demanded, bribes from companies seeking construction contracts, tax breaks, or licenses of any kind. City councilmen and policemen took kickbacks from illegal gambling rings, houses of prostitution, and bars operating without liquor licenses. Dozens of investigative reporters wrote articles scrutinizing and exposing corruption in New York, Philadelphia, Chicago, St. Louis, Minneapolis, and other cities, which riled up the public to demand that something be done to hold public officials to a basic standard of honesty. The articles roused reform-minded citizens to run for public office pledging to clean up city hall. Tom L. Johnson won election as a progressive mayor in Cleveland, Samuel M. "Golden Rule" Jones in Toledo, Hazen S. Pingree in Detroit, and Seth Low in New York. And all of them succeeded in rooting out much (but by no means all) of the corruption. Some progressive mayors curbed corruption by establishing nonpartisan commissions that independently monitored public officials, while others converted utility companies (electric, gas, water) into publicly run departments of the city government.

Reformers pushed state legislatures to pass laws establishing building codes for tenement housing; laws limiting working hours in the textile, railroad, and mining industries; and legislation banning child labor. Regardless of progressive attempts to improve working and living conditions, however, industries found numerous ways to circumvent the laws, and the courts frustrated reformers by frequently striking down many progressive laws as unconstitutional—ruling that governments had no authority to regulate free enterprise.

The most significant political reform of the era, though, was the culmination of the long struggle for women's suffrage. During the last quarter of the nineteenth century two groups, the American Woman Suffrage Association and the National Woman Suffrage Association, led the campaign for women's rights. While the AWSA concentrated on the main goal, the more radical NWSA expanded the struggle beyond gaining the vote and promoted equal rights for women in the workplace, in politics, and in the eyes of the law. In 1890 the two groups combined as the National American Woman Suffrage Association (NAWSA), and they did achieve limited success in swaying several western state legislatures to grant women's suffrage; but by 1900 it became increasingly apparent that the state-by-state strategy was never going to achieve complete success.

During the first years of the twentieth century the torch of leadership in the women's movement was passed from Elizabeth Cady Stanton and Susan B. Anthony to a new generation of leaders, notably Carrie Chapman Catt, Harriot Stanton Blatch, Lucy Burns, and Alice Paul. All four women organized protest marches and applied increasing pressure on Congress to pass the women's suffrage amendment (first introduced to Congress in 1878 by Susan B. Anthony). From 1907 to 1910 Alice Paul studied in England, where she was influenced by Christabel Pankhurst and the more radical women suffragettes of Britain. When she returned to the States, Paul brought with her some of the more militant tactics— picketing, vigils, hunger strikes—that she had learned in England. On the day before Woodrow Wilson's inauguration in 1913, Paul organized a parade in Washington, DC, to pressure Wilson to support women's suffrage. She also formed the National Woman's Party in 1916 to campaign against anti-suffrage politicians, and in January 1917 she organized an ongoing series of protests at the White House. For more than a year women held a silent vigil rebuking Wilson for not supporting women's suffrage. After the United States declared war on Germany, the demonstrators' signs frequently, and irreverently, referred to the president's speeches in which he justified America's entry into the war as a noble effort to extend democracy to Europeans who had no say in their government. "Kaiser Wilson," one such sign cheekily proclaimed, "20,000,000

FIGURE 2.1. Suffragists parading in New York City, May 4, 1912. Photograph titled "Youngest Parader in New York City Suffragist Parade," by the American Press Association.
Credit: Public domain; courtesy of Library of Congress.

American Women Are Not Self-Governed. Take the Beam out of Your Own Eye." The protesters were daily derided, mocked, harassed, and even physically abused by passersby and policemen. Embarrassed by the picketers, Wilson ordered their arrest, but Paul continued her protest in prison by going on a hunger strike. She was force-fed and eventually released but went right back to the picket line. In the end, in 1918, an exasperated Wilson announced a change of position and urged Democrats in Congress to vote for the women's suffrage bill. The bill made it through both houses by June 1919, and in August 1920, when Tennessee became the thirty-sixth state to ratify the Nineteenth Amendment, it became the law of the land. And so, forty-eight years after Susan B. Anthony was arrested for casting a vote in Rochester, New York, seventy-two years after Elizabeth Cady Stanton and Lucretia Mott penned the Declaration

FIGURE 2.2. Alice Paul, c. 1915. Militant suffragist; National Chairman, Congressional Union for Woman Suffrage; Member, Ex-Officio, National Executive Committee, Woman's Party. Alice Paul was arrested several times while protesting at the White House. In jail she went on a hunger strike and was force-fed by correctional officers. In 1923 she introduced the Equal Rights Amendment to Congress.

Credit: Women of Protest: Photographs from the Records of the National Woman's Party. Public domain; courtesy of Library of Congress.

of Sentiments, and 144 years after Abigail Adams had exhorted her husband not to forget "the Ladies" in the "new Code of Laws," American women finally won the right to vote.[3]

* * *

Reformers also sought to remedy social ills such as the rampant discrimination faced by immigrants and African Americans, while others sought to diminish poverty, domestic violence, and crime by waging war on alcohol. There were also reformers who went beyond secular humanism and drew on Christian morality to improve American society.

Between 1889 and 1893 the first settlement houses were established: Jane Addams's Hull House in Chicago, Robert A. Woods's South End House in Boston, and Lillian Wald's Henry Street Settlement in New York. Settlement houses were essentially community centers set up to alleviate the appalling conditions in urban slums, especially those overflowing with immigrants. Volunteer workers, mostly women, toiled to aid immigrants from rural areas of Europe who were having difficulty adjusting to urban life in the United States. They provided shelter and taught English, cooking, sewing, and hygiene, seeking to ease immigrants' path into American society. Soon the volunteers found that the work done in the settlement houses was simply not enough. Consequently, they lobbied local governments to improve sanitation, to finance more schools, and to pass laws regulating child labor and tenement housing. They became experts at gathering statistical data that could be used to sway lawmakers to enact socially progressive legislation. Settlement-house workers also solicited private charities and benefactors to sponsor libraries, playgrounds, and daycare centers.

The basic philosophy underlying the movement, according to Jane Addams, was "the solidarity of the human race," and the goal was "to aid in the solution of the social and industrial problems which are engendered by the modern conditions of life in a great city . . . [and] attempt to relieve, at the same time, the overaccumulation at one end of society and the destitution at the other; but it assumes that this overaccumulation and destitution is most sorely felt in the things that pertain to social and educational privileges."[4]

Because settlement-house workers witnessed firsthand the debilitating effects of alcohol on the working class, many of them became staunch activists in the temperance crusade. The temperance movement had been going strong for decades, with people such as Frances E. Willard and Carrie Nation and organizations such as the Woman's Christian Temperance Union, the Anti-Saloon League, and the Prohibition Party aggressively lobbying local governments to enact laws restricting alcohol. For women who experienced abuse from alcoholic husbands it was primarily a feminist issue, for conservative Protestants it was a moral issue, and for many rural folk it was linked to nativism. Most of the new immigrants flocking to the United States came from southern and eastern European countries where wine and beer was part of daily life. Some nativists supported temperance as a way to dissuade immigrants from Jewish, Roman Catholic, and Eastern Orthodox areas from coming to America. The temperance crusade is, in fact, a prime example of the overlapping motives that sometimes form the basis of dissent. Despite their diverse goals, radicals, reformers, and reactionaries all took part in the temperance movement.

The most legendary prohibitionist was Carrie Nation. In 1900, convinced she was doing God's will, Carrie Nation launched her "Hatchetation" campaign. She would regularly march into a saloon, carrying her Bible and singing hymns, and wielding a hatchet, proceed to destroy the place. She smashed liquor bottles, chopped up the bars, and lectured the owners and patrons on the evils of alcohol. "Men," she proclaimed, "I have come to save you from a drunkard's fate!"[5] She was arrested thirty times. In between incarcerations she toured the country lecturing in churches, vaudeville halls, and college campuses and earned enough money to pay her fines and legal costs. By the time of her death in 1911 she had literally destroyed dozens of bars and saloons.

While Carrie Nation was carrying on her entertaining campaign, thousands of women and men joined the crusade to eliminate alcohol. By the second decade of the twentieth century the temperance movement had gained considerable political clout. The argument continually put forth was that the elimination of alcohol would eliminate alcoholism, which in turn would reduce the number of people losing their jobs and sinking into lives of poverty and crime. By 1916 sixteen state legislatures had prohibited the sale of alcohol; and then in 1919 the Eighteenth Amendment was ratified, outlawing the sale of alcohol in the United States as of January 17, 1920.

By 1900 it was clear to many in the African American community that Booker T. Washington's[6] 1895 injunction that Blacks should not concern themselves with civil and political rights as long as they worked to lift themselves up economically was not a particularly effective strategy. In 1900 alone more than one hundred African Americans were lynched, many of whom *had* moved up the economic ladder. No one knows exactly how many Black people were murdered, for there are no reliable statistics, but historians estimate that between 1901 and 1914 more than a thousand lynchings took place. Racism was obviously too deeply entrenched in American society for white people to accept Black people as equals.

In 1905 W. E. B. Du Bois, William Monroe Trotter, John Hope, and more than thirty other prominent Black intellectuals met in Niagara Falls, Canada, to hammer out a strategy to secure African American civil rights. Denouncing Booker T. Washington's "accommodationism," they demanded the abolition of the Jim Crow laws, the reinstatement of the right to vote where that right had been contravened by literacy tests and poll taxes, equal educational and economic opportunity, and the right to protest for their civil rights.[7] The following year they met again in Harpers Ferry and further developed the strategy to secure civil rights, and in 1909 they became the National Association for the Advancement of Colored People (NAACP).

The NAACP was the first of the major civil rights organizations. Its chief focus was to use the judicial system to overturn the 1896 *Plessy v. Ferguson* decision that had established the "separate but equal" doctrine legalizing segregation, and also to bring lawsuits challenging civil rights violations at the state and local level. Within a few years the NAACP had chapters in many states, with thousands of members. The NAACP had very little impact during the first decades of its existence, but it did give hope to millions of African Americans who understood that, for the first time, there was an organization that was actively fighting for their rights.

Underlying these and many other reforms of the early twentieth century was the Social Gospel movement, which brought a moral dimension to protest by applying Christian principles to reform. Traditionally, clergymen counseled their poor parishioners that their suffering was God's will and that they would get their reward in heaven, but Walter Rauschenbusch, a Baptist pastor in New York's Lower East Side, rejected this approach. It is all well and good, he reasoned, to minister to people's souls, but it was just as essential to apply Christian principles to daily life and to do everything possible to make life better for the needy in the here-and-now. Rauschenbusch put his Social Gospel views into practice. In the Hell's Kitchen section of Manhattan he opened soup kitchens that gave aid and comfort to the poor and the homeless. In 1907 he published *Christianity and the Social Crisis* and in 1912 *Christianizing the Social Order*, in which he criticized capitalist exploitation of workers as being unchristian and argued for the Social Gospel and the establishment of a welfare state.

At the same time, Father John A. Ryan, responding to the papal encyclical *Rerum Novarum* (in which Pope Leo XIII declared that the state had an obligation to guarantee the rights of workers), became a leading advocate for the Catholic social justice movement. Ryan argued that workers have the right to livable wages and reasonable working hours. He wrote, in *Distributive Justice: The Right and Wrong of Our Present Distribution of Wealth* (1916), that ethics and economics were inextricably entwined and that the government's duty was to ensure that workers were treated equitably. He called for a minimum wage and criticized the culture of consumption that was pervasive in the United States.

Charles Sheldon's novel *In His Steps* (1898) popularized the Social Gospel for an evangelical audience.[8] In it Sheldon argued that business leaders who were confronted with decisions about working conditions and wages or politicians debating a law for workers' compensation should first ask themselves one question before they made their decision: "What would Jesus do?" The message was clear. Would Jesus run a sweatshop? Would he try to extract the maximum labor from workers for minimum pay? Such sentiments had a profound impact on conservative Christians, who normally thought of reform as an expression of radical politics, persuading many to get involved.

* * *

Writers and journalists throughout the country applied their analytical skills to an obsessive effort to root out and expose the ills of society. Some writers worked for the tabloid press, and part of their motivation was to produce sensational, scandalous stories that sold newspapers. But many of them were themselves progressives who were legitimately outraged at the corruption, abuse, and exploitation they uncovered, as well as the apathy of the public. Their intention was to awaken the nation's conscience and propel Americans into action. President Theodore Roosevelt called them "muckrakers" because he thought they were too busy wallowing in the muck of scandal and ignored the positive side of American society, but at the same time they did influence him to act.

Lincoln Steffens wrote a series of investigative articles for *McClure's Magazine* (collected and published as *The Shame of the Cities* in 1904) about the relationship between corrupt politicians and unscrupulous business leaders. Ida M. Tarbell wrote a scathing indictment of the Standard Oil Company, exposing John D. Rockefeller's ruthless business practices. Publisher S. S. McClure's editorials hammered at the immorality of business leaders, landlords, politicians, judges, lawyers, and even workers and educators.

But the most influential of all the muckraking publications was Upton Sinclair's best-selling novel *The Jungle* (1906). Sinclair, a socialist, wrote the book as a paean to socialism. Sinclair described, in shocking detail, the unsanitary conditions rampant in the meat-packing industry and the appalling exploitation that destroyed an immigrant family. At the end of the novel, Sinclair makes a case for socialism as the cure for capitalism. But that was not the message readers took from the book. The public was gripped by Sinclair's graphic descriptions of the butchering of the cattle, the sickening methods for producing ground beef and stuffing sausages, the processing of contaminated meat from diseased cattle that had died on the way to the slaughterhouse, and the maiming of overworked men operating the meat grinders. As Sinclair later put it, "I aimed at the public's heart, and by accident I hit it in the stomach."[9] President Roosevelt (carnivore that he was) was so sickened when he read the book that he stopped eating meat for several months until he got Congress to pass the Pure Food and Drug Act.

One of the worst abuses of the age was the exploitation of children in factories and mines. It was a common practice to hire child workers in order to cut production costs. In textile mills their small hands could reach into the power looms to extract defective threads, in mines boys as young as eight years old were employed sorting coal, and in all cases they were paid less than adults. Children frequently lost fingers and hands in factory accidents, developed fatal respiratory diseases in mines, worked ten hours and more a day for less than fifty cents, and forfeited any opportunity for education. Many were literally worked to death. One investigator wrote an article about a young girl, Roselie Randazzo, who died of a hemorrhage coughing up blood while working in the unsafe air of an artificial flower factory.

In the 1880s and 1890s Florence Kelley, who worked with Jane Addams at Hull House, brought cases to the Illinois courts seeking to get the state to outlaw child labor. In 1901 Kelley moved to New York, where she led the National Consumers League. Its purpose was to encourage consumers to buy products only from companies that met minimum wage and safety standards. The league's slogan was "investigate, agitate, legislate." Kelley also organized consumer boycotts of sweatshops and other industries that exploited child labor; she pioneered the practice of assembling scientific and statistical data to influence courts and legislatures, and she came up with numerous creative ideas to eradicate child labor: for example, compulsory education and requiring labels on manufactured goods certifying that children were not used in its production.

Mary Harris "Mother" Jones was a liberal organizer for the Knights of Labor and the United Mine Workers of America, but by the turn of the century she became a socialist and was one of the founders of the Industrial Workers of the World. In 1903, at the age of seventy-three, she went to the Kensington neighborhood of Philadelphia to show her solidarity with seventy-five thousand textile workers who had walked off the job demanding shorter hours and increased wages. Ten thousand of the striking workers were children. "Every day," she wrote, "little children came into Union Headquarters, some with their hands off, some with

FIGURE 2.3. The mill children on Mother Jones's famous march from Philadelphia to Oyster Bay protesting child labor, 1903.
Credit: Public domain.

the thumb missing, some with their fingers off at the knuckle. They were stooped things, round shouldered and skinny." Although state law prohibited employing children under the age of twelve, many of them were only ten years old. "I asked the newspaper men why they didn't publish the facts about child labor in Pennsylvania. They said they couldn't because the mill owners had stock in the papers. 'Well, I've got stock in these little children,' said I, 'and I'll arrange a little publicity.'"[10]

And so Mother Jones organized the children for a protest march from Philadelphia to Oyster Bay, Long Island. "I decided to go with the children to see President Roosevelt to ask him to have Congress pass a law prohibiting the exploitation of childhood. . . . I thought too, out of politeness, we might call on Morgan in Wall Street who owned the mines where many of these children's fathers worked." In Trenton, New Jersey, the police were ordered to stop the march, but instead "they just smiled and spoke kindly to the children, and said nothing at all about not going into the city." The children marched into the city, where Mother Jones spoke to the crowd, "and it was the wives of the police who took the little children and cared for them that night, sending them back in the morning with a nice lunch rolled up in paper napkins."[11]

The march's next stop was Princeton, where Jones told a gathering of professors and students that she would speak to them about higher education. "'Here's a text book on economics,' I said pointing to a little chap, James Ashworth, who was ten years old and who was stooped over like an old man from carrying bundles of yarn that weighed seventy-five pounds. 'He gets three dollars a week and his sister who is fourteen gets six dollars. They work in a carpet factory ten hours a day while the children of the rich are getting their higher education.'" In New York City they got donations from a crowd when she delivered a speech about the evils of child labor. "I showed them Eddie Dunphy, a little fellow of twelve, whose job it was to sit all day on a high stool, handing in the right thread to another worker. Eleven hours a day he sat on the high stool with dangerous machinery all about him. All day long, . . . for three dollars a week."[12]

When the protesters finally got to Oyster Bay, President Roosevelt refused to greet them. Still, the children's march raised public awareness. "Our march," Mother Jones declared, "had done its work. We had drawn the attention of the nation to the crime of child labor. And while the strike of the textile workers in Kensington was lost and the children driven back to work, not long afterward the Pennsylvania legislature passed a child labor law that sent thousands of children home from the mills, and kept thousands of others from entering the factory until they were fourteen years of age."[13]

In 1904 anti-child-labor activists founded the National Child Labor Committee (NCLC) to lobby Congress to enact anti-child-labor legislation. In 1908 the NCLC commissioned the photographer Lewis W. Hine to travel the country documenting child labor. Hine was horrified at what he discovered, and his photographs remain a powerful and disturbing reminder of the terrible conditions under which children, some as young as five years old, worked. For years Hine exhibited his photos and urged audiences around the country to vote for politicians who took a stand against child labor. "Perhaps you are weary of child labor pictures," he said. "Well, so are the rest of us, but we propose to make you and the whole country so sick and tired of the whole business that when the time for action comes, child labor pictures will be records of the past."[14] In 1912 President Taft signed the bill creating the United States Children's Bureau and appointed Julia Lathrop as its chair to "investigate and report upon all matters pertaining to the welfare of children and child life among all classes of our people."[15]

Despite the efforts of Jones, Addams, Kelley, Hine, and so many others, it was not until the New Deal in the 1930s that child labor was effectively regulated at the federal level, when another Roosevelt signed the Fair Labor Standards Act prohibiting child labor under the age of fourteen and setting strict limits on the hours and type of work for children between the ages of fourteen and eighteen.

Progressive reformers also targeted the working conditions of New York City's garment industry, which employed thousands of young

FIGURE 2.4. Mother Jones, 1915. Photograph of the labor activist Mother Jones (1837–1930) attending the 1915 hearings of the federal Commission on Industrial Relations at New York City Hall.

Credit: Photograph by Bain News Service. Public domain; courtesy of Library of Congress.

women (mostly Italian and Jewish immigrants) in hundreds of sweat-shops throughout lower Manhattan. These women worked long, fifty-six hour weeks, in unsafe, miserable conditions for one dollar a day making dresses and blouses. The companies, seeking to maximize profits, forced the women to rent their sewing machines (sometimes even requiring that they pay for the electricity) and made them take their breaks at their stations. In 1909 nearly twenty thousand garment workers walked off their jobs, demanding better working conditions. Supported by the International Ladies' Garment Workers Union and dozens of the city's clergymen, the women won. But not all the cloth-ing manufacturers improved working conditions, and many of the sweatshops remained unsafe. The Triangle Shirtwaist Company, for example, still required employees to take their breaks at their sew-ing machines, and to ensure they did the managers routinely kept the doors to the workshop locked so the women could not even go out into the hallway.

On March 25, 1911, a fire broke out in the eighth-floor workshop. Most of the doors were locked; but even those that were unlocked swung in-ward, and the press of panicked workers trying to escape prevented the doors from opening. The women were trapped. With flames and smoke engulfing them many women, in threes and fours, holding hands, leapt to their deaths. "They jumped with their clothing ablaze," one newspa-per reported. "The hair of some of the girls streamed up aflame as they leaped. Thud after thud sounded on the pavements."[16] When it was all over, 146 women were dead. None of the managers died.

The public was outraged. The governor established a commission to in-vestigate working conditions throughout the state. The commission's find-ings, after five years, eventually led to the enactment of legislation that set safety standards for the workplace, prohibited the employment of children under fourteen, and limited women's working hours to fifty-four per week. From 1911 on it became clear that the government needed to establish regu-lations that would improve the safety of the workplace for all workers. It took a long while, but eventually, in 1971, the federal government established the Occupational Safety and Health Administration (OSHA).

One of the most shocking incidents underscoring the need for labor reform was the Ludlow Massacre. The miners at the Colorado Fuel and Iron Company (owned by the Rockefeller family) lived in company towns, were paid in company scrip, and were forced to shop in company stores. In 1913 they went on strike, demanding the recognition of their union—the United Mine Workers of America (UMWA)—an eight-hour day, the right to choose where to live and shop, and finally to be paid for such "dead work" as shoring up the mines and laying track (miners were paid by the ton of coal they mined). As soon as they struck, the company evicted the strikers from the towns. Twelve hundred miners set up a tent city near the mines so they could prevent scab workers from being brought in. The company hired the Baldwin-Felts Detective Agency to break the strike. The detectives began routinely patrolling the encampment in an armored vehicle, arbitrarily shooting into the tents. On April 20, 1914, the governor sent in the National Guard to disperse the strikers. During the ensuing melee seventeen people were killed.

"The Ludlow camp is a mass of charred debris," the *New York Times* reported the following day, "and buried beneath it is a story of horror imparalleled [*sic*] in the history of industrial warfare. In the holes which had been dug for their protection against the rifles' fire the women and children died like trapped rats when the flames swept over them."[17] And an outraged Mother Jones could not restrain her righteous fury. "The women and children fled to the hills," she wrote. "All day long the firing continued. Men fell dead, their faces to the ground. Women dropped. The little Snyder boy was shot through the head, trying to save his kitten. A child carrying water to his dying mother was killed." The fighting continued for fourteen hours. "Night came. A raw wind blew down the canyons where men, women and children shivered and wept. Then a blaze lighted the sky. The soldiers, drunk with blood and with the liquor they had looted from the saloon, set fire to the tents of Ludlow with oil-soaked torches. The tents, all the poor furnishings, the clothes and bedding of the miners' families burned." Finally it ended. "The wretched people crept back to bury their dead. In a dugout under a burned tent, the charred bodies of eleven little children and two women were found—unrecognizable. Everything lay in ruins. . . . Oil and fire and guns had robbed men and women and children of their homes and slaughtered tiny babies and defenseless women."[18]

United Mine Worker officials urged mineworkers throughout Colorado to rise up in arms and defend themselves. For ten days guerrilla warfare broke out as nearly a thousand miners attacked and destroyed mine property and killed guards. Dozens more were killed during the uprising, and order was restored only after President Woodrow Wilson deployed the U.S. Army. Estimates of the number of dead ranged from sixty to two hundred. Hundreds of strikers were arrested. Twenty-two National Guardsmen were court-martialed after thousands of people demonstrated in front of the state capitol in Denver demanding that they be tried for murder. In the end, the strike was broken, the UMWA did not gain recognition, most of the striking workers were fired, and no National Guardsmen served time in prison.

The federal government set up the Commission on Industrial Relations to investigate the affair, interrogated the people involved, including John D. Rockefeller, Jr., and concluded that many of the union's demands should be implemented, that child labor in the mines should be abolished, and that a national eight-hour day should be implemented. Rockefeller himself was so shaken by the event (and the negative publicity) that he hired labor-relations experts and instituted a series of reforms to improve working and living conditions, including building recreational facilities and paved roads in the towns, upgrading safety and health standards in the mines, and permitting miners to unionize.

* * *

Most of the progressives seeking to reform society were middle-class moderates, but there was a smaller group of radical dissenters who desired

deeper, more fundamental changes. In fact, they sought a complete transformation of the way things were. Socialists, for example, demanded the
public ownership of factories, mines, and railroads; free education; fair
wages; and humane working conditions. Declaring that "the capitalist
system has outgrown its historical function, and has become utterly incapable of meeting the problems now confronting society," and denouncing
"this outgrown system as incompetent and corrupt and the source of
unspeakable misery and suffering to the whole working class," the Socialist Party Platform of 1912 called for a radical upheaval of the American
system of government. "The Socialist party is the political expression of
the economic interests of the workers. . . . It proposes that, since all social
necessities to-day are socially produced, the means of their production
and distribution shall be socially owned and democratically controlled."
Thus the plutocracy that ran America must be thrown out, and a system
of "collective ownership and democratic management of railroads, wire
and wireless telegraphs and telephones, express service, steamboat lines,
and all other social means of transportation and communication and of
all large scale industries," including banking, mining, natural resources,
must immediately be inaugurated. This was only the beginning. Among
the many other demands the Socialists put forward were the establishment of a minimum wage, a shorter workweek, safety inspection in mines
and factories, women's suffrage, and the abolition of child labor.[19]

Eugene V. Debs was the party's candidate for president five times between 1900 and 1920. Business leaders, bankers, and politicians fretted
about Debs's increasing popularity and the surging growth of the Socialist Party. By the second decade of the century the party had well
over one hundred thousand members actively engaged in politics, and
Debs won nearly a million votes in both the 1912 and 1920 elections. In
speeches all over the country Debs consistently fought for the rights of
labor, women, children, and the downtrodden. "While there is a lower
class," Debs famously proclaimed, "I am in it; while there is a criminal
element, I am of it; while there is a soul in prison, I am not free!" By
1916, as the United States moved ever closer to involvement in the Great

War, he became a powerful antiwar activist. War, Debs believed, was a capitalist plot to preserve the political and economic status quo by pitting international workers against each other. "Years ago I declared that there was only one war in which I would enlist and that was the war of the workers of the world against the exploiters of the world. I declared moreover that the working class had no interest in the wars declared and waged by the ruling classes of the various countries upon one another for conquest and spoils."[20]

Although Debs never came close to challenging the Republican or Democratic candidates on the national level, socialist support was strong enough in certain immigrant, working-class, and Populist communities that local socialist candidates did score some successes. Socialists elected mayors in several cities as well as Meyer London in New York and Victor L. Berger in Wisconsin to the House of Representatives.

In 1905 a band of radical union organizers founded the Industrial Workers of the World (IWW). The purpose of the IWW was to ensure the representation of *all* workers regardless of ethnicity, race, gender, or skill, whether citizens or undocumented migrant workers. The "Wobblies," as they were popularly called, proudly extended "a fraternal hand to every wage-worker, no matter what his religion, fatherland, or trade." Moreover, they advocated that workers overthrow the state, abolish the wage system, and seize the means of production. "The working class and the employing class," the preamble to the IWW constitution declares, "have nothing in common. There can be no peace so long as hunger and want are found among millions of the working people and the few, who make up the employing class, have all the good things of life." The exploitation of workers is not merely an American problem but an international problem. "Between these two classes a struggle must go on until the workers of the world organize as a class, take possession of the means of production, abolish the wage system, and live in harmony with the Earth."[21]

When the IWW coordinated a strike, the leadership insisted on the complete solidarity of the striking workers. Previous strikes, such as those of the Knights of Labor and the American Railway Workers

Union, failed because strikers did not maintain cohesion but became a powerless, disorganized mob. Within the IWW's first few years it organized dozens of strikes with mixed success. IWW restaurant and hotel workers in Nevada were successful in winning an eight-hour day, while sawmill workers in Pennsylvania secured a pay raise and a nine-hour day. Occasionally the Wobblies turned violent when authorities deployed security forces to crush a walkout. During an eleven-week strike in McKees Rocks, Pennsylvania, in 1909, the company requested the Pennsylvania State Constabulary (referred to as the "American Cossacks" by the strikers) to break the strike. The confrontation led to a standoff in which several strikers and constables were killed and fifty wounded before it finally ended with a victory for the strikers.

One of the founding members of the IWW was William "Big Bill" Haywood. Haywood had been a member of the Western Federation of Miners before getting involved with the IWW. In 1907 he was arrested and tried for participating in the assassination of an antilabor former governor of Idaho. But Haywood's lawyer, the noted defense attorney Clarence Darrow, got one of the defendants (the confessed bomb thrower) to admit that he was paid off by the Western Mine Owners' Association. Haywood was acquitted.

In 1912 more than twenty-thousand textile workers in Lawrence, Massachusetts, walked off the job in opposition to the reduction of their wages (which were already an abysmal sixteen cents an hour). When the mill owners called in the police, violence broke out, and a number of strikers were killed. The workers asked for the IWW's assistance, and soon Big Bill Haywood arrived. Haywood suggested that the workers send their children to New York City for the duration of the strike in order to garner public sympathy and support. Socialist families in New York agreed to take them in, and when scores of hungry, destitute children marched from the train station through the middle of Manhattan, reporters were on hand to write heart-wrenching stories about their plight. "I have never found children who were so uniformly ill-nourished, ill-fed, and ill-clothed," one witness to the march ex-claimed.[22] The resulting publicity led embarrassed Lawrence officials to forbid any other children from leaving the city. When a group of moth-ers and children tried to board a train in Lawrence, the police beat them back. When newspaper stories around the world expressed outrage at the heartless actions of the city officials and the company, the governor of Massachusetts was forced to step in on the workers' side and settle the strike.

Perhaps the most famous Wobbly was the Swedish immigrant and songwriter Joel Haggland. When he arrived in the United States in 1902, Haggland was deeply disappointed that the hoped-for success prom-ised to immigrants seemed beyond his grasp. For a number of years he drifted around the country looking for work, eventually joined the IWW, changed his name to Joe Hill, and, using his musical talent, be-came a leading recruiter and organizer for the union.

His technique was to gather a crowd outside a factory at the end of a shift by singing a few songs. Then he and fellow organizers would hand out literature and make short speeches extolling the benefits of joining the Wobblies. Hill, in effect, was one of the country's first protest singers. His songs all had an anticapitalist, prounion message. Usually, he took a popular tune or hymn to grab people's attention and added new lyrics to get them thinking, as in "The Preacher and the Slave." Sung to the tune of the hymn "Sweet Bye and Bye," the song began with an attack on Christianity's collusion with the robber barons:

> Long-haired preachers come out every night,
> Try to tell you what's wrong and what's right;
> But when asked how 'bout something to eat,
> They will answer with voices so sweet:
> You will eat, Bye and bye,
> In that glorious land above the sky;
> Work and pray, live on hay,
> You'll get pie in the sky when you die.

And it ended with the Wobblies' socialist message:

> Workingmen of all countries, unite,
> Side by side we for freedom will fight:
> When the world and its wealth we have gained
> To the grafters we'll sing this refrain:
> You will eat, bye and bye,
> When you've learned how to cook and to fry.
> Chop some wood, 'twill do you good,
> And you'll eat in the sweet bye and bye.[23]

In January 1914 while Hill was in Utah on an IWW recruitment mission, two men killed a grocer and his son during a robbery. Joe Hill was arrested for the crime. Though he steadfastly proclaimed his innocence in the courtroom, Hill was convicted on circumstantial evidence and sentenced to death. Immediately Big Bill Haywood organized mass demonstrations protesting the conviction. It was clear to all members of the IWW and even to huge numbers of the general public that the trial was a setup and that big business and the state of Utah were out to destroy Hill and discredit the IWW. For months the protests spread around the nation and around the world. There were demonstrations in New York and London and other major cities. Helen Keller and Elizabeth Gurley Flynn (both socialists and members of the IWW) protested the verdict, and even President Wilson urged the governor of Utah to commute Hill's sentence. Despite the public outcry, Hill was executed by firing squad in November 1915. Just before his execution he sent a telegram to Haywood urging the IWW and his supporters worldwide: "Don't waste any time in mourning. Organize."[24] Later in the twentieth century union organizers as well as musicians and protest singers from Woody Guthrie and Pete Seeger to Billy Bragg and Bruce Springsteen drew inspiration from Hill.

One of the most notorious radicals of the time was Emma Goldman. A Russian immigrant who promoted anarchism, socialism, and

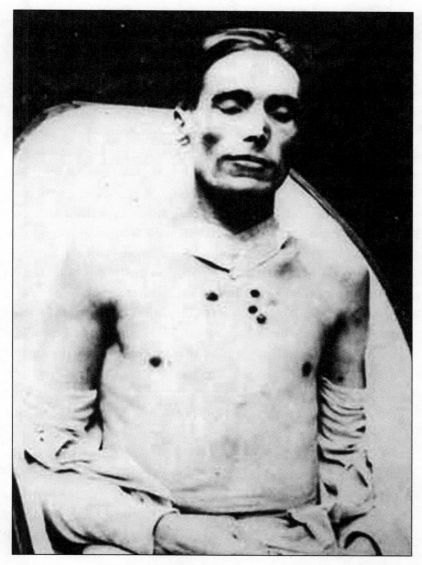

FIGURE 2.5. Joe Hill, 1915. The socialist IWW organizer Joe Hill was executed by firing squad in Utah on what most activists believed were trumped-up charges of murder. Hundreds of thousands of people around the world protested his conviction and execution.
Credit: Public domain; courtesy of J. Willard Marriott Library.

communism, Goldman was such an outspoken critic of American capitalism that she was relentlessly harassed by law enforcement officials. In 1892 Goldman was suspected of being involved in plotting with her lover, Alexander Berkman, the assassination of Henry Clay Frick during the Homestead Strike, and in 1901 she was arrested and questioned intensively in connection with the assassination of William McKinley by an anarchist who had confessed he was inspired by one of Goldman's speeches. Along with championing workers' rights, she was a radical feminist. In a 1911 essay, "Marriage and Love," Goldman argued that women's fight for suffrage, even if successful, was not going to accomplish any real change unless the underlying evils of capitalism itself were addressed. In capitalist society, she contended, women were treated as commodities. Marriage was nothing more than an economic arrangement; in fact, marriage was nothing more than legalized prostitution, an institution dedicated to keeping women subservient. "Marriage and love have nothing in common," she wrote; "they are as far apart as the poles; are, in fact, antagonistic to each other." Women cannot earn enough money to live independently, and so they must find a man to support them. Marriage condemns women to a life of servitude. "The moral lesson instilled in the girl is not whether the man has aroused her love, but rather . . . Can the man make a living? Can he support a wife? That is the only thing that justifies marriage. Gradually this saturates every thought of the girl; her dreams are not of moonlight and kisses, of laughter and tears; she dreams of shopping tours and bargain counters. This soul-poverty and sordidness are the elements inherent in the marriage institution. The State and the Church approve of no other ideal, simply because it is the one that necessitates the State and Church control of men and women."[25]

It is true, Goldman acknowledged, that things are changing, that more and more women are entering the workforce, and that soon women may gain the right to vote. But in capitalist society, where workers are exploited, what sort of progress is this? If and when women gain all the benefits that men have, will there be real progress? She suspected that the only result would be that women would then have "the equal right with men to be exploited, to be robbed, to go on strike; aye, to starve even."[26] Still, she never wavered from her demand for "freedom for both sexes, freedom of action, freedom in love and freedom in motherhood."[27] Many thousands of Americans attended Goldman's speeches and read her essays, and many thousands were inspired by her message and imported her views into their daily lives. Greenwich Village, New York, where Goldman lived, was a vibrant enclave of cultural rebels, or "Bohemians," who rejected conventional morality. Avant-garde writers and painters, poets and dancers—Max Eastman, Isadora Duncan, and many others—published articles and poetry, exhibited paintings, produced experimental plays and dance, and yearned for the day when complete, uninhibited freedom would dawn in the United States. Such Bohemian views, however, horrified and frightened the majority of

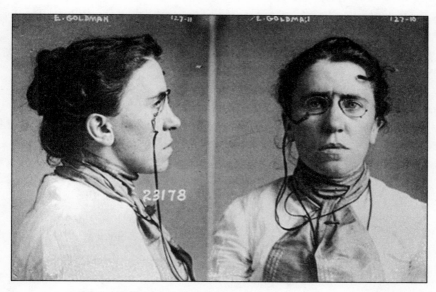

FIGURE 2.6. Emma Goldman's mug shot after she was arrested in 1901 to be interrogated concerning the assassination of President William McKinley. Anarchist, socialist, activist, and revolutionary, Goldman was involved in just about every radical cause of her time.
Credit: Public domain; courtesy of Library of Congress.

Americans, especially after the outbreak of World War I and the triumph of the Bolsheviks in Russia. Still, Goldman did not keep quiet or lower the tone of her rhetoric. Her defiant and ceaseless dissent eventually led in 1919 to her deportation back to Russia, where she found, to her horror, that free speech was considered a bourgeois superstition.

* * *

By the time of the 1912 presidential election, the issues raised by progressives and radicals—the enormous power of monopolies, the plight of workers, political corruption, women's rights, and the role of government—were the focus of public discourse. The Democratic Party's candidate, Woodrow Wilson, running on a program he called "The New Freedom" advocating federal regulation of the economy, new legislation to improve working conditions, and strict measures to break up the trusts, won the election. President Wilson lowered the protective tariff, authorized a graduated income tax, established the Federal Trade Commission to prosecute companies accused of stifling competition, and enacted other progressive reforms. But despite his economic progressivism, socially he was a conservative. He dragged his feet on the crucial issue of women's suffrage, and he brought Jim Crow to Washington. In nearly all federal agencies and departments, lunchrooms, restrooms, and offices were officially segregated, and African American administrators were transferred or dismissed. Black people who had been working side by side with white people in federal offices suddenly found themselves shunted aside. Wilson believed that the separation of races was ordained by God. Instituting segregation as official federal policy, he said, was not "a movement *against* Negroes": "I sincerely believe it to be in their interest."[28] Wilson ignored the protests of the NAACP and Black leaders and even, to their dismay, praised the 1915 feature film *Birth of a Nation* (a shockingly racist glorification of the Ku Klux Klan) as a masterpiece. "Have you a 'new freedom' for white Americans," the civil rights activist William Monroe Trotter acidly asked him at a meeting in the White House, "and a new slavery for your African-American fellow citizens?"[29]

* * *

For the most part progressives, whether Republican or Democrat, believed in the American credo of equality, they sought to end exploitation and protect the victims of industrialism through governmental intervention. Most progressives were scientific in their approach to the problems created by industrial growth and many also brought a moral, Christian element to their campaigns. Whether they based their philosophy on Reform Darwinism or the Social Gospel, progressives were on a mission to reform society. Muckrakers attempted, with some success, to jolt Americans out of their apathy and push the government to do something about political corruption, poverty, and the unchecked greed of the moneyed interests. Women fought for, and won, the vote. Temperance advocates successfully persuaded the federal government to prohibit the sale of alcohol. African Americans embarked on a campaign to reverse the *Plessy v. Ferguson* "separate but equal" decision and formed the first influential civil rights organization.

At the same time, radicals felt a far more drastic approach was needed to overcome the evils of capitalism. Socialists such as Eugene V. Debs and anarchists such as Emma Goldman believed that the system was too corrupt to be reformed and that capitalism itself had to be overthrown and a new society created from its ashes. Although radicals did not get the new world they hoped for, they did push moderate reformers' goals to be more inclusive; and this, in effect, influenced moderates to achieve more than they perhaps would have without radical prodding. Furthermore, although never more than a minority movement, the radicals of the Progressive era did lay the basis for American radicalism of the twentieth century, especially during the 1930s and 1960s, when radical thought again came to the forefront.

3

War and Its Dissidents

The flag is most intimately connected with military achievement, military memory. It represents the country not in its
intensive life, but in its far-flung challenge to the world. The
flag is primarily the banner of war; it is allied with patriotic
anthem and holiday. . . . A nation's patriotic history is solely
the history of its wars, that is, of the State in its health and
glorious functioning. So in responding to the appeal of the
flag, we are responding to the appeal of the State, to the sym-
bol of the herd organized as an offensive and defensive body,
conscious of its prowess and its mystical herd strength.
—Randolph Bourne, "War Is the Health of the State," 1918

When Europeans enthusiastically marched off to war in the summer of
1914 after the assassination of Archduke Franz Ferdinand, most Americans reacted with disbelief. It seemed preposterous that modern nations
would go to war over outmoded notions of monarchy. At the outset
President Wilson announced that the United States would remain neutral, and he urged Americans to remain neutral even in their private
thoughts. Americans, for the most part, had no wish to get involved, and
certainly the knowledge that the Atlantic Ocean insulated the United
States from the European conflict assured Americans that we would not
get drawn in.

As the 1916 election approached, Wilson worried that the Republicans
might nominate the formidable Theodore Roosevelt. In order to solidify
the progressive vote, he began a calculated push to enact many of the
stalled bills that progressives had been advocating. For example, he got
Congress to pass the Keatings-Owen Child Labor Bill, which outlawed

interstate commerce in goods produced by children under the age of fourteen. He also got a Workmen's Compensation Bill passed as well as the Adamson Act, which established the eight-hour day for railway workers. These reforms had long been a part of the progressive agenda, but it was the looming election that finally induced politicians to support these measures. This illustrates one of the less dramatic, more modest ways that dissent brings about change. Dissenters are often a few steps ahead of their time and consequently are forced to wait for public opinion and political circumstances to catch up with them. Progressive activists such as Mother Jones, Florence Kelley, and Jane Addams had worked hard for years focusing public awareness on the need for such reforms, and now, within a few months and a few acts of Congress, change was rapidly coming to pass. Wilson's electoral strategy paid off. By promoting progressive legislation and campaigning to keep the country out of war, he won the votes of progressives, moderates, and anti-interventionists. The election was close, but Wilson was reelected.

Despite Wilson's campaign pledge to keep the U.S. out of the war, however, the president asked Congress for a declaration of war in April 1917 after German submarines resumed sinking American merchant ships that were supplying Britain with war matériel.

* * *

The war had an enormous impact on the home front, and that impact ushered in new attitudes about social relations, especially for women and African Americans, and it raised questions about the nature of American freedom and the meaning of democracy. All of this set in motion trends that fueled dissent and dominated political discourse for the rest of the century.

The large number of men entering the military created a labor shortage. This was a boon for workers, especially for minority groups that suffered discrimination. Millions of women landed better-paying jobs during the war as factory workers, agricultural workers, secretaries, nurses, and drivers. Some joined the army, mostly as nurses or secretaries. But as soon as the war was over, most jobs evaporated or were taken away from women and offered to returning veterans. Still, the war focused attention on women's rights and began to revolutionize the age-old assumptions about gender relationships and women's place in society.

African Americans too found that the war meant new opportunities. As the demand for workers increased in the all-important war-production industries, many companies sent agents into the Deep South to recruit Black sharecroppers. By 1918 a "Great Migration" was well under way as hundreds of thousands of African Americans left their homes, and the Jim Crow laws, for jobs in the industrial plants of Chicago, Detroit, Cleveland, and other northern cities. This Great Migration to the "Promised Land" lasted far beyond the war. Indeed, the flow of African Americans northward swelled during the 1920s and 1930s and well beyond into the post–World War II era.

Many African Americans took W. E. B. Du Bois's advice to "forget about special grievances and close our ranks shoulder to shoulder with our own fellow white citizens . . . that are fighting for democracy"[1] and enlisted in the army. Their hope was that they would be accepted more readily into American society if they proved themselves on the battlefield. Unfortunately, such acceptance did not happen. The 367,000 who entered the military found themselves segregated and shunted mostly into quartermaster and labor regiments where they worked to supply white troops and performed the least desirable tasks; 42,000 did serve in combat battalions, but most did not.

Despite the patriotic efforts of African Americans during the war, they continued to be faced with violent racism. There were forty-eight lynchings in 1917 and sixty-three in 1918, and these were *not* confined to the South. There were also race riots in several northern cities. In 1917 in East St. Louis, Illinois, dozens of Blacks were killed when employers brought in African American workers in an effort to break a union. Thousands of Blacks fervently protested against this outrage. They organized what they called a Silent Protest Parade, and on July 28, 1917, ten thousand African Americans marched down Fifth Avenue in New York City. "Mr. President," the signs they carried asked, "Why Not Make America Safe for Democracy?" White Americans were shocked at this bold display of insolence.

Shortly after the war in 1919, a major riot took place in Chicago. It was precipitated when whites drowned a Black teenager who had inadvertently crossed the invisible line segregating a Lake Michigan beach. The ensuing riot lasted for nearly a week and spread throughout the city. Five hundred people were injured and thirty-eight killed before the National Guard restored order. Lynchings and racial violence spread through all parts of the country well into the postwar period. In 1921 the worst of these disturbances took place when whites torched a Black neighborhood in the Greenwood section of Tulsa, Oklahoma. This was a prosperous African American business district frequently referred to as "Black Wall Street." When the rampage was over, more than three hundred African Americans had been murdered. It was clear that progress for African American citizens as well as the demographic impact of the Great Migration was stirring up deep-seated fears and intense resistance to change on the part of many white Americans.

Still, despite persistent racism and the savagery of white supremacist violence, for most African Americans the Great Migration offered hope and opportunity. Economically and psychologically those who went north were better off than those who stayed in the South. For many African Americans the opportunity to vote, to educate their children, and to be able to walk down a street without fear of being kidnapped or lynched was truly uplifting. By 1920 over half a million had moved north. Before the war 90 percent of America's Black population lived below the Mason-Dixon line. After the war that percentage had fallen to 80 percent. And over the next three decades the percentage dropped even further as ever-larger numbers of African Americans abandoned the South.

* * *

The war, of course, had its protesters. In fact, it was the most heavily pro-tested war in American history up to that time, and it prompted many citizens to examine the nature of patriotism and what it means to be an American. Hundreds of thousands spoke out against the war, against the draft, and against Wilson's efforts to suppress dissent. Right from the beginning Wilson knew that it would not be easy to unite public opinion behind the war. He was also well aware that roughly 20 percent of Americans had German roots and were not keen on going to war against Germany, just as most Irish Americans (also about 20 percent of the population) were not keen on fighting on Britain's side. If any-thing, both groups favored Germany. And so the president established the Committee on Public Information, headed by George Creel, to shape public opinion, stifle antiwar opposition, and convince Americans that the war was necessary in order to preserve American principles. Creel enlisted advertising men and academics, journalists and artists, to depict Germans as the enemies of freedom and democracy. "Four Minute Men" were hired to give "spontaneous," four-minute, prowar speeches on street corners and in theaters. Posters were widely distributed depicting Germans as ruthless barbarians, apes, and monsters. One poster showed a caricature of a fiendish German soldier impaling a Belgian baby on his bayonet. Other posters portrayed attractive young women being ravished and brutalized by Germans. The Kaiser was depicted as the "Beast of Berlin." Newspaper articles and short documentaries screened in movie theaters denounced Germans as a bloodthirsty race. By appeal-ing to and manipulating the unconscious fears and angst that Sigmund Freud's psychological studies had uncovered, the Committee on Public Information elevated propaganda to an art.

So many Americans got into the patriotic spirit that it became a sport to test other Americans whose patriotism was suspect to prove their loyalty. Flag-waving mobs frequently forced alleged German sympathiz-ers to march down the street repeatedly kissing the Stars and Stripes. Congress, in an attempt to promote patriotism and quash mounting antiwar dissent, approved the Espionage and Sedition Acts in 1917 and

1918, respectively. Along with prohibiting spying and surveillance, the Espionage Act also banned any attempt to interfere with the draft (demonstrating at a draft office, encouraging men to dodge the draft, or in any way aiding them in avoiding conscription or helping them desert), as well as making disparaging "false statements" about the military. Periodicals that were critical of the war or the government's policy in waging the war were banned from the mails. The Sedition Act prohibited any statements (printed or spoken) that could be construed as critical of the administration, the military, or the war. It condemned anyone who would "willfully utter, print, write, or publish any disloyal, profane, scurrilous, or abusive language about the form of government of the United States, or the Constitution of the United States, or the military or naval forces of the United States, or the flag of the United States . . . or shall willfully utter, print, write, or publish any language intended to incite, provoke, or encourage resistance to the United States, . . . or willfully advocate, teach, defend, or suggest the doing of any of the acts or things in this section enumerated."[2] In 1918 alone more than two thousand American citizens were arrested under the Sedition Act.

The Espionage and Sedition Acts reveal how deeply Washington saw dissent as a threat. Many protesters found that denouncing the war got them into a great deal of trouble. And they found that the civil liberties they believed were sacrosanct were not nearly as well protected as they assumed. Ordinary Americans, Quakers, intellectuals, radicals, many feminists, and some politicians spoke out adamantly against the war and just as adamantly against official efforts to stifle dissent. Some of these people were public figures, most were unknown, many were arrested.

During the Senate debate on the declaration of war, Senator Robert M. La Follette argued that the war was being foisted on the American people. "The espionage bills, the conscription bills, and other forcible military measures . . . is the complete proof that those responsible for this war fear that it has no popular support."[3] La Follette, however, was only one of six senators who voted against the declaration. As he was leaving the Senate chamber, someone handed him a coil of rope, presumably so he could save the country the cost of a trial for treason by hanging himself. Still, he was not intimidated, and he kept up his criticism against the war and against the administration's attempt to suppress antiwar dissent.

La Follette later delivered a blistering address in defense of free speech and dissent. "Since the declaration of war, the triumphant war press has pursued those Senators and Representatives who voted against war with malicious falsehood and recklessly libelous attacks, going to the extreme limit of charging them with treason against their country." Such attacks were also being directed at ordinary citizens in an attempt to coerce them into silence and acquiescence in an unjust war. "The mandate seems to have gone forth to the sovereign people of this country that they must be silent while those things are being done by their Government which most vitally concerns their well-being, their happiness, and their lives." This was deplorable. American citizens must not be "terrorized" in this way. He produced several affidavits of Americans being subjected to unlawful arrest merely for expressing opposition to the war. "Private residences," he declared, "are being invaded, loyal citizens of undoubted integrity and probity arrested, cross-examined, and the most sacred constitutional rights guaranteed to every American citizen are being violated." Of course, he conceded that citizens recognize that in time of war security measures are needed that might chip away at some civil liberties, but he emphasized, *the right to control their own Government . . . is not one of the rights that the citizens of this country are called upon to surrender in time of war*" (La Follette's emphasis). In wartime the American citizen "must be most watchful of the encroachment of the military upon the civil power. . . . More than all, the citizen and his representative in Congress in time of war must maintain his right of free speech. More than in times of peace it is necessary that the channels for free public discussion of governmental policies shall be open and unclogged." The most important right the American people enjoy is the right "to discuss in an orderly way, frankly and publicly and without fear, . . . every important phase of this war; its causes, and manner in which it should be conducted, and the terms upon which peace should be made." Any attempt to stifle free speech, public discussion of the war, or even criticism of the administration's policies, is "a blow at the most vital part of our Government."[4]

Many of those who dared to dissent did find themselves in considerable trouble with the law. In June 1918 Socialist Party leader Eugene V. Debs was arrested under the provisions of the Sedition Act for a scathing antiwar speech he gave in Canton, Ohio. "Wars throughout history," Debs reflected, "have been waged for conquest and plunder." When feudal lords in the Middle Ages sought to increase their domains, "they declared war upon one another. But they themselves did not go to war any more than the modern feudal lords, the barons of Wall Street go to war." It was the serfs, the peasants, who fought and died in the battles back then. "The poor, ignorant serfs had been taught . . . to believe that when their masters declared war upon one another, it was their patriotic duty to fall upon one another and to cut one another's throats for the profit and glory of the lords and barons who held them in contempt." This has not changed. Now, just as then, it is the master class that profits from war, the working class that dies in wars. "They have always taught and trained you to believe it to be your patriotic duty to go to war and to have yourselves slaughtered at their command. But in all the history of the world you, the people, have never had a voice in declaring war, and strange as it certainly appears, no war by any nation in any age has ever been declared by the people."[5]

The Great War, Debs insisted, is an imperialist war for the benefit of American businessmen and financiers—the Wall Street gentry—whom he likened to the Junkers, the autocratic Prussian ruling class that was the force behind German aggression. These "Wall Street Junkers" were lying about the war's goals when they say it is a war to make the world safe for American democracy. The war is really about profits, nothing else. They wrap themselves up in patriotism and intimidate the people by questioning the patriotism of anyone who does not wholeheartedly support the war. "These are the gentry who are today wrapped up in the American flag," Debs scoffed, who shout their claim from the housetops that they are the only patriots, and who have their magnifying glasses in hand, scanning the country for evidence of disloyalty, eager to apply the brand of treason to the men who dare to even whisper their opposition to Junker rule in the United Sates. No wonder Sam Johnson declared that "patriotism is the last refuge of the scoundrel." He must have had this Wall Street gentry in mind, or at least their prototypes, for in every age it has been the tyrant, the oppressor and the exploiter who has wrapped himself in the cloak of patriotism, or religion, or both to deceive and overawe the people.

These deceivers are the real traitors, Debs insisted, not those who criticize the war, not those who stand up for liberty and justice. Those are the real patriots.[6]

Shortly after Debs delivered this speech, he was arrested, tried, and sentenced to ten years in prison. Along with his prison term he was stripped of his American citizenship. "I have been accused of obstructing the war," Debs said when he was permitted to speak to the jury before sentencing. "I admit it. Gentlemen, I abhor war. I would oppose war if I stood alone."[7] But then he also confessed that he believed in the Constitution. "Isn't it strange that we Socialists stand almost alone today in upholding and defending the Constitution of the United States? The revolutionary fathers who had been oppressed under king rule understood that free speech and the right of free assemblage by the people were fundamental principles in democratic government. . . . I believe in the right of free speech, in war as well as peace."[8]

Debs served nearly three years of his sentence, and despite losing his American citizenship, he was nominated as the Socialist Party's candidate for president in 1920 and conducted his entire campaign from behind bars. During the three years he was in prison, thousands of Americans (even those who abhorred Debs's socialist views) sent letters and petitions to the president and Congress calling for Debs (as well as others who had been jailed for antiwar dissent) to be pardoned. "A government that will deliberately take away the inalienable rights of natural

FIGURE 3.1. The Socialist Party leader Eugene V. Debs leaving the federal penitentiary in Atlanta, Georgia, on Christmas Day 1921. He had been imprisoned in 1918 under the Sedition Act for giving a speech against participation in the First World War. President Warren G. Harding commuted his sentence to time served in December 1921. "While there is a lower class," Debs declared, "I am in it; while there is a criminal element, I am of it; while there is a soul in prison, I am not free!"
Credit: Photograph by Underwood & Underwood. Public domain; courtesy of Library of Congress.

born citizens," one woman wrote Wilson, "throttle free speech, institute espionage and intimidation systems, cannot be held in low enough contempt by its subjects."[9] Debs's views and imprisonment led to a vital and energetic national debate about the nature of free speech, the validity of the First Amendment, and how to balance national security needs with the fundamental rights guaranteed in the Bill of Rights—a debate that still rages in the United States. Attorney General A. Mitchell Palmer advised Wilson to commute Debs's sentence, but Wilson refused to do so. It was the new (Republican) president, Warren G. Harding, who released Debs from prison on Christmas morning 1921. Eventually, in 1976 (fifty years after Debs's death), Congress restored his citizenship.

Another prominent antiwar dissenter was Randolph Bourne. Bourne was a man of impressive intellect. An influential spokesman for his generation, he contributed articles to the *Atlantic*, the *New Republic*, the *Dial*, and *Seven Arts*, in which he encouraged the nation's youth to question conventional social roles, personal relationships, and American values. He also wrote essays criticizing corporate capitalism and condemning the Wilson administration's policy of suppressing dissent. His uncompromising opposition to America's entry into the Great War alienated so many of his contemporaries that he was fired from the *New Republic* and was put under surveillance by the Justice Department. Bourne could never accept President Wilson's conviction that the war would be the "war to end wars" or that it would "make the world safe for democracy," nor could he approve of the intellectuals who supported and condoned the war, especially those who wrote propaganda for Creel's Committee on Public Information. To Bourne, American participation in the war revealed that the United States, despite its deeply held belief in democracy, was no better than any nondemocratic nation.

Although Bourne's voice was silenced when he died at the age of thirty-two in the 1918 flu pandemic, his antiwar essays "War and the Intellectuals" and "War Is the Health of the State" remain two of the most articulate indictments of war—indictments that are applicable to any war. In these essays, especially the latter, Bourne analyzes the characteristics of the state, the psychology of a people at war, the nature of patriotism, and why it becomes necessary for the state to stifle dissent.

In "War and the Intellectuals" Bourne reproached the intellectuals and academics who supported the war or worked for the government or collaborated with the Creel committee in spreading prowar, anti-German propaganda. "The American intellectuals, in their preoccupation with reality," he wrote, "seem to have forgotten that the real enemy is War rather than imperial Germany." It is wrong to try to convince Americans, as Wilson has tried to do, that the war is "a holy crusade. What shall we do with leaders who tell us that we go to war in moral spotlessness or who make 'democracy' synonymous with a republican form of government? There is work to be done in still shouting that all the revolutionary by-products will not justify the war or make war anything else than the most noxious complex of all the evils that afflict men."[10]

But it is in Bourne's posthumous essay "War Is the Health of the State" that he offers the most profound analysis of the historical role and the psychological basis of war. Bourne is writing about the Great War, but his conclusions can be applied to all wars. "Wartime brings the ideal of the State out into very clear relief," Bourne observed, "and reveals attitudes and tendencies that were hidden. In times of peace the sense of the State flags in a republic that is not militarized. For war is essentially the health of the State. The ideal of the State is that within its territory its power and influence should be universal. As the Church is the medium for the spiritual salvation of man, so the State is thought of as the medium for his political salvation." When a state goes to war, it gathers power and energy from the people's urgent need to feel protected, to feel one with the state. Bourne's definition of the state is that it "is the organization of the herd to act offensively or defensively against another herd similarly organized. The more terrifying the occasion for defense, the closer will become the organization and the more coercive the influence upon each member of the herd. War sends the current of purpose and activity flowing down to the lowest level of the herd."[11] During peacetime people go about their lives without a sense of their connection to the state, but war awakens them to this connection, arouses their sense of loyalty, and makes them feel empowered.

The people do not, however, have power. Citizens in a democracy believe they have a voice in the operation of their government, but they have had no say whatsoever in the policies that have led to war. Those policies are exclusively in the domain of the executive branch of government. When it comes to foreign policy, "the Government, with no mandate from the people, without consultation of the people, conducts all the negotiations, the backing and filling, the menaces and explanations, which slowly bring it into collision with some other Government, and gently and irresistibly slides the country into war." The executive officer of a nation (whether president, prime minister, chancellor, or king) convincingly puts forward moral reasons for the necessity of war: that the enemy is evil or that going to war will create a better future. Such arguments win over the people and their representatives. "The result is that, even in those countries where the business of declaring war is theoretically in the hands of representatives of the people, no legislature has ever been known to decline the request of an Executive, which has conducted all foreign affairs in utter privacy and irresponsibility, that it order the nation into battle." It is clear to Bourne that "all foreign policy, the diplomatic negotiations which produce or forestall war, are equally the private property of the Executive part of the Government, and are equally exposed to no check whatever from popular bodies, or the people voting as a mass themselves." Even when people realize this, something magical happens when war is declared. Suddenly, in a wave of patriotic fervor, "the mass of the people," even the intellectual classes, "through some spiritual alchemy, become convinced that they have willed and executed the deed themselves. They then, with the exception of a few malcontents, proceed to allow themselves to be regimented, coerced, . . . and turned into a solid manufactory of destruction toward" the enemy.[12]

War is the health of the state because it "automatically sets in motion throughout society those irresistible forces for uniformity, for passionate cooperation with the Government in coercing into obedience the minority groups and individuals which lack the larger herd sense. The machinery of government sets and enforces the drastic penalties; the minorities are either intimidated into silence, or brought slowly around by a subtle process of persuasion which may seem to them really to be converting them." At this stage inevitably "minorities are rendered sullen, and some intellectual opinion bitter and satirical. But in general, the nation in wartime attains a uniformity of feeling, a hierarchy of values culminating at the undisputed apex of the State ideal, which could not possibly be produced through any other agency than war. . . . Loyalty—or mystic devotion to the State—becomes the major imagined human value."[13] Any critical thinking, any questioning of the meaning of loyalty, is considered treason.

Bourne analyzes the "filial mysticism" that the citizenry invests in the state. When a people go to war, there is a deep-seated need for security. People want protection. And just as they looked to their fathers and mothers for protection when they were children, in wartime they look to the state for protection. Thus the state is strengthened.

> It is not for nothing that one's State is still thought of as Father or Motherland, that one's relation towards it is conceived in terms of family affection. The war has shown that nowhere under the shock of danger have these primitive childlike attitudes failed to assert themselves again, as much in this country as anywhere. If we have not the intense Father-sense of the German who worships his Vaterland, at least in Uncle Sam we have a symbol of protecting, kindly authority, and in the many Mother-posters of the Red Cross, we see how easily in the more tender functions of war service, the ruling organization is conceived in family terms. A people at war have become in the most literal sense obedient, respectful, trustful children again, full of that naïve faith in the all-wisdom and all-power of the adult who takes care of them, imposes his mild but necessary rule upon them and in whom they lose their responsibility and anxieties. In this recrudescence of the child, there is great comfort, and a certain influx of power.[14]

And so the State is our protector, and any criticism, any dissent, is reviled and treated as treason. "In this great herd-machinery, dissent is like sand in the bearings." People seek unanimity of opinion. When everyone is pulling together, there is a deeper sense of security. Unity means security. "Any interference with that unity turns the whole vast impulse towards crushing it. Dissent is speedily outlawed, and the Government, backed by the significant classes and those who . . . identify themselves with them, proceeds against the outlaws. . . . The herd becomes divided into the hunters and the hunted, and war-enterprise becomes not only a technical game but a sport as well."[15]

Much of Bourne's writings speak directly to the Committee on Public Information's propaganda work and the laws restricting freedom of speech and press. Bourne himself, had he not died in December 1918, might very well have been imprisoned, as Debs was, under the Sedition Act. "War Is the Health of the State" is one of the most eloquent and intelligent analyses of the relationship between the citizen and the state. Along with Thoreau's "Resistance to Civil Government" and Martin Luther King, Jr.'s "Letter from Birmingham Jail," it is indispensable reading for dissenters or anyone interested in dissent.

Hundreds of thousands of ordinary Americans, workers, immigrants, political radicals, feminists, and middle-class citizens protested in a variety of ways against U.S. involvement in the Great War and against the efforts on the part of the government to suppress dissent by restricting free speech. In Minnesota thousands of farmers attended public gatherings organized by socialists to protest the war and the draft. In Wisconsin thousands also participated in antiwar/antidraft demonstrations. There were antiwar parades in Boston in the summer of 1917. In local elections that year, antiwar socialist candidates made a remarkably good showing—in New York State, for example, ten socialists were elected to the state assembly, and the socialist mayoral candidate in New York City received 22 percent of the vote.

Americans protested against the war even though they risked imprisonment under the provisions of the Espionage and Sedition Acts. One citizen was sent to jail when she proclaimed that "the government is for the profiteers," and another was arrested for calling President Wilson "a wooden-headed son of a bitch."[16] A socialist printer in Philadelphia, Charles Schenck, was sentenced to six months in prison for printing and distributing antiwar and antidraft leaflets. Sixty-five thousand Americans refused to serve in the armed forces on the grounds that they were conscientious objectors, while thousands more refused to register for the draft. In South Dakota Fred Fairchild was imprisoned for a year after publicly proclaiming that if drafted, he would not serve. "They could shoot me, but they could not make me fight," he said.[17] Underscoring

Bourne's observation that in order to stifle dissent, "the herd becomes divided into the hunters and the hunted," more than one hundred thousand Americans joined the vigilante American Protective League (APL) to root out "slackers" and subversives and anyone who criticized the war or the president or refused to buy liberty bonds. They intercepted people's mail and tapped their telephones. APL vigilantes proudly claimed that they had uncovered three million disloyal Americans. Sometimes speaking out proved deadly. The IWW labor organizer Frank Little gave a fiery antiwar speech urging American workers to resist the draft and fight the capitalists, not the Germans. Shortly afterward six masked men dragged him from his home in Butte, Montana, tortured him, and hanged him from a railroad trestle. They fastened a sign to his body proclaiming, "Agitator Called Our Troops 'Scabs in Uniform' and Denounced American Government."[18] The murderers were never caught.

* * *

After the war Americans faced an uncertain future. Many believed that getting involved in the war was a disaster. The United States had not heeded George Washington's admonition to stay out of European affairs. The lesson was clear—the United States must remain neutral, must stay within the confines of the Western Hemisphere. The United States did not ratify the Versailles Treaty, nor did it join the League of Nations— dashing Wilson's naïve vision that the war would prove to be the war to end all wars. The Bolshevik Revolution raised the specter of revolution in the United States; the fear that communism might spread to these shores frightened millions of Americans, yet at the same time the Russian Revolution, with its vision of a working-class utopia, also inspired many American workers to join the struggle for better wages and working conditions. As a result, in 1919 a wave of labor unrest coupled with a frightening Red Scare swept over the country. Americans soon discovered that it was not going to be easy to return to the old prewar days.

Wilson's idealistic comments about fighting for political and economic freedom gave American workers the misleading impression that the president would actively support workers' rights, but he did not. In January 1919 shipyard workers walked off their jobs in Seattle. This precipitated a general strike of one hundred thousand workers. By February the city had ground to a halt. Committees of strikers kept some essential city services running, but most had stopped. The strike finally ended when the mayor called in federal troops. Strikes spread around the country in a variety of industries. There were strikes of textile workers, telephone operators, policemen, coal miners, and even actors. In some labor disputes the conservative American Federation of Labor, despite its fear of radicalism, combined with the socialist Industrial Workers of the World in an uneasy alliance.

The most momentous of the strikes was the steel strike that started in Chicago in September and spread to Pittsburgh. Workers demanded an eight-hour day, increased wages, and union recognition. More than three hundred thousand steelworkers, many of them immigrants, participated in the strike. The owners countered by manipulating and inflaming native-born steelworkers' anti-immigrant prejudice, which helped management break the strike.

Approximately four million workers participated in a total of four thousand strikes in 1919. Labor unrest unsettled the public, and just as in the period after the Haymarket affair, middle-class Americans equated unionism with radicalism, anarchism, socialism, and communism. To be sure, the radical IWW participated in the strikes, but most workers only demanded better wages and hours, not socialism. They simply wanted to reform the system, not overthrow it. Still, the strikes exacerbated the fear of communism.

And then came a wave of terrorist attacks. A few months after the mayor of Seattle had called for federal troops to crush the general strike, a package containing a bomb was sent to his residence. (It was discovered before it exploded.) Radicals targeted other politicians and public figures. An anarchist planted a bomb on the doorstep of Attorney General A. Mitchell Palmer in Washington, DC. (Unfortunately for the bomber, the only person he killed was himself when the bomb exploded prematurely.) Anarchists also attempted to assassinate John D. Rockefeller and Supreme Court Justice Oliver Wendell Holmes, Jr.

The nation was jolted. Americans, unaware that there was little connection between communists and the anarchists responsible for the bombings, believed that violent radicals were the vanguard of a worldwide communist conspiracy to topple the United States. Attorney General Palmer formed the General Intelligence Division within the Department of Justice and appointed the young J. Edgar Hoover as its director. Starting in November Palmer seized the opportunity to combat the left and authorized hundreds of raids against suspected radicals. In multiple cities around the country, Palmer's agents illegally broke into people's homes in the middle of the night and arrested them. Palmer targeted socialists, anarchists, communists, and immigrants from eastern Europe and Russia. One of the attorney general's goals was to destroy the anarchist immigrant group, the Union of Russian Workers; another was to destroy the socialist IWW. Both goals were accomplished. Thousands of leftists, usually beaten up in the process, were arrested. On a single night in January 1920, more than four thousand suspected "reds" were arrested in coordinated raids in thirty-three American cites. Socialists who had been elected to state office were expelled from their seats. More than 250 radical aliens, including Emma Goldman, were deported. The Palmer Raids also fanned the flames of intolerance as many Americans eagerly joined in the "red hunt." Vigilante bands singled out "radical terrorists," harassed them, beat them, and in a few cases, lynched them. Patriotic organizations sprouted in the fertile soil of the anticommunist crusade (among them the United States Flag Organization and the American Legion), dedicated to promoting the "American way" and ferreting out subversives.

Of course, not all Americans succumbed to the hysteria. Many liberals, intellectuals, and legal scholars, as well as ordinary people, protested against the abuses of civil liberties and the outrageous assault on the Bill of Rights. Alarmed at this attack on the Constitution, Crystal Eastman and Roger Baldwin founded the American Civil Liberties Union in 1920 "to defend and preserve the individual rights and liberties guaranteed to every person in this country by the Constitution and laws of the United States."[19] By the spring of that year, it was transparently clear to increasing numbers of people that the Palmer Raids were a serious abuse of civil liberties. Palmer's zeal (and the fact that he had one eye on the 1920 presidential nomination) led him to overstep so many bounds that the Red Scare finally imploded. Assistant Secretary of State Louis Post became critical of Palmer and insisted that legal rights must be provided for the detainees, and over the remainder of the year most of the six thousand who were arrested were released. Attorney General Palmer also lost credibility when he falsely claimed that radical terrorists were planning a massive uprising on May 1, 1920. He put police forces around the nation on high alert, but nothing happened.

The Red Scare had peaked. Still, despite the fact that the sweeping arrests came to an end, the scare persisted, as two Italian immigrants, Nicola Sacco and Bartolomeo Vanzetti, were about to experience. In April 1920 a security guard and a paymaster were killed during a holdup at a South Braintree, Massachusetts, shoe factory. Soon thereafter Sacco and Vanzetti were arrested for the crime. It was obvious to most observers that the men were accused of the crime because they were anarchists and because they were immigrants. Both men were associated with the followers of the Italian anarchist Luigi Galleani, who was suspected of being involved with the bombing of the attorney general's residence in June 1919, and both had avoided the draft during the war, facts that further doomed them in the eyes of the public.

The trial was a farce. No real evidence was offered as to their guilt, witnesses changed their testimony, while others verified the defendants' alibis. The biased judge referred to them as "those anarchist bastards" and instructed the jury that although Vanzetti "may not have actually committed the crime attributed to him, [he] is nevertheless culpable, because he is the enemy of our existing institutions."[20] Throughout the proceedings it was apparent that the two men were being railroaded because of their political beliefs and their nationality. They were convicted and sentenced to the electric chair. For the next seven years, as their lawyers appealed the case, a worldwide campaign for their release was waged. Liberals, intellectuals, lawyers, and writers in the United States and Europe, including Dorothy Parker, John Dos Passos, H. G. Wells, and George Bernard Shaw, protested the verdict and called for a new trial. As the appeals process wound down, tens of thousands of protesters around the world participated in massive demonstrations and vigils against the impending executions. "I have had to suffer," Vanzetti said before their execution, "for things that I am guilty of. I am suffering because I am a radical, and indeed I am a radical; I have suffered because I am an Italian, and indeed I am an Italian."[21]

* * *

When the United States emerged from the Great War, it was on the verge of becoming a global power. The U.S. was the world's largest creditor, American heavy industries were dominating world markets, and American diplomats had an important influence on shaping the peace. And yet the experience of the war turned Americans inward and fostered the desire to find security in isolation from the world. It was as though the United States was rejecting the invitation to become a major player on the world's stage. The American reaction to the Bolshevik Revolution further underscored the fear of engagement with the world. The Red Scare and the Sacco and Vanzetti case foreshadowed one of the most toxic trends of the next decade: intolerance.

During World War I thousands of Americans found the courage to protest, and they found many ways to do so. Some refused to register for the draft. Some left the country. Some formed the American Civil Liberties Union to guard against infractions of the Bill of Rights. Some went to prison. Some gave speeches. Some wrote essays. The legacy of these protesters ensured that dissent was more deeply embedded than ever in the American consciousness. For the rest of the twentieth century, American dissenters continued to draw inspiration from the protesters of 1917–1920.

4

Culture Wars in the Jazz Age

No woman can call herself free who does not own and control her body. No woman can call herself free until she can choose consciously whether she will or will not be a mother.
—Margaret Sanger, 1920

Despite the booming economy of the 1920s, disillusion, insecurity, and uncertainty began to eat away at the nation's psyche. The war had been a terrible shock. How could God have let it happen? The experience of the war—the carnage, the devastation, the surfacing of such inhumane brutality—was a profound challenge to traditional values. The belief in God, the belief in progress, even the belief in science all came under attack. Darwin's theory of evolution had laid bare the animal origins of humans, Nietzsche's famous dictum that "God is dead" struck at the heart of religious faith, Freud's analysis of the tremendous hold the unconscious mind has on human behavior undermined the belief in human reason and rationality, and Einstein's theory of relativity and Heisenberg's uncertainty principle showed that science itself was open to question. All this buttressed the existential philosophers' view that there is no teleological meaning to life. In the 1920s it seemed that there was no certainty, no security, nothing to hold onto. Many Americans willingly embraced these modern ideas, but many others were aghast and steadfastly strove to return to a bygone, simpler era, when belief was not challenged. It is this conflict between a world of accelerating technological advances, automation, consumerism, changing social and gender relationships, and revolutionary philosophies challenging the existence of God on one side and the deeply entrenched conservatism that resisted the new trends that defined the decade on the other side. The Roaring Twenties, dubbed "the Jazz Age" by writer F. Scott Fitzgerald, was characterized by this clash between traditionalism and modernism. It was an age of bifurcation. Dissent was everywhere. Liberal dissenters denounced the forces of reaction, while conservative dissenters denounced the forces that were taking the United States in a direction they did not want to go.

Warren G. Harding, the new president, promised to return the country to normalcy. But normalcy was irretrievably in the past. While Europe was struggling to rebuild, the United States was experiencing an astounding rate of economic growth. Business expanded, exports rose, unemployment declined, wages increased, and Americans had a voracious appetite for new consumer products. Automobiles, aviation, advertising, radio broadcasting, and the cinema all boomed in the 1920s, while Americans filled jazz clubs to listen to African American music and dance halls to dance the trendy Charleston. And although the Eighteenth Amendment prohibited the sale of alcohol, rural bootleggers as well as urban crime bosses such as Al Capone provided booze illegally to anyone who wanted it. Americans flocked in huge numbers to speakeasies, where they consumed vast quantities of bootleg liquor. The one good thing about Prohibition, humorist Will Rogers reportedly quipped, was that it was better than no alcohol at all.

* * *

After more than a century of protest, women found their horizons expanding. In most respects women's position in society and especially in the family did not change drastically, but employment opportunities were opening up, and the "new woman" was beginning to emerge.

Socially, women's role *did* change. After gaining the right to vote, many young women rejected the old Victorian ways of thinking and acting and dressing and adopted a new, confrontational style. They discarded the restricting clothing their mothers had worn—the Victorian dresses that covered all parts of the body—in favor of knee-length, close-fitting, seductively suggestive dresses. Underscoring women's equality with men, they sought ways to present a more boyish figure, wore undergarments to flatten breasts, bobbed their hair short, and copied behaviors that were traditionally reserved for males. They smoked in public (a behavior that before the war would have horrified most people) and went to dance halls and speakeasies where they danced wildly, flirted openly, spoke candidly about sex, and acted in ways aimed at highlighting their liberation.

Despite all the looseness and apparent independence, women's freedom was somewhat illusory. Although large numbers of women, especially in cities such as New York, were employed, they were not earning enough to support themselves. Whether they worked low-paying menial and service jobs—as secretaries, sales clerks, telephone operators—or competed with men for teaching jobs or managerial work, they did not receive equal wages. In banks, business offices, department stores, law firms, and schools, women worked side by side with men but were paid at a much lower rate. When women protested, they were told that men received more because they had families to support.

The upshot was that despite women's earnings, they were not self-sufficient. They were still dependent on men. Married women depended on their husband's income. Single women usually lived at home, where they did not have to pay rent. It was clear, as the English writer Virginia Woolf put it in *A Room of One's Own*, that women would never be completely emancipated until they were economically independent of men. Until they could afford to support themselves, until they could afford a room of their own, women would never be free. Women had been jubilant when the Nineteenth Amendment was ratified, but their experience in the 1920s revealed that the right to vote was not enough to ensure equality. Feminists, led by Alice Paul, introduced the Equal Rights Amendment in 1923, designed to guarantee full equality under the law. It was a straightforward statement—"Equality of rights under the law shall not be denied or abridged by the United States or by any state on account of sex"—but it was voted down. Lawmakers continued to introduce the amendment for decades, but Congress showed little interest in passing it until the 1970s.[1]

One of the leading activists of the era was Margaret Sanger. A committed feminist, Sanger was especially concerned with reproductive rights and the legal restrictions on birth control that posed a life-threatening danger, especially for poor immigrant women. In 1912, she began writing a column in the socialist *New York Call*, "What Every Girl Should Know," seeking to educate women on matters of sexual health. She also worked in a women's health clinic on the Lower East Side, where she was exposed to poor women seeking medical aid for botched abortions. Most of the patients sought advice on how to avoid pregnancy, but federal law prohibited the dissemination of birth-control information. The Comstock Law (1873), for example, forbade sending birth-control information through the mail, while other laws stipulated that even members of the medical profession were not allowed to give verbal advice to patients about birth control. One day, Sanger later recalled, an immigrant woman named Sadie Sachs came into the clinic to receive treatment for a hemorrhage resulting from an illegal abortion. When she was about to be released, she implored the physician in charge to tell her how to avoid becoming pregnant. They were a poor family, she said, but as soon as she would return home, her husband would want to have sex, and they simply could not afford another mouth to feed. The doctor flippantly replied that Sachs should tell her husband "to sleep on the roof."[2] Sanger was taken aback but kept silent. Several months later Sadie Sachs returned to the clinic after another bungled back-alley abortion. This time, however, she died, and Margaret Sanger vowed that she would never again remain silent.

In 1914 Sanger began publishing a radical feminist magazine, the *Woman Rebel*, for the sole purpose of advancing women's rights, especially reproductive rights. Each issue provided explicit information on birth control and contained articles proclaiming women's right to control their own bodies. Within a few months Sanger was arrested for violating the Comstock Law, but charges against her were eventually dropped, and

FIGURE 4.1. The activist, socialist, and feminist Margaret Sanger, December 31, 1921. "No woman can call herself free who does not own and control her body. No woman can call herself free until she can choose consciously whether she will or will not be a mother."
Credit: Photograph by Underwood & Underwood. Public domain; courtesy of Library of Congress.

in 1916 she opened a birth-control clinic in Brooklyn. She was arrested again and this time spent a month in jail. By the time Sanger founded the American Birth Control League in 1921, she and her supporters had enough influence that Congress passed a law that permitted *a physician* to offer birth-control advice if medical reasons warranted. This was only a partial victory, but Sanger was astute enough to capitalize on it and make it work even better for the cause. In 1923 she opened a clinic staffed with female doctors and eventually set up clinics in other cities throughout the country where birth control became available to anyone who wanted it. In 1939 Sanger founded the Birth Control Federation of America, the forerunner of the Planned Parenthood Federation of America, and before her death in 1966 she was instrumental in the research and development of the birth-control pill. Although she embraced controversial views about eugenics that have been rightly criticized, Sanger was America's most successful proponent of reproductive rights.

For Sanger birth control was a vital feminist issue. The right to vote was not enough. Women, she believed, would never be free until they had control over their own bodies. If they did not, their lives would continue to be dictated by men. When would a woman have time to pursue her own educational and creative goals if she was perpetually pregnant and forced into the role of caring for one child after another? If that was what a woman wanted, that was fine—as long as it was the path she chose. But if it was not what she wanted, then she *must* be free to choose the path she envisions. The only way to achieve this is to have complete reproductive control. Sanger was not in favor of abortion per se. She argued that if birth control was available to the public, then the abortion rate would fall drastically. Contraception was a way to avoid abortion. There have always been ways for educated and upper-class women to gain access to contraceptives, because of their privileged position in society. But the poor and immigrants did not know how to acquire the information, and as a result "women of the impoverished strata of society" are forced to "violate those laws of their inner beings which tell them not to bring children into the world to live in want, disease and general misery. They break the first law of nature, which is that of self preservation. Bound by false morals, enchained by false conceptions of religion, hindered by false laws, they endure until the pressure becomes so great that morals, religion and laws alike fail to restrain them. Then they for a brief respite resort to the surgeon's instruments."[3]

Women must protest. They must "assert themselves upon this fundamental right. . . . These laws were made by men and have been instruments of martyrdom and death for unnumbered thousands of women. Women now have the opportunity to sweep them into the trash heap." It is only by making birth control available that motherhood can become the fulfilling experience it should be. "When motherhood becomes the fruit of a deep yearning, not the result of ignorance or accident," Sanger wrote optimistically in 1920, "its children will become the foundation of a new race. There will be no killing of babies in the womb by abortion, nor through neglect in foundling homes, nor will there be infanticide. Neither will children die by inches in mills and factories. No man will dare to break a child's life upon the wheel of toil."[4]

Along with birth control women activists also continued to push the federal government for anti-child-labor legislation, safer workplaces, and an eight-hour day. Additionally, with the suffering wrought by the Great War still foremost in people's minds, thousands of American women joined pacifist organizations, notably the Women's International League for Peace and Freedom (WILPF). Under the leadership of Jane Addams and Carrie Chapman Catt the crux of its campaign was to lobby Congress to apply for U.S. membership in the League of Nations. The WILPF was actively opposed to the National Defense Act of 1920, which provided for the maintenance of a standing army of 280,000 men. The way to prevent war, the WILPF maintained, was not through military preparedness but through being involved in global diplomacy, nipping disputes in the bud before they became international crises, and through complete disarmament. Because of its antiwar position the WILPF was accused by right-wing critics of being a communist-run front. Some conservatives even came up with a color-coded radicalism chart showing how "red" the individual members of the WILPF were. Henry Ford joined in the red-baiting by publishing the "Spider Web Chart" in the *Dearborn Independent* in 1924, purportedly exposing the web-like connections between the WILPF and various communist and socialist organizations.

As a result of these attacks, the WILPF failed in its campaign to convince the United States to join the League of Nations, but its influence was considerable—considerable enough that Secretary of State Frank B. Kellogg signed (even though he regarded it as meaningless) the Kellogg-Briand Pact renouncing war as an instrument of international relations.

* * *

Women, of course, were not the only activists in the Roaring Twenties. Americans from all classes and political persuasions energetically spoke out for causes they deemed vital for the public good. Dissenters of the left—women and men, Blacks and whites—protested racism, rampant consumerism, and the business-as-usual attitudes that permeated the nation in the aftermath of the Great War, while dissenters of the right protested the rapid societal changes they deemed too radical. Conservatives, for example, appalled at what they considered the libertine behavior of the "new woman," regularly harassed and ostracized women who adopted the flapper lifestyle.

One influential way that dissent against American materialism was expressed was through literature. H. L. Mencken, Ernest Hemingway, F. Scott Fitzgerald, Gertrude Stein, Sinclair Lewis, John Dos Passos, Eugene O'Neill, and other notable writers were disheartened by Americans' obsession with accumulating money. From blistering satires and parodies to more subtle commentaries and poignant stories about what it means to be an American, these writers voiced their disillusionment with the United States. Some, such as Stein and Hemingway, were so disillusioned that they moved to Paris. Creative artists, these expatriates believed, were nurtured and valued in Europe, whereas the crass, stultifying materialism of the United States crushed the human spirit and poisoned creativity. Hemingway in *The Sun Also Rises* and *A Farewell to Arms* portrayed characters wrecked by the meaningless horrors of war and the vagaries of life; F. Scott Fitzgerald in *The Great Gatsby* described people caught up in soul-destroying materialism. The heroes of so many of the "Lost Generation's" novels had grown up, as Fitzgerald put it in *This Side of Paradise*, "to find all Gods dead, all wars fought, all faiths in man shaken."[5]

One of the most popular writers of the decade was Sinclair Lewis, who specialized in novels satirizing small-town middle-class America and chamber of commerce "boosterism." Two of his most successful novels, *Main Street* and *Babbitt*, were exposés of the smug provincialism that permeated the United States. Lewis's characters were utterly conventional and banal; they were self-righteous bigots who strove only for material goods, spoke in clichés and platitudes, and never came up with an original thought. Many Americans saw themselves in the pages of Lewis's novels but, to Lewis's dismay, missed the sarcasm and did not realize they were being parodied.

Even more scathing in ridiculing middle-class American values was the journalist H. L. Mencken. Mencken was the ultimate curmudgeon. He took on nearly every aspect of the status quo and did so with scurrilous, outrageous humor (that bordered on libel) but equally remarkable perceptiveness. The only things Mencken valued were free speech and critical thinking because "the most dangerous man, to any government is the man who is able to think things out for himself, without regard to the prevailing superstitions and taboos. Almost inevitably he comes to the conclusion that the government he lives under is dishonest, insane and intolerable."[6] Everything about America—Democrats, Republicans, socialists, politicians, the common man, women, Victorian morality, democracy, religion, prohibition—were targets of his ridicule. However, as Mencken himself observed, "it is inaccurate to say that I hate everything. I am strongly in favor of common sense, common honesty, and common decency. This makes me forever ineligible for public office."[7]

In the magazine Mencken founded, the *American Mercury*, and in thousands of newspaper articles, he described Americans as unsophisticated, uncultured idiots. Americans never looked deeper than the surface. They were the most gullible people in the world, blindly believing everything politicians and advertisers told them. Labeling them the "booboisie," Mencken frequently declared that no one ever lost money betting on the stupidity of the American people.

As for democracy, which Mencken defined as the "pathetic belief in the collective wisdom of individual ignorance,"[8] he admitted that at least it is "the most charming form of government ever devised by man" and should not be dismissed out of hand. Still, it is important to keep in mind that democracy "is based upon propositions that are palpably not true and what is not true, as everyone knows, is always immensely more fascinating and satisfying to the vast majority of men than what is true." The average American believes in democracy, Mencken wrote, because he

> gets a feeling that he is really important to the world—that he is genuinely running things. Out of his maudlin herding after rogues and mounte-banks there comes to him a sense of vast and mysterious power—which is what makes archbishops, police sergeants, the grand goblins of the Ku Klux and other such magnificoes happy. And out of it there comes, too, a conviction that he is somehow wise, that his views are taken seriously by his betters—which is what makes United States Senators, fortune tellers and Young Intellectuals happy. Finally, there comes out of it a glowing consciousness of a high duty triumphantly done which is what makes hangmen and husbands happy.

But Mencken gets more serious when he attacks what he considers a most dangerous tendency in a democracy—during times of a national crisis, when a democracy's natural instinct is to stifle dissent. Democracy is "a self-limiting disease," Mencken contends, but even worse it is "self-devouring":

> One cannot observe it objectively without being impressed by its curi-ous distrust of itself—its apparently ineradicable tendency to abandon its whole philosophy at the first sign of strain. I need not point to what

happens invariably in democratic states when the national safety is men-
aced. All the great tribunes of democracy, on such occasions, convert
themselves, by a process as simple as taking a deep breath, into despots
of an almost fabulous ferocity. Lincoln, Roosevelt and Wilson come instantly to mind. . . . Democracy always seems bent upon killing the thing
it theoretically loves. . . . I offer the spectacle of Americans jailed for reading the Bill of Rights. . . . Try to imagine monarchy jailing subjects for
maintaining the divine right of Kings! Or Christianity damning a believer
for arguing that Jesus Christ was the Son of God![9]

* * *

African American writers and intellectuals joined the chorus of
voices that increasingly criticized American society and values. And,
of course, they brought a racial perspective to the discourse. Marcus
Garvey, a Jamaican émigré who came to the United States in 1916, had
a vital impact on getting African Americans to rethink how to deal
with the dilemma of being Black in America. Garvey was the founder
of the United Negro Improvement Association (UNIA), and from his
headquarters in Harlem he urged Blacks, all over the world, to join the
association and form a powerful bloc to fight against oppression and
racism. In rousing speeches Garvey claimed that the time had come for
Blacks to take charge of their own destiny. Whites would never willingly grant equality to Blacks; therefore Blacks *must* take charge of their
own lives. America was a white man's country, Garvey declared, and
would never fully accept Blacks. He urged African Americans not to
cooperate with whites and not to strive for integration but instead to
demand power to regulate their own communities. Garvey coined the
phrase "black power" and advocated a "back to Africa" movement. He
also coined the phrase "black is beautiful," exhorting Blacks to be proud
of their innate beauty and the uniqueness of Africanness. They should
forgo any effort to blend into white society; they should not adopt
white clothing and hairstyles and mannerisms but should emphasize
their African heritage. "No Negro," Garvey said, "let him be American,

European, West Indian or African, shall be truly respected until his race as a whole has emancipated itself, through self-achievement and progress, from universal prejudice." It was essential that Blacks create their own culture and literature, their own society and government. Only then would whites take them seriously. "Until then, we are but wards of a superior race and civilization, and the outcasts of a standard social system."[10]

Garvey designed a red, green, and white flag to symbolize the Pan-Africa movement, composed a national anthem, and sold shares in a steamship company (the Black Star Line—a wordplay on Britain's White Star Line) that would build ships to take American Blacks to Africa. African Americans, however, were not interested in moving to Africa, the Black Star Line did not build any ships, and Garvey's business venture failed. Although his ways of raising money were extremely controversial (notable African Americans such as W. E. B. Du Bois and A. Philip Randolph accused him of trying to defraud poor Blacks), and although he was convicted of mail fraud and deported back to Jamaica, Garvey had an important impact on racial politics in the United States. Most of his followers, and there were hundreds of thousands of them, were heartened by his message, and "Garveyism" helped deepen a sense of pride and solidarity in the Black community and was an influence on the Civil Rights Movement that emerged after World War II. "We were created equal," Garvey repeatedly told his audiences, "and were put into this world to possess equal rights and equal privileges, and the time has come for the black man to get his share."[11] Garvey's wife, Amy Jacques Garvey, even before she married him, was a committed civil rights activist. She traveled thousands of miles around the United States delivering speeches that advanced the UNIA message and edited a page in the Negro World devoted to articles about the status of Black women in America and worldwide.

Other esteemed African Americans had a different vision. A. Philip Randolph and Chandler Owen believed that socialism was the answer. It was the only political system that could overcome capitalist exploitation and had the potential to create an egalitarian society free of racism. The two men published a radical magazine, the *Messenger*, urging Blacks to join unions and convert to socialism if they wanted to gain economic, social, and political equality. In 1925 Randolph founded the Brotherhood of Sleeping Car Porters to represent the interests of the thousands of porters—most of whom were Black—who worked on the nation's passenger trains. Randolph successfully negotiated with the Pullman Company to gain recognition for the union and improvements in wages and job security for its members.

Just as important as the efforts of Black activists seeking political and economic remedies for racism was the impact of the Harlem Renaissance. As hundreds of thousands of African Americans moved north during the Great Migration, many creative writers, musicians, and artists gravitated toward New York's Harlem. Writers such as Langston Hughes, Zora Neale Hurston, Jean Toomer, and Claude McKay wrote novels and poetry, short stories and plays, expressing what it means to be Black in a racist society. Like the expatriate writers of the Lost Generation, the Harlem Renaissance writers articulated their discontent through critically acclaimed literature that not only offered a discerning commentary on American life but also persuaded white America that Black America had something of profound significance to offer. As their books reached a wide audience, many of the stereotypes and assumptions that whites had about Blacks were shattered. African Americans were not submitting to racism; they were proud, they were forceful, and they were not afraid to fight back. "If we must die," McKay wrote, "let it not be like hogs / Hunted and penned in an inglorious spot. . . . / Like men we'll face the murderous, cowardly pack, / Pressed to the wall, dying, but fighting back!"[12] It was clear to both African Americans and whites that Black literature was the equal of anything white writers had to offer. The key to great writing, Hughes wrote in his essay "The Negro Artist and the Racial Mountain," was to be completely honest and to write fearlessly. "We younger Negro artists," he wrote, "now intend to express our individual dark-skinned selves without fear or shame. If white people are pleased we are glad. If they aren't, it doesn't matter. We know we are beautiful. And ugly too. . . . If colored people are pleased we are glad. If they are not, their displeasure doesn't matter either. . . . We . . . stand on the top of the mountain, free within ourselves."[13]

Music reached an even wider audience than literature and went a long way to opening America's mind (through its ears) to the vibrancy of Black culture. Two forms of music that derived directly from the African American experience, jazz and the blues, became popular in the 1920s. Whites flocked to Harlem to listen to Duke Ellington, Louis Armstrong, and other jazz musicians. They purchased 78 rpm records of these artists as well as of such blues singers as Ma Rainey and Bessie Smith and guitarists Blind Lemon Jefferson and Mississippi John Hurt. The uncommon rhythms and syncopations, harmonies and playing style, seemed exotic and alluring and, above all, liberating. Jazz was the perfect soundtrack for the 1920s, expressing musically the revolt against traditionalism and the exaltation of the modern. In some respects, the allure of jazz, as well as the blues, began to create an atmosphere that fostered racial understanding and tolerance.

* * *

Whereas liberal writers, intellectuals, and African Americans condemned racism, consumerism, and conservatism, conservatives condemned the rapid changes that were taking place as dangerous to American values—so dangerous that American identity was in jeopardy. The ending of the Red Scare did not eradicate fear and paranoia. Xenophobia entrenched itself ever more deeply in the United States as the decade wore on. Millions of rural and small-town whites were repulsed by anything and anybody they considered un-American, and many of them were so angry that they joined the Ku Klux Klan. Conservatives also feared that forces of modernization and the theories of Sigmund Freud threatened family values and that the teaching of Darwin's theory of evolution was undermining faith in God. The only way to resist a potential disaster, they reasoned, was to return to the fundamentals of

Christianity and restore the "old-time religion." On the whole, significant numbers of Americans were so alarmed by the rapidly changing
world that they dug in their heels and did all they could to resist change
and return to the more familiar, more secure world of their fathers.

Urban Americans, for the most part and out of necessity, accepted
the diversity of religions and ethnicities that exemplified city living. But
those who lived outside the cities resisted such pluralism. America's
white Anglo-Saxon heritage, they believed, was gravely endangered by
the influx of so many Catholic and Jewish immigrants. A formidable
nativist movement, which rivaled that of the Know-Nothings seventy
years before, demanded that the government in Washington close
America's doors to the hundreds of thousands of immigrants flocking
to the United States. In 1921, responding to such demands, Congress
set a quota system that strictly limited the number of immigrants from
eastern and southern Europe and in 1924 passed the National Origins
Act which limited immigration even further as well as prohibiting all
immigration from Asia.

The anti-immigration fervor was one manifestation of the rising racism, anti-Semitism, and bigotry that seemed to obsess the nation. The
rebirth of the Ku Klux Klan was another. The second Klan was founded
in 1915 by William J. Simmons, shortly after the release of D. W. Griffiths's
film venerating the Reconstruction-era Ku Klux Klan, *Birth of a Nation*.
This time the Klan was not confined to the South, nor was its focus only
on Blacks. Along with its white supremacy views and commitment "to
protect and defend the Constitution of the United States," the Klan was
anti-Catholic, anti-Semitic, antiforeigner, antifeminist, anti-Bolshevik,
and anti–modernist Protestant. In fact, it was against anything that it
did not regard as "100 percent pure Americanism." The urban North-
east was a favorite target of KKK hostility. New York City, because of
its large foreign population, was the "most un-American center on the
American continent," the Klan's leader, Simmons, told a convention of
the Kamelia—a women's Klan-like organization. "The foremost political and social economist of the world," Simmons said, "recently made a

survey of New York City and after listening to its babel of tongues, after feeling its hot breath of anarchy, after touching its seething restlessness, he calmly turned away and said that Petrograd in its dust and desolation, was a picture of New York City of the future." And "New England," he continued, "is settled by French Roman Catholics, Canadians who continue to speak the French language, maintain parochial schools and multiply with amazing rapidity."[14]

By the mid-1920s the KKK had over three million members (some estimates go as high as six million) and had hundreds of chapters throughout the United States. Oregon, Pennsylvania, Maine, Indiana, and many other northern states boasted numerous Klan chapters. More midwesterners joined the Klan than southerners. The Klan was so popular during the decade that tens of thousands of Klansmen marched in massive protest parades in the nation's capital in 1925 and 1928, campaigning against all threats to "Americanism."

Klansmen intimidated Blacks, Jews, and Catholics by boycotting businesses that hired them; burning crosses on their lawns, hoping to harry them out of town; beating them; and in some cases lynching them. The Klan also viewed itself as the protector of family values and the purity of women by ferreting out "loose women" for punishment. In Alabama, for example, Klansmen frequently staked out the secluded spots where young couples met for a romantic rendezvous. They would catch the unlucky couple, strip them to the waist, tie them to a tree, and whip them as punishment for their "immoral behavior."

It was the Klan's own immoral behavior, though, that brought it down. A series of financial scandals in which it was disclosed that several Klan leaders had been swindling members discredited the organization. But the tipping point came when David Stephenson, the Grand Dragon of the Klan in Indiana, was convicted in a sensational trial for raping and murdering a young woman. Almost immediately thousands of Klansmen dropped out of the organization, and by 1930 membership had declined to less than ten thousand. Although this second iteration of the Klan died out, anti-Semitism, racism, and bigotry did not.[15]

FIGURE 4.2. Formation of Ku Klux Klan parade in Washington, DC, August 8, 1925. The Klan held marches in the nation's capital several times in the 1920s, with the participation of tens of thousands of hooded Klansmen and women. They demanded "100% Pure Americanism" and denounced African Americans, Jews, Catholics, immigrants, liberals, flappers, modernist Protestants, and all those who did not fit their vision of a white-dominated America.
Credit: Photograph by the National Photo Company. Public domain; courtesy of Library of Congress.

Conservatives also protested the modern forces threatening traditional values by returning to the fundamental evangelical roots of Protestant Christianity. The moral depravity of the cities, the changing role of women, the flagrant defiance of Prohibition, and the widespread acceptance of the theory of evolution were all anathema to rural and small-town Americans. In response, millions of Americans were "born again" at the revival meetings and radio broadcasts of such flamboyant evangelical preachers as Billy Sunday and Aimee Semple

McPherson. In emotionally charged sermons Sunday and McPherson emphasized the fundamentals of the Trinity, the Virgin Birth, the divinity of Christ, and the Resurrection. To fundamentalists, scientific theories, especially the theory of evolution, which contradicted the literal truth of the Bible, were simply wrong. Furthermore, "modernist" theologians' efforts to interpret scripture figuratively so as to accommodate the theory of evolution were just as dangerous to faith as the theory itself. In addition to evolution, fundamentalists denounced as sins promiscuity, alcohol, tobacco, profanity, nightclubs, burlesque, and all forms of liberal freethinking. When Prohibition went into effect, fundamentalists rejoiced. The corruption and violence caused by bootlegging and organized crime, however, was proof that the fight against "demon rum" was far from over and convinced them they had to keep fighting against the evils of alcohol.

In 1925 the evangelical crusade against "Darwinism" reached its high point in Dayton, Tennessee. Shortly after the passage of Tennessee's antievolution law, the American Civil Liberties Union offered its services to any teacher who would challenge the law. John Scopes, a tenth-grade science teacher, agreed to be the guinea pig. On May 7, 1925, Scopes was arrested for teaching a lesson on evolution. The ensuing "Monkey Trial" was the ultimate clash between opposing voices of dissent. Traditionalists and fundamentalists were determined to prevent the scientific community's attempt to impose ideas that threatened deeply held religious beliefs. Modernists and liberals were just as determined to prevent what they saw as a clumsy attempt to proscribe the free exchange of thought. Fundamentalists fought to protect religion and the "faith of our fathers," the ACLU to protect free speech and the separation of church and state.

Clarence Darrow, the most famous trial lawyer in the country, volunteered his services to the ACLU's team defending Scopes. Darrow was an outspoken liberal, an ardent defender of free thinking who opposed capital punishment, traditional morality, and the narrow-minded intolerance of the "slave religion" of Christianity. The Christian view of sin and salvation, Darrow believed, was "dangerous," "wicked," and even "silly." "It is not the bad people I fear so much as the good people. When a person is sure that he is good, he is nearly hopeless; he gets cruel—he believes in punishment."[16]

The perennial Democratic presidential candidate William Jennings Bryan volunteered for the prosecution team. Bryan was a fundamentalist Christian who believed that the Bible was the divinely inspired word of God and that it should be taken literally. But a major part of Bryan's motivation in taking on the theory of evolution was his political progressivism: if he could prove Darwin wrong, it would undermine the Social Darwinist argument against progressive legislation. The Darwinian view posited that man was an animal, that natural selection was cruel, that there was no purpose to existence. The biblical view was that man was created in God's image, and though he was sinful, redemption was possible. For progressives such as Bryan, it was essential to promote a worldview of decency and integrity and to disprove the gloomy cruelty of the Darwinian world. Bryan opposed the theory of evolution "because I fear we shall lose the consciousness of God's presence in our daily life." Furthermore, "the Darwinian theory represents man as reaching his present perfection by the operation of the law of hate—the merciless law by which the strong crowd out and kill off the weak."[17] For these reasons the theory must be challenged.

From the outset the trial was a media circus. Hundreds of correspondents filed daily reports, Chicago radio station WGN broadcast the proceedings live, and thousands of sightseers participated in the carnival-like festivities. Itinerant preachers denounced Darwin and handed out copies of the Bible while evolutionists denounced narrow-mindedness and handed out offprints from *The Origin of the Species*. Enterprising individuals entertained the public by putting trained chimpanzees dressed in business suits through their tricks and sold monkey dolls and all manner of simian souvenirs.

"Civilization," Darrow told a packed courtroom as the trial began; "is on trial. The prosecution is opening the doors for a reign of bigotry equal to anything in the Middle Ages. No man's belief will be safe if they win."[18] The highpoint of the trial came when Darrow surprised the courtroom by calling Bryan to the stand as a *defense* witness. Since the judge would not allow scientific experts to testify, the defense would argue the case with the help of a biblical expert. First, Darrow got Bryan to affirm under oath that every word of the Bible was the literal truth. Then he proceeded to read passages from the Bible to expose the paradoxes of literalism. If there were only four people on Earth at the beginning (Adam, Eve, Cain, and Abel), where did Cain's wife come from? How could the sun have stood still when Joshua commanded it to, when even fundamentalists knew that it was the earth that revolved around the sun? Darrow's incessant badgering finally forced Bryan to acknowledge that there were passages open to interpretation and that he himself even believed that the twenty-four-hour days of creation were metaphorical days of indeterminate length.

The outcome of the trial was that Scopes was found guilty and Tennessee's antievolution law remained on the books until 1967. However, the literal interpretation of the Bible was discredited, and it opened the possibility for even conservative Christians to acknowledge that God created the heavens and the earth *through* some sort of evolutionary process. Science and religion were not necessarily incompatible. Although fundamentalists still challenge the Darwinian view in the twenty-first century, and controversy continues to swirl around the subject, scientific skepticism has dominated scholarship and science education ever since the "Monkey Trial."

* * *

The underlying theme of the Roaring Twenties was the sharp division within American society between the forces of modernism and the forces of traditionalism. The expanding popularity of Darwin's, Einstein's, and Heisenberg's scientific theories, Freud's psychological hypotheses, and European existentialism; the rapid technological developments and the expansion of a consumer culture; the Great Migration of African Americans into northern cities; the emergence of the "modern woman"—all of these changes underscored the philosophical divide that was rapidly widening and that made the 1920s a watershed decade separating modern America from its more naïve past. Many Americans embraced the modernist future wholeheartedly. But many others recoiled from it by putting up a powerful and sometimes effective resistance to the forces they believed would destroy traditional American values and religion. In a sense the 1920s was an early chapter in conservatism's reaction to modernity, a cycle that repeats throughout the latter half of the twentieth century and still continues.

5

Depression and War

These Punch and Judy Republicans, whose actions and
words were dominated by the ventriloquists of Wall Street,
are so blind that they do not recognize, even in this perilous
hour, that their gold basis and their private coinage of money
have bred more radicals than did Karl Marx or Lenin.
—Father Charles Coughlin, 1936

For the American people the Great Depression was a catastrophe of
unprecedented proportions. With more than five thousand banks
failing between 1930 and 1932, significant numbers of Americans questioned the ability of laissez-faire economics to extricate the nation from
the depression. Unemployment was a staggering 25 percent. And even
those who were employed worked for reduced wages or reduced hours.
Untold numbers took to the highways seeking jobs in other communities, only to find that there were no jobs. "Okies"—impoverished farmers
from the dust bowl of Kansas, Oklahoma, and northern Texas—went
west to California, where they hoped to find jobs picking fruit, only to
find disappointment and further hardship. Migrants set up shantytowns
of makeshift corrugated steel and plywood shacks (irreverently called
"Hoovervilles") in garbage dumps on the outskirts of the unwelcoming
cities and towns that refused them admittance. Middle-class families
defaulted on their mortgages, and banks repossessed their houses.

While the depression affected most Americans, minority groups
suffered disproportionately. African Americans, North and South, remained at the bottom of the economic ladder. When a job did become
available, whites were hired before African Americans were even considered. In the South white-supremacist organizations saw to it that whites

received preferential treatment over Blacks in even the lowest-paying jobs. In California and the Southwest, Latinos faced severe discrimination and harassment. Thousands of Mexican migrant workers who had been brought into the region as cheap labor during the 1920s were rounded up and deported, even those who were legally in the country.

In the spring of 1932, World War I veterans captured the nation's attention when they marched on Washington demanding the immediate payment of the retirement bonuses they were promised by 1924 legislation. These bonuses were not due until 1945, but the unemployed veterans desperately needed financial assistance. Nearly twenty thousand veterans from all ethnic and racial backgrounds descended on Washington to push Congress to pass the bonus bill. For several weeks the Bonus Army demonstrated at the Capitol and the White House, but when the bill was defeated, most of the protesters gave up and returned home. Several thousand, however, vowed to keep up the pressure and remain in the shantytown they had set up at Anacostia Flats near the Capitol building until Congress reversed its decision. The police tried to remove the demonstrators, shots were fired, two people were killed, and then President Herbert Hoover, embarrassed by the Bonus Army, ordered in the U.S. Army. What followed was a bizarre scene with General Douglas MacArthur leading tanks and troops up Pennsylvania Avenue to torch the encampment. In the ensuing chaos hundreds of panicked demonstrators were injured, and the shantytown was leveled.

People around the country, already critical of President Hoover's aloof attitude in dealing with the depression, were appalled. Photographs and newspaper accounts of veterans being violently removed from their encampment by heavily armored troops shocked Americans. "What a pitiful spectacle," one newspaper reported. "The mightiest government in the world chasing unarmed men, women and children with Army tanks. If the Army must be called out to make war on unarmed citizens, this is no longer America."[1]

* * *

FIGURE 5.1. The Bonus Army, July 1932. More than ten thousand World War I veterans from all over the country and from all ethnic and racial backgrounds took part in a protest march on Washington in June–July 1932. When Congress refused to pass the bonus bill, they occupied land near the Capitol building to pressure Congress to accede to their demands. President Hoover sent in the U.S. Army under the command of General Douglas MacArthur to evict the protesters.
Credit: Photograph by Harris & Ewing. Public domain; courtesy of Library of Congress.

As the election of 1932 approached, dread and foreboding gripped the land. Something needed to be done. President Hoover seemed incapable of solving the problem. Would the Democratic candidate, Franklin Delano Roosevelt, who pledged "a New Deal for the American people,"[2] be up to the task of reversing the downward slide? Americans certainly hoped so. They flocked to the polls and gave him the largest margin of victory in presidential election history up to that point.

During his first hundred days FDR introduced (and Congress passed) more legislation than any of his predecessors had done. He signed into law acts establishing the Federal Deposit Insurance Corporation, the Securities and Exchange Commission, and a veritable alphabet soup of legislation to deal with the depression: the AAA, CCC, NIRA, TVA. Most Americans were hopeful that FDR would restore the economy (and by the end of 1933 nearly two-thirds of Americans believed that the nation was on the road to recovery). However, the president's bold, controversial measures were so unprecedented that soon there was a rising cacophony of dissenting voices. For conservatives the New Deal was a threat to American values and the free market system. Bankers, businessmen, industrialists, and right-wing newspaper publishers believed that Roosevelt's policies were nothing more than socialism in disguise. Roosevelt, they believed, was trying to transform the United States into a socialist state. By the summer of 1934 their antagonism to the New Deal turned into open defiance. A group of business leaders established the Liberty League, ostensibly an "educational" association for the promotion of "American ideals" but primarily dedicated to the goal of electing anti–New Deal men to Congress. They were, however, unsuccessful in both 1934 and 1936. But as the decade wore on, the Liberty League began to chip away at FDR's support and remained adamantly determined to put an end to relief programs as well as to transfer government-planned initiatives, such as the Tennessee Valley Authority, to the private sector.

For the Liberty League, congressional Republicans, and most conservatives, every New Deal program was an attack on liberty and individualism; the expansion of federal authority and government planning would lead to socialism and communism. These "economic royalists" (as FDR referred to them) were appalled that the president took the United States off the gold standard, they demanded that Roosevelt discontinue his deficit-spending spree, and they especially despised the president for reversing the government's customary role of siding with business and instead supporting unions and workers' rights. The newspaper mogul William Randolph Hearst became an ardent antagonist of the New Deal when Roosevelt supported an inheritance tax. From 1935 on Hearst instructed his reporters to refer to the New Deal as the "Raw Deal" and the inheritance tax as the "soak-the-successful tax." Colonel Robert Rutherford McCormick, owner of the influential *Chicago Tribune*, regularly demonized Roosevelt in his newspaper as the archenemy of capitalism and American democracy. The writer and activist Elizabeth Dilling attacked the New Deal as a socialist plot to take over the United States. The "Socialist administration" in Washington, Dilling wrote, has made sure that "economic serfdom has become a grim reality in the United States."[3] Dilling admired Adolf Hitler for rooting out communists in Germany, and like Hitler, she equated Marxism and "Jewry"—communism, she believed, was a Jewish conspiracy, and FDR, his cabinet, and even the First Lady, were in its thrall.

What the right did not fully understand was that FDR had to sound more left-wing than he indeed was, so that the more radical elements among his supporters were not attracted to the populist demagoguery of such adversaries as Huey Long or Father Coughlin or to the platforms of socialists such as Norman Thomas or communists such as William Z. Foster. The president for his part was deeply frustrated over "the failure of those who have property to realize that [he was] the best friend the profit system ever had."[4]

It is no surprise that in a country that was essentially conservative, peopled with individuals with a deep distrust of centralized authority, Roosevelt's approach to tackling the depression faced formidable criticism from those whose chief articles of faith were free enterprise and individual liberty. But many of Roosevelt's most vocal critics, ironically, were those who criticized him from the left: populists, socialists, communists, and radicals who believed that the depression was a clear signal that capitalism had failed and that what the United States needed was a new economic structure. Indeed, in terminology that foreshadowed the Occupy movement of 2011–2012, leftists incessantly denounced Wall Street's influence on Washington. Concentrated wealth and power, they claimed, had ruined the country. The system was set up to benefit the wealthy at the expense of the middle and lower classes. It was time to change this.

One of FDR's most influential critics was Senator Huey "Kingfish" Long. Long campaigned for Roosevelt in the 1932 election, but by 1934 he was stridently protesting that the New Deal did not go nearly far enough in tackling the problems that lay at the core of the depression. Roosevelt, he declared, should throw the full weight of the presidency into redistributing wealth and breaking the stranglehold of power wielded by bankers and big business. In February 1934 he delivered a speech on the Senate floor in which he proposed his "Share Our Wealth" program to destroy the power of the moneyed interests and eliminate poverty. "There is nothing wrong with the United States," Long declared.

> We have more food than we can eat. We have more clothes and things out of which to make clothes than we can wear. We have more houses and lands than the whole 120 million can use if they all had good homes. So what is the trouble? Nothing except that a handful of men have everything and the balance of the people have nothing if their debts were paid. There should be every man a king in this land flowing with milk and honey instead of the lords of finance at the top and slaves and peasants at the bottom.[5]

Long proposed that no individual be permitted to earn more than $1 million a year. Any amount over that sum would be taxed at 100 percent. Each citizen would receive a guaranteed annual income of $2,500. He called for full employment of everyone, a thirty-hour week, thirty days of paid vacation, and free college education for every American who wanted to attend college.

Millions of Americans enthusiastically responded to Long's populist appeal. By early 1935 he was routinely calling the depression the "Roosevelt depression," and it was obvious that he was gearing up to challenge FDR for the Democratic nomination in 1936. But although Long's demagoguery gained him many followers, he had also trod on many toes during his political career. In September 1935 the son-in-law of one of Long's political enemies in Louisiana confronted Long in the corridor of the state capitol in Baton Rouge and assassinated him. "God, don't let me die!" Long said, mortally wounded. "I have so much to do!"[6]

After the stock market crashed Father Charles Coughlin, the host of a popular radio show, shifted his message from spiritual guidance to political attacks on President Hoover and Wall Street. He supported Roosevelt in 1932 and during the early days of the new administration proclaimed "the New Deal is Christ's Deal."[7] Coughlin was hoping to ingratiate himself with the Roosevelt administration as a sort of unofficial adviser, but when Coughlin realized that FDR was spurning his advances, he shifted his stance. By 1934 Coughlin was using his radio pulpit to denounce FDR's policies as inadequate for extricating the nation from the depression and punishing the moneyed interests. As many as forty-five million Americans listened weekly to the "Radio Priest" condemning the New Deal, FDR, and capitalism. Coughlin founded the National Union for Social Justice as an organization to promote a new economic system that would find a middle way between the twin evils of capitalism and communism. Capitalism, he argued, was finished. And communism was a dead-end that would destroy individualism and religion. "My friends, the outworn creed of capitalism is done for. The clarion call of communism has been sounded. I can support one as easily as the other. They are both rotten! But it is not necessary to suffer any longer the slings and arrows of modern capitalism any more than it is to surrender our rights to life, to liberty and to the cherished bonds of family to communism. . . . Away with both of them!"[8]

Coughlin called for the nationalization of banks, a currency based on both gold and silver, and the type of corporatist economics implemented by fascist Italy. His criticism of Roosevelt and the New Deal was laced with sarcasm. "No man in modern times," he said, "received such plaudits from the poor as did Franklin Roosevelt when he promised to drive the money-changers from the temple—the money-changers who had clipped the coins of wages, who had manufactured spurious money, and who had brought proud America to her knees." But Roosevelt betrayed the American people. He was still too cozy with the mandarins of finance. "Alas! The temple still remains the private property of the money-changers. The golden key has been handed over to them for safekeeping—the key which now is fashioned in the shape of a double cross!"[9]

During the 1936 election campaign Coughlin referred to FDR as "Franklin Double-Crossing Roosevelt," and called him "the great betrayer and liar." His vitriol increased as Election Day neared. He called Roosevelt an "anti-God" communist (while at the same time accusing Roosevelt of being in league with the money-changers), a "scab president," and an "upstart dictator," and he implied that it would not be a bad thing if Roosevelt were assassinated. This was too much for his superiors in the church, and Coughlin was ordered to issue a public apology.[10]

Still, Coughlin's attacks on Roosevelt intensified during FDR's second term. By this time, with much of the world taking notice of what was transpiring in Hitler's Germany, the Radio Priest descended into anti-Semitism. The president, Coughlin asserted, was carrying out the policies of Jewish bankers and industrialists and the Jewish members of his cabinet. He began calling the New Deal the "Jew Deal." Coughlin's anti-Semitism proved to be his undoing. Shortly after Kristallnacht in Germany in 1938, when Jewish synagogues and businesses were destroyed during the "night of broken glass," Coughlin proclaimed that the Jews were only being paid back for their persecution of Christians. Even after Hitler invaded Poland, he continued his anti-Semitic diatribes while praising Hitler. Finally, in 1940 the radio networks were so appalled at his pro-Nazi, anti-Semitic remarks that they took his show off the air.

The populist critique of the New Deal clearly had a radical tinge to it, but other dissidents were even more radical in their denunciation of FDR's attempt to save the free enterprise system. Many of those who were devastated by the depression were drawn to socialism. For these individuals it seemed that the severity of the depression was proof that capitalism had failed and that the only way to escape from the boom/bust cycle was through a planned economy. The anarchist Emma Goldman continued writing blistering attacks on capitalism and called for a government that would truly recognize the worth of the individual. Society does not exist to support the interests of the moneyed classes, as it does under a capitalist system, Goldman contended; it exists to elevate the individual. Anarchy, for Goldman, was the answer. "Of all social theories Anarchism alone steadfastly proclaims that society exists for man, not man for society. The sole legitimate purpose of society is to serve the needs and advance the aspiration of the individual."[11]

In the Midwest, hard-hit farmers, disenchanted with the Democrats for not proposing radical solutions, formed third parties to promote their interests. In Minnesota activists formed the Farmer-Labor Party and campaigned for Floyd Olson for governor. The party's platform proclaimed that "capitalism has failed" and demanded that "all the natural resources, machinery of production, transportation, and communication, shall be owned by the government."[12] Olson deprecated the liberal label. "I am a radical," he proudly proclaimed. "You bet your life I'm a radical. You might say I'm radical as hell!"[13] In Wisconsin thousands of farmers supported the equally radical Progressive Party and elected Philip La Follette as governor and Robert M. La Follette, Jr., as senator. "We are not liberals!" the new governor said. "Liberalism is nothing but a sort of milk-and-water tolerance. . . . I believe in a fundamental and basic change." Without explaining exactly what he meant, Philip La Follette called for a "cooperative society based on American traditions."[14]

More threatening, however, was the increasing popularity of the Communist Party. The Great Crash was proof to many radicals that American capitalism was through and a new political/economic structure modeled on that of Stalin's Russia was a necessity. In 1932 the presidential candidate of the Communist Party USA, William Z. Foster, won over one hundred thousand votes. By 1934 the party boasted a card-carrying membership of approximately thirty thousand and became increasingly vocal in condemning the New Deal. "Roosevelt's program," the party's general secretary, Earl Browder, contended, "is the same as that of finance capital the world over." The National Recovery Administration, communists insisted, was a "fascist slave program," and there must be no compromise with capitalism.[15] The entire system needed to be overthrown.

From coast to coast, communists of various factions (not limited to the Communist Party), organized strikes of agricultural workers, truck drivers, transportation workers, longshoremen, miners, and autoworkers. Some strikes escalated into riots. In May 1934 in Minneapolis, communists helped lead a Teamsters' strike of 20,000 people during which scores of strikers were shot and two died. A few months later, a strike of San Francisco stevedores led to a citywide general strike that effectively closed down all business in the city for several days until the police, backed by 4,500 National Guardsmen, finally brought the strike to an end. Later that year, 325,000 textile workers walked off their jobs in South Carolina, took control of the mills, immobilized the looms, and battled the police and guards. Seven were killed and twenty wounded before the strike ran its course.

Even moderate, less radical labor militancy increased, despite the fact that New Deal programs were slowly providing more jobs and better conditions for workers. Workers initiated new tactics that were effective in having their demands met and their unions recognized. Perhaps the most successful innovation was the "sit-down" strike. Instead of walking out of the plant (which invariably resulted in owners bringing in scabs to keep production going), striking workers occupied it. This meant that the workers themselves were in control of the factory, not management. Such worker-controlled grassroots activism spread to other industries and forced management to recognize and bargain with unions. Workers of the fledgling United Auto Workers union (UAW) were victorious at Goodyear and Firestone in Akron, Ohio, and at Fisher Body, General Motors, and Ford in Michigan. In 1937 alone, nearly one million labor activists demanding union recognition participated in more than two thousand strikes. In response to these disputes, President Roosevelt urged the automobile manufacturers to recognize and negotiate with the UAW, while Congress passed the Wagner Act establishing the National Labor Relations Board. The NLRB was empowered to oversee union activity, to determine the makeup of bargaining units, to prohibit "unfair business practices" (such as firing workers for joining the union), and to force employers to sit down at the bargaining table with union representatives.

Although the Great Depression saw a considerable upsurge of radicalism in the United States, that radicalism did not take root sufficiently to survive long after the depression. One reason for this, as historian Alan Brinkley observes, is that there had never been a serious left-wing radical tradition in the United States. "The rhetoric of class conflict," Brinkley maintains, "echoed only weakly among men and women steeped in the dominant themes of their nation's history." The American Revolution and most protest movements throughout the nineteenth century were primarily motivated by a distrust of centralized authority. "Opposition to centralized authority and demands for the wide dispersion of power had formed the core of American social and political protest, the nation's constricted version of a radical tradition, for more than a century."[16] This distrust lay behind the reform movements of the 1830s and 1840s as well as the free-labor/free-soil ideology of the 1850s. By the time of the Great Depression, the old dominant forces had been replaced by a new paradigm. Wall Street, big business, and the finance industry were the new centralized authority, and the protests against concentrated wealth and power were an echo of the American political tradition of opposition to the forces that prevented a wider dispersal of economic opportunity and therefore of power. This tradition, and not the Marxist ideology of class struggle, was the foundation of the protests of the 1930s.

* * *

Along with direct political action, speeches, and demagoguery, dissent in the 1930s was also expressed through literature, music, and the arts. As the depression deepened, creative artists described the harsh realities that the hardest-hit Americans faced in their daily lives. Writers, photographers, and artists focused public attention on the breadlines, the dust bowl, the dispossessed migrants, and the Hoovervilles that had become an indelible part of the American landscape. Raising consciousness through social realism, they hoped, would spur the government and the private sector to take more significant action in alleviating suffering and getting people back on their feet. Some of the most poignant images we have of the 1930s are the photographs of Walker Evans, Dorothea Lange, and Margaret Bourke-White depicting the despair of destitute Americans. Erskine Caldwell's novel *Tobacco Road* tells the story of white tenant farmers in Georgia, John Steinbeck's *The Grapes of Wrath* describes the countless misfortunes faced by the Joad family as they traveled from the dust bowl of Oklahoma to the promised land of California, lured by the false hope of finding decent-paying jobs as fruit pickers, Richard Wright's *Native Son* relates the story of an impoverished young African American man living in Chicago's South Side who finds there is no escape from poverty and racism, and on a more political level, John Dos Passos's trilogy *U.S.A.* relentlessly blames the capitalist system for causing the depression. Murals and paintings by artists such as Thomas Hart Benton, John Steuart Curry, and Isaac Soyer were another form of social protest that portrayed the harsh realities of poverty as well as hopeful images of a more prosperous America that they hoped would soon come to pass.

In 1932 Myles Horton and Jim West founded the Highlander Folk School in Monteagle, Tennessee. The school was a grassroots educational institution offering a variety of workshops that addressed social issues in the region and sought to get people involved in direct action campaigns for the purpose of creating a more humane society. Throughout much of its first decade, the school concentrated on labor activism. The faculty taught miners and textile workers effective collective action strategies, such as picketing and the sit-down strike, and techniques for organizing successful recruitment drives. One of the features of Highlander was the emphasis on music. Harking back to the tradition of Joe Hill and the Wobblies, Highlander taught workers inspirational prounion songs that would promote solidarity and optimism on picket lines and protest marches. One of the songs it introduced to activists was an African American hymn titled "I'll Overcome Someday." (After World War II Highlander shifted its main focus to civil rights activism, and the hymn was secularized when Pete Seeger, Guy Carawan, and others quickened the tempo, wrote new verses, and changed the title to "We Shall Overcome.")

While volunteers at Highlander recognized the power of music in voicing dissent and promoting social change, the disorder and hard times of the Great Depression also produced a growing coterie of musicians and songwriters who used their talent to fortify and propagate political activism. Alfred Hayes and Earl Robinson paid homage to Joe Hill in a song they hoped would inspire workers to stand up for their rights. "I dreamed I saw Joe Hill last night," they wrote, "alive as you and me." Florence Reese wrote "Which Side Are You On?"—a resounding union song that was sung for decades at labor rallies and strikes and civil rights marches. But it was Woody Guthrie who had the most extensive impact as a writer of protest songs.

During the depression, as Guthrie hitchhiked and rode the rails around the country, he found himself very much engaged with the unemployed, the migrant workers, and the Okies desperately seeking any kind of job that would bring in some money. Angered by the discrimination and exploitation migrant workers faced in California, Guthrie began writing and performing songs at Hoovervilles, union meetings, migrant camps, protest rallies, and even on the radio. He wrote what he

FIGURE 5.2. Woody Guthrie, March 8, 1943, playing his guitar with a sticker that reads, "This Machine Kills Fascists." Guthrie wrote hundreds of protest songs and was a major force on the evolution of music as a means of expressing dissent. His influence was enormous and continues to this day—from Pete Seeger, Joan Baez, Bob Dylan, and Phil Ochs to Bruce Springsteen, John Mellencamp, and countless other artists.
Credit: Photograph by Al Aumuller. Public domain; courtesy of Library of Congress.

called his "Dust Bowl Ballads," songs such as "Hard Travelin'," "Blowin' Down This Old Dusty Road," "I Ain't Got No Home," "Tom Joad," and "Pastures of Plenty," detailing the stories of poor migrant workers; union songs such as "Union Maid," "Ludlow Massacre," and "Union Burying Ground," extolling unionization; and political protest songs such as "Pretty Boy Floyd," "Jesus Christ," and "Do Re Mi," attacking the hypocrisy and dishonesty of the establishment. In "Pretty Boy Floyd" Guthrie portrays the notorious bank robber as a modern-day Robin Hood who steals from the bankers and gives money to the poor. Guthrie wryly observes that he's seen all sorts of people as he's traveled around the land, "Some will rob you with a six-gun / And some with a fountain pen."

In "Jesus Christ" Guthrie ponders how people would respond if Jesus Christ returned to preach his message in the United States today, and he concludes that the preachers and the bankers and the cops would crucify him all over again. In "Do Re Mi" Guthrie observes that California was not exactly the "promised land" that existed in the minds of the thousands of Okies fleeing the dust bowl. The migrants arriving in California looking for jobs discovered all too soon the truth of Guthrie's lyrics that they were not going to make it unless they had the dough.

Guthrie's songs were always topical, often controversial and provocative, touching on the real-life misfortunes of the poor. Many of the songs were taken directly from his personal experience and the stories he read in newspapers. When a plane carrying illegal Mexican migrant workers who were being deported crashed over Los Gatos Canyon on the way to Mexico, Guthrie was appalled that the radio and newspapers reported that the victims "were just deportees." When he read this, Guthrie was inspired to write "Deportee," a heartfelt song protesting the exploitation of migrant workers.

He wrote his most famous song, "This Land Is Your Land," as a rejoinder to Irving Berlin's "God Bless America," which Guthrie considered the epitome of American sanctimoniousness. In the first version of the song the repetitive refrain he invoked was "God blessed America for me." Later he changed it to "this land was made for you and me." He also wrote several radical verses (later dropped from recordings of the song) that made it clear he believed America belonged to *all* the people, even the ones who wait in line outside relief offices, not just wealthy landlords and banks and corporations.

Many people accused Woody Guthrie of being a communist. He often made fun of these accusations by denying he was a "red," even though he had always been "in the red" all his life. Although he was attracted to communism, he did not join the Communist Party because he believed it was too authoritarian, especially its antireligious stance. Guthrie was too much of an individualist to adhere to strict party lines. When World War II broke out, Guthrie aimed his militant songs at the Nazis. He was always opposed, as he wrote in his autobiography, to "Hitlerism and fascism homemade and imported."[17] He pasted a notice on his guitar's soundboard proclaiming, "This Machine Kills Fascists." Guthrie considered himself a true American patriot, a man who sincerely believed in what the United States stood for. And when he felt American ideals were endangered, whether by Nazis or by business leaders and bankers, he spoke out strongly and eloquently in song. His songs were heard by millions of Americans, stirred people's consciousness, and were an enduring legacy that influenced Pete Seeger, Bob Dylan, Bruce Springsteen, Ani DiFranco, and hundreds of other artists who wrote songs of political protest and social activism later in the century.

* * *

By 1936 ominous events in Asia and Europe were increasingly demanding America's attention. In East Asia, imperial Japan had occupied Manchuria and invaded China. In Africa the Italian dictator Benito Mussolini overran Ethiopia and turned it into an Italian colony. In Spain fascists led by Francisco Franco (with support from Mussolini and Hitler) started a civil war against the democratically elected government. And in Germany Adolf Hitler violated the Versailles Treaty by rearming Germany and militarizing the Rhineland. Whereas Britain and France, unwilling to risk another war, tolerated Hitler's belligerent rhetoric and behavior, FDR regarded the German dictator as a major threat to world peace and was convinced that if Hitler was not reined in, war would be inevitable. Roosevelt believed that the only way to preserve world peace was by actively engaging in diplomacy. The problem was that the cornerstone of American foreign policy was isolationism, reaffirmed by America's disillusionment with getting involved in the Great War. Congress's response to the growing crisis in Europe was a series of Neutrality Acts between 1936 and 1939 that prohibited the United States from selling arms to belligerents, even those countries that needed to defend themselves against aggression.

And so, as the European peace deteriorated, Roosevelt embarked on the daunting task of educating the American public of the dangers of noninvolvement. Every move the president made to change America's course met with stiff opposition from isolationists in both parties. Progressives and liberals opposed any policy that would lead to American involvement because they feared it would undermine New Deal reforms. Business leaders and investors were isolationist because war would disrupt access to markets. But at the same time, many Republicans and conservative southern Democrats who seldom saw eye-to-eye with Roosevelt on domestic issues sided with him on foreign policy because they believed that the United States would never be more than a second-rate power in a world dominated by the Axis.

The advent of war in Europe in 1939 strengthened the isolationists' hand. Americans, above all, did not want to be dragged into another European conflict, and a potent antiwar/neutrality movement swung into high gear. Roosevelt's call for a special session of Congress at the end of September to reconsider neutrality legislation galvanized isolationist forces. Senator William Borah of Idaho warned that tampering with neutrality laws would surely drag the United States into the war. The Radio Priest, Father Coughlin, and the esteemed aviation hero Charles Lindbergh relentlessly blasted Roosevelt's efforts to circumvent the Neutrality Acts and aid the victims of Nazi aggression. "The destiny of this country," Lindbergh argued, "does not call for our involvement in European wars. One need only glance at a map to see where our true frontiers lie. What more could we ask than the Atlantic Ocean on the east and the Pacific on the west . . . ?"[18] Millions of Americans sent letters and telegrams to Congress and the White House opposing any revision in the neutrality laws. Like Lindbergh, they believed that the Third Reich did not endanger "Fortress America."

Such opposition continued throughout 1940 and 1941 as Roosevelt sought ways to support Britain. In Chicago a group of anti-interventionist activists founded the America First Committee to coordinate the protests against FDR's course of action, which would

inevitably drag the United States into the war. When Roosevelt introduced the Lend-Lease Bill in order to bypass the restrictions on selling
military supplies to Britain, the America First Committee stepped up its
attacks. Such a policy, they declared (rightly), would only lead the U.S.
Navy to protect the convoys of goods going to England, and this in turn
would lead to a shooting war with Nazi submarines. The antiwar "Mothers' Crusade" held a "pray-in" at the Capitol while Congress voted on
the Lend-Lease Bill and then, when the bill was approved, picketed the
White House demanding the president kill Lend-Lease, "not our sons."
At the same time, America First organized additional rallies around the
country. The antiwar activism delayed the passage of the Lend-Lease
Bill, but Roosevelt eventually signed the bill into law in January 1941.
Lindbergh and other America Firsters continued to give speeches all
over the country. "In time of war," Lindbergh said at an April rally in
New York, "truth is always replaced by propaganda. I do not believe
we should be too quick to criticize the actions of a belligerent nation
[Germany]. . . . But we in this country have a right to think of the welfare of America first. . . . When England asks us to enter this war, she is
considering her own future, and that of her Empire. In making our reply,
I believe we should consider the future of the United States and that of
the Western Hemisphere." President Roosevelt and his interventionist
cronies, Lindbergh claimed, are destroying American democracy. "It is
they who are undermining the principles of Democracy when they demand that we take a course to which more than eighty percent of our
citizens are opposed."[19]

* * *

In less than two hours on December 7, 1941, the Japanese were able
to accomplish what FDR had been trying to accomplish for over two
years—unite the American people behind the war.

The war ended the Great Depression. Unemployment was over. Anyone who wanted a job found one. Millions went to work in defense
industries. The demand for workers and soldiers provided endless

opportunities for everyone and accelerated social change, especially for women and minorities. Manufacturers and industrialists sent agents south of the border to recruit Mexican workers for their factories. Women's roles expanded as they were offered good-paying jobs in the defense industry that had previously only been open to men. And millions of Americans enlisted in the armed forces or were drafted. More than two hundred thousand women served in the army and navy. Thousands of Native Americans and Mexican Americans volunteered for the military, more than two million African Americans registered for the draft, and nearly a million of them served in segregated regiments, where they committed themselves to fighting for the "Double V Campaign"— victory abroad against fascism, victory at home against racism.

Five months before Pearl Harbor, A. Philip Randolph, the president of the Brotherhood of Sleeping Car Porters, gained an audience with the president and informed him that if African Americans were not hired on an equal-opportunity basis in the defense industries, he would lead a massive protest march on Washington. Worried that calling attention to racism in the United States at such a moment would be a propaganda victory for the Nazis, FDR issued an executive order that prohibited discrimination in the defense industry and established the Fair Employment Practices Commission. In this way dissent, although merely the threat of a protest march, modified official federal racial policy. This was only the beginning. The experience of African American soldiers, pilots, and sailors in combat had a profound impact on their lives and proved to be one of the key factors in the rise of the postwar Civil Rights Movement.

Despite the pride African American soldiers felt in serving the nation they continued to protest against the racism, segregation, and unequal treatment they experienced on a daily basis in the military. When FDR proclaimed that the United States was fighting "to make a world in which tyranny and aggression cannot exist; a world based upon freedom, equality, and justice; a world in which all persons regardless of race, color, and creed may live in peace, honor, and dignity,"[20] an African

American soldier, Private First Class Charles Wilson, sent an angry letter of protest. "Dear President Roosevelt," he wrote, it is quite clear that the United States itself is undemocratic as long as "jim crow and segregation is practiced by our Armed Forces against its Negro members." Segregation means that "totally inadequate opportunities are given to the Negro members of our Armed Forces . . . to participate with 'equality' . . . 'regardless of race and color' in the fight for our war aims." He went on to describe the inferior conditions in the segregated barracks that African American soldiers had to endure. "How can we convince nearly one tenth of the Armed Forces, the Negro members," he reasoned, "that your pronouncement of the war aims of the United Nations means what it says, when their experience with . . . the United States of America, is just the opposite?"[21]

The most egregious example of racial discrimination occurred in POW camps where African American troops served as guards. Routinely, prisoners of war were taken to nearby farms to be used as forced labor. When the guards took the POWs back to the camps in the evening, they usually stopped for food at a diner along the way. While the POWs would be served inside, their African American guards had to get their food handed to them out of the kitchen window. This happened not only in the South but in the North as well. "The people of Salina [Kansas]," one African American soldier recalled after the war, "would serve these enemy soldiers and turn away black American G.I.'s."[22]

On the home front, hundreds of thousands of African Americans, lured by good pay and job security, moved to industrial centers. This migration triggered a number of race riots. One riot in Detroit lasted several days, during which twenty-five Blacks and nine whites were killed. Other riots took place in New York; Los Angeles; Beaumont, Texas; and Mobile, Alabama. In the face of such violence, Blacks became more militant. Hundreds of thousands joined the NAACP (membership jumped from 50,000 in 1940 to 405,000 by the end of the war), and in 1942 a new civil rights organization was founded: the Congress of Racial Equality (CORE). Unlike the NAACP, which confronted racism primarily through legal action, CORE organized and coordinated civil disobedience actions. One of the first was the "Don't Shop Where You Can't Work" campaign urging the public to boycott stores, restaurants, and theaters in northern cities such as New York that did not employ African American workers. In 1944 fourteen Black intellectuals published *What the Negro Wants*, a manifesto calling for voting rights in the South and full integration into the American way of life. World War II made it patently obvious that there was an inherent contradiction in fighting for freedom in a segregated military and a segregated nation. By the end of the war, African Americans and white liberals envisioned an integrated society in which the U.S. recommitted itself to the nation's ideals of liberty and equality for all.

* * *

Although most Americans supported the "Good War," many thousands protested against the war, against the draft, and against infringements on civil liberties and civil rights. Most isolationists and members of the America First Committee ceased protesting against Roosevelt's policies immediately after Pearl Harbor, but many of them simply shifted their protest to focus on war strategy, arguing that the United States should throw the bulk of its might into the Pacific Theater fighting the "yellow peril" rather than the president's "Germany first" strategy. This expression of the deep-seated racism that persists in American society, coupled with the Japanese attack on Pearl Harbor, ignited an outbreak of anti-Japanese hysteria. This was especially problematic on the West Coast, where more than one hundred thousand Japanese Americans lived. Americans jumped to the conclusion that Japanese Americans could not be trusted, that their loyalty was not to the United States but to Imperial Japan. Rumors spread that the Japanese living in California were spies, saboteurs, traitors; they were planning to guide Japanese warplanes to targets in California; they were hatching plots to blow up dams and hydroelectric power stations. Both the governor and attorney general of California called for their removal. Many whites saw it as a golden opportunity to acquire Japanese farms, orchards, businesses, and homes at bargain-basement prices. Anti-Japanese prejudice reached the boiling point. The respected *New York Times* columnist Walter Lippmann reported that "it is a fact that communication takes place between the enemy at sea and enemy agents on land."[23] The commander of the army's Western Command, General John DeWitt, urged Washington to remove the Japanese from the West Coast. "A Jap's a Jap," he declared; "it makes no difference whether he is an American citizen or not."[24] Public pressure was put on Roosevelt to do something, and in February 1942 FDR signed Executive Order 9066 authorizing the internment of Japanese Americans on the West Coast. Without due process, without any charges being filed, without writs of habeas corpus, more than 110,000 Japanese Americans were forced out of their homes and sent to internment camps. More than half of them were *nisei*, born in the United States, American citizens. Civil liberties were disregarded. The NAACP, the Communist Party, the Socialist Party, the American Jewish Committee—organizations that had traditionally fought for civil rights protections—were embarrassingly silent.

But there *was* dissent against this policy. Japanese Americans who were interned resisted through strikes, refusal to take loyalty oaths, and even riots. Some refused to report for evacuation and were arrested. Some of those who were arrested took their cases to the Supreme Court. Gordon Hirabayashi, Minoru Yasui, and Fred Korematsu all challenged the constitutionality of the executive order. "The thing that struck me immediately," Minoru Yasui said about the evacuation order, "was that the military was ordering the civilian to do something. In my opinion, that's the way dictatorships are formed. And if I, as an American citizen stood still for this, I would be derogating the rights of all citizens. By God, I had to stand up and say, 'That's wrong.' I refused to report for evacuation."[25] As a result, he was arrested and served nine months in solitary confinement. "The insidious danger," he wrote his sister from his cell, "of creating a precedent of confining American citizens behind barbed wire fences and machine guns when they have committed no crime seemed reprehensible to me. . . . But surely as the attack on Pearl Harbor endangered our democracy, . . . [the] evacuation of American citizens on the basis of race is just as dangerous a threat to democracy!" Thus it was clear to Yasui that it was his *patriotic* duty, as a loyal American, to fight the internment policy. "Caucasian Americans are no better nor worse than I, for we are all human beings. It is only the principles of liberty, democracy and justice, and the adherence to these principles that made America great, and as a loyal American who can suffer his native land to do no wrong, I must hold true to those principles."[26] In 1943 in *Yasui v. United States* the Supreme Court upheld the evacuation order and denied Yasui's appeal.

* * *

Between 1941 and 1945 thirty-seven thousand pacifists were given "conscientious objector" classifications, while seven thousand others refused to participate in any way in the war and wound up serving prison sentences. Some were sent to Civil Public Service (CPS) work camps where they toiled nine hours a day, six days a week. They came from all walks of life. "We had PhDs," one inmate recalled later, "we had winners of Fulbright prizes, we had guys who had a third-grade education, we had stockbrokers, we had ballet dancers, we had atheists, we had fundamentalists . . . every possible kind of human being was there."[27] Some of the conscientious objectors worked as assistants in mental institutions; some worked as "fire jumpers" (combating forest fires); some worked as caregivers for juvenile delinquents; and some even volunteered for hazardous medical experiments to find cures for hepatitis, malaria, typhus, and other infectious diseases as well as for studies on the effects of starvation in order to improve the treatment of starvation victims.

Two of the draft resisters imprisoned during World War II, David Dellinger and Bayard Rustin, went on to become major players in the two principal dissent movements of the 1960s—Rustin in civil rights and Dellinger in the mobilization against the war in Vietnam. Dellinger was a young progressive activist who was inspired by the example of Mahatma

Gandhi and the writings of the Social Gospel advocate Reinhold Niebuhr. Dellinger had visited Germany in 1936 and 1937 and was disgusted with American complicity in the rise of Adolf Hitler. Sperry Gyroscope sold important aviation navigation technology to the Luftwaffe, DuPont was in cahoots with German explosive manufacturers, Pratt and Whitney had a brisk trade in selling aircraft engines to the Third Reich. "It was clear to me during this period," Dellinger wrote, "that England, France, and the United States were working with Hitler not only for the profits to be gained by U.S. banks and corporations, but also with the major aim of influencing the Nazis to expand militarily to the east, destroying, or at least crippling, the Communist enemy."[28] It was only after the Nazi-Soviet Nonaggression Pact that American financiers began to turn against Hitler. When the war broke out in Europe, Dellinger helped organize and take part in antiwar demonstrations, and then in 1941 he refused to register for the draft. He was arrested and sentenced to prison. While in prison he continued his activism by leading protests and staging hunger strikes against the practice of segregating white inmates from Black.

One such protest was a spontaneous act shortly after Dellinger began serving his sentence. Prisoners were allowed to view movies on Saturday nights. The first time he entered the prison theater, he accompanied an African American inmate. "The guard pointed to the white section for me and the black section for him, but I sat next to my friend in the black section. It was not a planned protest, just the instinctive, natural thing to do. Soon I was carried out and placed in a solitary cell in the maximum security 'troublemakers' cell block."[29]

Bayard Rustin was imprisoned for two years in the Lewisburg Federal Penitentiary in Pennsylvania, where, like Dellinger, he organized boycotts, strikes, and antisegregation protests. Immediately after the war, Rustin became an anticolonial/anti-imperialist activist demanding the end of colonial rule in Africa and Asia. In the 1950s Rustin was a leading force in the Civil Rights Movement, joining Martin Luther King, Jr., in the Montgomery bus boycott and, most famously, organizing and coordinating the 1963 March on Washington.

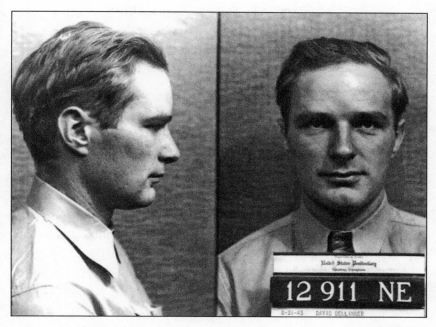

FIGURE 5.3. The antiwar protester David Dellinger, August 31, 1943, in prison for resisting the draft during World War II. Dellinger went on to participate in many other protests after his release, including acting as one of the organizers of the anti–Vietnam War demonstrations at the Democratic Convention in Chicago, 1968.
Credit: Photograph by the Federal Bureau of Prisons. Public domain.

What is perhaps most astonishing about the World War II antiwar movement is that there were so many conscientious objectors. The war had virtually zero organized opposition. The Socialist and Communist Parties as well as most anarchist groups that had previously taken antiwar positions were unanimous this time in their support for the war. To them it was a "people's war" against fascism. Of all the wars the United States has ever fought, none had such support as World War II. Pacifists were viewed as cowards. And so it took extraordinary courage on their part to dissent. One conscientious objector, Desmond T. Doss, who served as a medic but refused to carry a gun and was therefore subjected to the ridicule and hostility of his fellow soldiers, showed exceptional courage when he saved the lives of seventy-five men as a medic during a fierce battle in Okinawa. At the end of the war, President Harry Truman awarded Doss the Congressional Medal of Honor.

* * *

Before the war, radical students and professors at the City College of New York (CCNY) organized a chapter of the Communist Party and sponsored a series of antifascist demonstrations denouncing America's indifference to the rise of Hitler, Mussolini, and Franco while publicly proclaiming their admiration for Soviet communism. In 1941 and 1942 the New York City Board of Higher Education and the college administration launched a campaign to destroy "communist subversion." They banned the Communist Party and other left-wing student organizations, expelled students, and fired faculty. Hundreds of protesters took to the streets blasting this inexcusable abrogation of freedom of speech, but to no avail.

On the heels of the CCNY protests, the House Committee on Un-American Activities inaugurated a systematic investigation of disloyal Americans. With the onset of the Cold War, increasing numbers of Americans were subpoenaed to give testimony before the committee. And then in 1950 Senator Joseph McCarthy enflamed the anticommunist hysteria with allegations that the reason for the worldwide expansion of communism was that the United States was infiltrated with traitors. The State Department was riddled with communists. Spies were everywhere. Disloyal Americans must be rooted out. Anyone who dissented against American policy or subscribed to left-wing ideology or pacifist beliefs was suspect.

6

Conformity and Dissent

Some of my ancestors were religious dissenters who came to America over 300 years ago. Others were abolitionists in New England of the 1840's and 50's.

For twenty years I have been singing folksongs of America and other lands to people everywhere. I am proud that I never refused to sing to any group of people because I might disagree with some of the ideas of some of the people listening to me. . . .

A good song can only do good, and I am proud of the songs I have sung. I hope to be able to continue singing these songs for all who want to listen, Republicans, Democrats, and independents. Do I have the right to sing these songs?
—Pete Seeger, statement at his sentencing for contempt of Congress, 1961

"From Stettin in the Baltic to Trieste on the Adriatic an iron curtain has descended on the Continent."[1] Thus Winston Churchill characterized the geopolitical reality of postwar Europe and coined the term that dominated the West's view of the Cold War. Soviet troops occupied an enslaved eastern Europe, while British and American forces were the occupiers in the free West. The tension between East and West, which intensified and spread around the globe at a dizzying pace, became the defining feature of international relations for the next forty-five years.

As the United States and the Soviet Union faced off against each other, rattling their swords and raising the rhetoric to a fearsome pitch, anxious Americans proudly rallied around the flag. By 1953 the division in Europe had hardened, the Soviet Union had successfully tested its own atomic bomb, China had gone communist, Congress was investigating communists and spies *within* the U.S. government, Julius and Ethel Rosenberg were tried, convicted, and executed as Soviet spies, a war had been fought in Korea, and a new, far more terrifying, nuclear arms race was under way.[2] The prevailing attitude was that Armageddon was just around the corner and that an evil, totalitarian foe was aiming to enslave the United States. Americans, joining together in universal revulsion for communism and their belief in the American way, proudly proclaimed that everything about the United States was noble while everything about the Soviet Union was evil. Yet, despite this patriotic unity, a powerful groundswell of discontent simmered just below the seemingly placid surface of the 1950s.

Like the 1920s, the 1950s was a decade of contrasts. Whereas the 1920s featured a conflict between modernism and traditionalism, the 1950s was a schizophrenic age split between confidence and paranoia. On one hand, the booming economy, suburban growth, and a plethora of new consumer goods produced an atmosphere of great optimism and faith in the future. Things were only going to get better. But on the other hand, the arms race, Cold War anxiety, and the paranoid fear of communism produced a sense of foreboding that it all might end at any moment in a nuclear holocaust. The growth of the middle class, home ownership, and the consumer society also, conversely, underscored that there were serious discrepancies in the United States, that there were numerous marginalized groups within American society, that contrary to conventional wisdom the American Dream was not fully available to all.

* * *

One way that dissent reared its head during the early years of the Cold War was in the reaction to the Second Red Scare that swept over the nation. As the House Committee on Un-American Activities (HUAC) and then later the Senate, led by Senator Joseph McCarthy, held hearings in an attempt to root out communist infiltration in the United

States, courageous Americans spoke out against what they regarded as a twentieth-century witch hunt.

Some of those who protested, not surprisingly, were the very people being investigated by Congress. John Howard Lawson, the president of the Screen Writers' Guild, was a case in point. Because the film industry was a particularly powerful force in shaping public opinion, Congress targeted Hollywood. Lawson (who had joined the Communist Party in the 1930s) was a screenwriter who, according to congressional investigators, was brainwashing Americans by slipping communist propaganda into his screenplays. When he appeared before HUAC, he denounced the committee itself for being "un-American" because of its flagrant contempt for the Bill of Rights. During his testimony Lawson attempted to read a statement criticizing the hearings, but the chairman refused to let him do so. A brief excerpt from the record conveys the chaotic atmosphere in the room as the chairman did everything in his power to prevent Lawson from reading his statement:

THE CHAIRMAN: Mr. Lawson, you will have to stop or you will leave the witness stand. And you will leave the witness stand because you are in contempt. That is why you will leave the witness stand. And if you are just trying to force me to put you in contempt, you won't have to try much harder. You know what has happened to a lot of people that have been in contempt of this committee this year, don't you?

MR. LAWSON: I am glad you have made it perfectly clear that you are going to threaten and intimidate the witnesses, Mr. Chairman.

(*The chairman pounding gavel.*)

MR. LAWSON: I am an American and I am not at all easy to intimidate, and don't think I am.

(*The chairman pounding gavel.*) . . .

THE CHAIRMAN: (*pounding gavel*) Mr. Lawson, just quiet down again. Mr. Lawson, the most pertinent question that we can ask is whether

or not you have ever been a member of the Communist Party. Now,
do you care to answer that question?

MR. LAWSON: You are using the old technique, which was used in
Hitler [*sic*] Germany in order to create a scare here—

THE CHAIRMAN: (*pounding gavel*) Oh—

MR. LAWSON: In order to create an entirely false atmosphere in which
this hearing is conducted— . . .

THE CHAIRMAN: (*pounding gavel*) Stand away from the stand—

MR. LAWSON: I have written Americanism for many years, and I
shall continue to fight for the Bill of Rights, which you are trying to
destroy.

THE CHAIRMAN: Officers, take this man away from the stand—[3]

In the disallowed statement, Lawson accused the committee of con-
ducting "an illegal and indecent trial" that was a "gross violation of the
Constitution of the United States, and especially of its First and Fifth
Amendments." What HUAC was really trying to do, Lawson insisted,
is "introduce fascism in this country. They know that the only way
to trick the American people into abandoning their rights and liberties is to manufacture an imaginary danger, to frighten the people into
accepting repressive laws which are supposedly for their protection." If
the committee is not stopped, freedom of thought and conscience will
be extinguished. "If I can be destroyed no American is safe. You can
subpoena a farmer in a field, a lumberjack in the woods, a worker at a
machine, a doctor in his office—you can deprive them of a livelihood,
deprive them of their honor as Americans."[4] But Lawson's protestations
were scornfully dismissed. He was convicted of contempt of Congress,
sentenced to a year in prison, and blacklisted.

Pete Seeger, a member of the popular music group the Weavers,
which had recorded a number of hit songs ("Goodnight Irene," "Kisses
Sweeter than Wine," "Sixteen Tons"), also ran afoul of HUAC. In August 1955 he was subpoenaed by the committee to testify about his political affiliations. Seeger, who had been a member of the Communist

Party, was responsible for introducing "We Shall Overcome" to civil
rights activists and was the composer of such protest songs as "If I Had
a Hammer" and "Where Have All the Flowers Gone?" Seeger's antiwar
views and firm commitment to civil rights, as well as his former Communist Party membership, made him an obvious target for a HUAC
investigation. Members of the committee interrogated Seeger about
his attendance and performances at communist rallies and meetings,
but Seeger refused to answer the questions, not on the grounds of the
Fifth Amendment, as so many defendants routinely pleaded, but on the
grounds of the First Amendment—that Congress had no right to ask
questions regarding personal political beliefs. "I am not going to answer
any questions," Seeger told the committee, "as to my association, my
philosophical or religious beliefs or my political beliefs, or how I voted
in any election, or any of these private affairs. I think these are very im-
proper questions for any American to be asked, especially under such
compulsion as this. I would be very glad to tell you my life if you want
to hear of it." When pressed repeatedly to admit that he sang his songs at
communist rallies, Seeger replied, "I have sung for Americans of every
political persuasion, and I am proud that I never refuse to sing to an
audience, no matter what religion or color of their skin, or situation in
life. I have sung in hobo jungles, and I have sung for the Rockefellers,
and I am proud that I have never refused to sing for anybody. That is the
only answer I can give along that line." The committee kept insisting that
Seeger answer the question.

MR. SEEGER: Except for the answer I have already given you, I have
no answer. . . . I am proud that I have sung for Americans of every
political persuasion, and I have never refused to sing for anybody
because I disagreed with their political opinion, and I am proud of
the fact that my songs seem to cut across and find perhaps a unifying
thing, basic humanity. . . .
MR. TAVENNER: My question was whether or not you sang at these
functions of the Communist Party. . . .

MR. SEEGER: I decline to discuss, under compulsion, where I have
sung, and who has sung my songs, and who else has sung with me,
and the people I have known. I love my country very dearly, and I
greatly resent this implication that some of the places that I have
sung and some of the people that I have known, and some of my
opinions, whether they are religious or philosophical . . . make me
any less of an American.[5]

Seeger, like Lawson, was convicted of contempt of Congress and sentenced to a year in prison. Seeger appealed, and the sentence was
overturned seven years later. But he was blacklisted and banned from
radio and television until 1967.

Another target of HUAC was the African American actor-singer Paul
Robeson. Starting in the 1930s, Robeson, who had achieved great fame
for his acclaimed performances in *Othello*, *The Emperor Jones*, and *Show
Boat*, traveled extensively abroad, where he assertively expressed his political views. He condemned segregation in the United States, denounced
the fascist dictators in Europe, and expressed support for the Loyalists in
Spain and his admiration of Soviet communism. Robeson was especially
impressed with his treatment in the Soviet Union, where he found that
he could walk the streets, eat in restaurants, and take public transportation without being subjected to racial discrimination. Communism,
Robeson declared, was more egalitarian than American democracy.
After World War II he continued to speak favorably of communism,
protested against the Jim Crow laws, and urged African Americans not
to participate in an "imperialist war" if the United States went to war
against the Soviet Union. In 1949 anticommunism was so extreme that
when Robeson was booked to perform a concert in Peekskill, New York,
all hell broke loose. Militant anticommunist protesters, wielding baseball bats, attacked concertgoers and forced the postponement of the
concert. The following week more than twenty thousand people were in
attendance at the open-air event when Robeson and other performers
finally took the stage. But when people were leaving at the end of the

concert, they were violently attacked. Hundreds of protesters screamed epithets at the performers and concertgoers, condemning them as unpatriotic, anti-American communists. With the police looking on, rock-throwing vigilantes, local residents as well as members of the American Legion and the Ku Klux Klan, attacked the cars and buses leaving the area. Dozens of people were severely injured. In the aftermath, producers canceled Robeson's bookings, and there were public burnings of his records.

In 1950 the State Department revoked Paul Robeson's passport. With Robeson unable to travel abroad and not being booked in American concert halls, his career came to a crashing halt. With the FBI keeping him under surveillance, Robeson sued the government to reinstate his passport. Finally, in 1956 he was summoned to testify before the House Committee on Un-American Activities. Despite the constant browbeating by members of the committee and despite his continued invocation of the Fifth Amendment, Robeson managed to lecture them on the meaning of "Americanism" and insisted that it was the committee, not he, that was unpatriotic. "Whether I am or not a Communist is irrelevant," he declared. "The question is whether American citizens, regardless of their political beliefs or sympathies, may enjoy their constitutional rights." Furthermore, he asked at another point, "what do you mean by the Communist Party? As far as I know it is a legal party like the Republican Party and the Democratic Party. Do you mean a party of people who have sacrificed for my people, and for all Americans and workers, that they can live in dignity? Do you mean that party?" Robeson admitted that he admired the Soviet Union. "In Russia," he said, "I felt for the first time like a full human being. No color prejudice like in Mississippi, no color prejudice like in Washington. It was the first time I felt like a human being. Where I did not feel the pressure of color as I feel [it] in this Committee today." One of the interlocutors then asked him why he did not stay in Russia, to which Robeson replied, "Because my father was a slave, and my people died to build this country, and I am going to stay here, and have a part of it just like you. And no

Fascist-minded people will drive me from it. Is that clear? I am for peace with the Soviet Union, and I am for peace with China, and I am not for peace or friendship with the Fascist Franco, and I am not for peace with Fascist Nazi Germans. I am for peace with decent people." He was a true patriot, Robeson insisted, unlike the members of the committee, the very existence of which goes against the most fundamental principles of the United States. "You gentlemen belong with the Alien and Sedition Acts, and you are the nonpatriots, and you are the un-Americans, and you ought to be ashamed of yourselves."[6] This was too much for the congressmen, and they abruptly adjourned the hearing.

Many Americans were appalled by the proceedings of HUAC as well as the McCarthy hearings in the Senate, and hundreds protested against the attempt to root out Americans with left-wing political beliefs, to destroy their careers, and to tarnish them as unpatriotic. The playwright Arthur Miller responded to the hearings with his play *The Crucible*, in which he drew on the 1692 Salem witchcraft trials as a thinly veiled allegory for the anticommunist witch hunt. Actors and actresses spoke out against HUAC. "As an American," Katharine Hepburn declared, "I shall always resist any attempt at the abridgement of freedom."[7] And Humphrey Bogart and Lauren Bacall led a score of actors in a march in Washington, DC, protesting HUAC's hounding of the Hollywood Ten—a cohort of movie producers, directors, and screenwriters, including Lawson, Ring Lardner, Jr., Edward Dmytryk, and Dalton Trumbo, who were targeted and blacklisted by the House Committee. Republican Senator Margaret Chase Smith of Maine courageously protested the McCarthy hearings. According to Smith, her fellow senator's crusade was endangering one of the most cherished American principles—freedom of conscience. In 1950 she issued a "Declaration of Conscience" in which she denounced Senator McCarthy and appealed to all Americans to stand up for the principles of democracy. "I think that it is high time for the United States Senate and its members to do some soul searching—for us to weigh our consciences—on the manner in which we are performing our duty to the people of America—on the manner in which we are using or abusing our individual powers and privileges." The Constitution, she pointed out, is about freedom of speech and the right to a jury trial. It is *not* about "trial by accusation" or character assassination. "Those of us who shout the loudest about Americanism in making character assassinations," she said,

> are all too frequently those who, by our own words and acts, ignore some of the basic principles of Americanism—
>
> > The right to criticize;
> > The right to hold unpopular beliefs;
> > The right to protest;
> > The right of independent thought.
>
> The exercise of these rights should not cost one single American citizen his reputation or his right to a livelihood nor should he be in danger of losing his reputation or livelihood merely because he happens to know some one who holds unpopular beliefs. . . .

The tactics employed by Senator McCarthy and others, Smith concluded, are worse than the evils they are trying to expose. They are "totalitarian techniques" that threaten the very existence of the United States and "that, if continued here unchecked, will surely end what we have come to cherish as the American way of life." As a dedicated Republican, Smith stressed that she longed for a Republican victory in the 1952 presidential election, after twenty years of a Democrat in the White House, because it "is necessary to the security of this country."

> Yet to displace it with a Republican regime embracing a philosophy that lacks political integrity or intellectual honesty would prove equally disastrous to this nation. The nation sorely needs a Republican victory. But I don't want to see the Republican Party ride to political victory on the Four Horsemen of Calumny—Fear, Ignorance, Bigotry and Smear.

I doubt the Republican Party could—simply because I don't believe the American people will uphold any political party that puts political exploitation above national interest.[8]

Even so, despite such pleas for sanity and rational discourse, hundreds of creative artists were blacklisted, and careers were destroyed. In addition to Pete Seeger and Paul Robeson, Charlie Chaplin, Leonard Bernstein, John Garfield, Orson Welles, Arthur Miller, Dashiell Hammett, Lillian Hellman, Lee Grant, and Aaron Copeland were among those blacklisted.

* * *

At the same time that American soldiers were fighting communism in Korea and anticommunist hysteria was gripping the nation at home, the United States was experiencing unprecedented prosperity. This created an eerie, nearly schizophrenic, fixation within the American psyche. Pride in the "American way of life" was at odds with the obsessive fear that the nuclear powers could unleash Armageddon on the world, which would in an instant destroy civilization. Patriotic Americans believed that the Soviet Union was a malevolent, godless, totalitarian society, while the United States represented all that was good and virtuous in the world. Such an attitude generated enormous pressure for conformity. The message was clear. Everyone should aspire to live the American Dream in a nice suburban house with a large picture window, have a stable job in a prosperous company, purchase consumer goods every week, faithfully watch television every night, value the American way, and be constantly vigilant against communism at home as well as abroad. But as the social critic John Keats pointed out, there was a "crack in the picture window" of suburbia.[9] Not everyone found happiness living the American Dream. Many found that material possessions did not bring contentment, while large numbers of Americans were too poor even to participate in the American Dream. The sociologists William Whyte and David Riesman condemned the conformity that had engulfed the United States. In *The Organization Man* Whyte argued that Americans were more concerned with fitting in than with standing out, that they had lost their ability to generate innovative ideas. And Riesman postulated in *The Lonely Crowd* that Americans were no longer "inner directed" individuals acting according to their deep-seated principles and morality but were "other directed," without original thoughts of their own, lacking inner values, and more concerned with pleasing others and "keeping up with the Joneses." Such insights were only the tip of the iceberg. Many Americans, in the midst of the conformist 1950s, resisted the impulse to conform.

Signs of dissent were apparent, if implicit, in art and music. Abstract expressionists such as Mark Rothko, Robert Motherwell, and Jackson Pollock painted canvases that ignored all the traditional conventions of visual art. Viewers did not know what to think of their paintings. Charlie Parker, Dizzy Gillespie, Thelonious Monk, and scores of other musicians took jazz to a new level of improvisation and individual inventiveness that puzzled listeners. Perhaps the musicians and artists themselves were not fully conscious that they were expressing in their own creative way a form of protest (or at least a nagging dissatisfaction) against the suffocating conformity of the era.

In literature too there were abundant signs of discontent, notably Arthur Miller's *The Crucible*, J. D. Salinger's *The Catcher in the Rye*, and Ray Bradbury's *Fahrenheit 451*. But it was in the Beat movement that a literature of dissent made a frontal assault on the political, social, and cultural orthodoxy of the times. William Burroughs, Allen Ginsberg, and Jack Kerouac formed the core of a phalanx of rebellious writers in New York City during the late 1940s. By the early 1950s in their writings (mostly unpublished at that time) and lifestyle they were a living reproof to the conformist, straitlaced mentality of the affluent society. Condemning the split-level American Dream, they denounced middle-class values, anticommunist hysteria, Cold War propaganda, and the unbridled materialism that dominated the era. To the Beats mainstream America was in denial about the millions of marginalized individuals who were ignored by television and the media—Blacks, Hispanics,

American Indians, homosexuals, drug addicts, ex-cons, creative artists, dropouts. And so in their poetry and novels they extolled the outcasts. Ginsberg was especially outspoken and unapologetic about his homosexuality and never missed an opportunity to celebrate it. In October 1955 he electrified the underground scene when he performed his poem "Howl" at the Six Gallery in San Francisco. "I greet you at the beginning of a great career," fellow poet and publisher Lawrence Ferlinghetti cabled Ginsberg after the performance.[10] When Ferlinghetti's City Lights Books published *Howl and Other Poems*, the San Francisco Police confiscated the books, arrested the clerk at City Lights Bookstore for selling an "obscene" book, and charged Ferlinghetti with obscenity. The publicity generated by the resulting trial was a marketing boon for the book. Everyone wanted to read it, even after the judge ruled that "Howl" was not obscenity but literature. "I saw the best minds of my generation destroyed by / madness, starving hysterical naked, / dragging themselves through the negro streets at / dawn looking for an angry fix," Ginsberg begins, and then he continues with a mesmerizing litany of American outcasts struggling to survive any way they can in the consumer society. He speaks of "angelheaded hipsters," "saintly motorcyclists," "visionary Indian angels," and the Old Testament deity Moloch, who demands the sacrifice of children.[11]

In another poem in the collection, "America," Ginsberg uses humor and history to effectively challenge Americans to reexamine their assumptions, their values, and the way they live their lives. Like Socrates, he implies that the unexamined life is not worth living. He extols the Wobblies, the Scottsboro Boys, communists, radicals, and marijuana while condemning tired Cold War clichés and *Time* magazine. "Are you going to let your emotional life be run by Time Magazine?" "America," Ginsberg says, "go fuck yourself with your atom bomb."[12]

In interviews, Ginsberg recalled that when he and Kerouac were young men, they were constantly lectured to about morality and ethics. Parents and teachers and politicians and clergymen were always telling them what was right and what was wrong, that marriage was good but premarital or homosexual sex was bad, that conformity and middle-class values were good but holding radical views and doing drugs was bad. And it occurred to them that the generation that was responsible for the Holocaust and Hiroshima had no right to lecture on morality. "In the forties the Bomb dropped, the entire planet was threatened biologically. . . . [We] suddenly [had] the realization, why are we being intimidated by a bunch of jerks who don't even know about life? Who are they to tell us what we feel and how we're supposed to behave and why take all that bullshit?"[13]

Jack Kerouac's *On the Road*, published in 1957, was an instant success, especially with the nation's youth. Young people (including Bob Dylan and Jim Morrison) responded to Kerouac's message of going against the grain, being in the here and now, and living life to the fullest. The journey, the road itself, not the destination, was the purpose of life. To Kerouac it was the downtrodden, the outsiders, who were the most exciting people. "The only people for me," Kerouac wrote, "are the mad ones, the ones who are mad to live, mad to talk, mad to be saved, desirous of everything at the same time, the ones who never yawn or say a commonplace thing, but burn, burn, burn."[14]

The fact that so many baby boomers read *On the Road* as well as "Howl" and other Beat works was a symptom of an undercurrent of rebellion that lay below the surface of the complacent 1950s. The writings of William Burroughs, Gregory Corso, Gary Snyder, and other Beat writers, with the emphasis on hipness, jazz, unconventional thinking, individuality, sexual freedom, drugs, and Zen Buddhism, had a significant influence on the generation that shaped the counterculture of the 1960s.

This undercurrent of rebellion was even evident at the same time with children who had no idea what conformity or nonconformity even meant. An irreverent comic book, *Mad Magazine*, captivated children and young adolescents. First published in 1953, *Mad* satirized everything about Cold War America, including pop culture. *Mad*'s socio-cultural effect appealed to adults as well, but for the children of the Cold War and atom bomb, *Mad* offered a subversive mockery of everything they were taught to respect and revere. The white-bread youth of the 1950s and early 1960s were (mostly) isolated from the rumblings of the Beats, bebop, and abstract expressionism for reasons of age or geography—but they did have *Mad*. For any young person who felt their reality and that shown on TV or newspapers differed greatly, *Mad* was both a balm and rallying-cry.

Mad was not the sole impetus for the countercultural rebellion of the 1960s, but its enormous popularity certainly aided the development thereof. *Mad* told its readers that advertisers were consummate liars, corporations and the government were detached from reality, and popular culture was pitched at the lowest common denominator—*Mad* itself included. In an age of deep moral rectitude and certainty, *Mad* insisted that nothing should be taken at face value and independent thought was critical. Despite its title, *Mad* was an ocean of sanity in the illogical wilds of Cold War suburbia.

* * *

The most conspicuous indication that young Americans were chafing at the oppressive conformity of middle-class American life was the arrival of rock and roll. In the early 1950s "race music" (as it was first called) was gaining in popularity. Record stores and radio stations were increasingly promoting African American rhythm and blues, but then interest in the music exploded in 1951 when a Cleveland radio station began airing disc jockey Alan Freed's *Moondog's Rock 'n' Roll Party*. Within a few years, hundreds of radio stations throughout the country featured rock and roll shows. By the mid-1950s American teenagers were hungrily consuming the music of Black artists such as Fats Domino, Little Richard, and Chuck Berry as well as whites such as Bill Haley, Jerry Lee Lewis, and above all, Elvis Presley. Presley was a phenomenon whose huge popularity hinted at cultural, racial, and sexual unrest. Adolescent girls were obsessed with Presley's music and overt (and somewhat ambiguous) sexuality, which flew in the face of conventional morality. They screamed so loudly at his concerts that it was impossible to hear him sing. Adults were horrified. They viewed Presley as a threat to morals and decency; they feared he would corrupt the nation's youth. But when Elvis performed on Ed Sullivan's popular television show in 1956, it was clear that, no matter how emphatically adults objected, rock and roll was here to stay.

Right-wingers loudly (and ludicrously) denounced rock and roll as part of the "international communist conspiracy to corrupt America's youth." But in a sense rock and roll was indeed "revolutionary" music—not in the sense that its goal was to overthrow the United States (and certainly not in the sense that the teeny-bopper lyrics emphasizing puppy love and teenage lust were at all political) but because the music itself, the visceral, uninhibited, sensual beat and the culture and lifestyle it represented, was inherently a powerful criticism of middle-class values and the repressive political culture of anticommunism. (A decade later, of course, rock and roll lyrics *did* become overtly political.) The rock and roll phenomenon in the 1950s, which inspired young people to religiously listen every day to the Top Forty hits on the radio and to watch *American Bandstand* on television, to purchase the latest hit singles and to line up to buy tickets to rock and roll concerts, was a clear indication that American teenagers had an indefinable longing for something that the material comforts of the affluent society were not providing.

* * *

America's restlessness and discontent, especially among young people, was one sign that all was not well in the affluent society. But the most important indicator that the American Dream was not quite living up to its billing was the emergence of the Civil Rights Movement. After a century of waiting for equal rights, African Americans refused to wait any longer. By the end of the decade, the modern Civil Rights Movement challenged the fundamental assumptions about the meaning of democracy and forced Americans to reevaluate their most basic and cherished principles.

There were signs, long before World War II, that the winds of change were impacting race relations in the United States. The founding of the NAACP, Marcus Garvey's United Negro Improvement Association, and the Harlem Renaissance were just a few of the important early steps in the long Civil Rights Movement. During the New Deal, First Lady Eleanor Roosevelt had pushed her husband hard to do more for African Americans in the programs he submitted to Congress. In 1939, when a concert at Washington's Constitution Hall featuring the famed African American opera singer Marian Anderson was canceled because the venue was a segregated facility, Eleanor Roosevelt made headlines when she arranged for Anderson to perform on the steps of the Lincoln Memorial on Easter Sunday. Seventy-five thousand people attended the widely publicized event, and it was not lost on the public that the First Lady was clearly a champion of civil rights. Many applauded her stance. Many hated her for it.

World War II was a transformative experience for African Americans soldiers. They saw a wider world and were welcomed as heroes in Europe as the Allied armies liberated Italy, France, Belgium, and the Netherlands. And when American troops crossed into Germany, African Americans were among those who entered the extermination camps, witnessing firsthand the consequences of Hitler's racist policies. But when Black GIs returned home, especially those returning to the South, they were not treated as conquering heroes. And the "Colored Only" and "Whites Only" signs were a galling reminder that though they had just played a part in the liberation of Europe and the destruction of fascism, not much had really changed at home. Tens of thousands of African Americans vowed that they were not going to take it anymore.

By the 1950s there was a rapidly growing Black middle class of physicians, lawyers, teachers, scientists, businessmen, and clergymen. African American role models became increasingly visible. Ralph Bunche was appointed the United States' first ambassador to the United Nations. Jackie Robinson broke the color line in major-league baseball and in doing so electrified the African American community (as well as millions of white Americans) and opened the way for Roy Campanella, Don Newcombe, Willie Mays, Ernie Banks, and eventually hundreds of others. Writers such as Ralph Ellison, Richard Wright, and James Baldwin were putting their mark on American literature. Musicians and performers such as Paul Robeson, Charlie Parker, and Louis Armstrong became household names. All this elevated African Americans to a more prominent place in the American consciousness.

When President Truman learned that a Black soldier, Isaac Woodard, was severely beaten by South Carolina police and heard about the lynching of other African American veterans returning home at war's end, he was galvanized into action. He appointed a Committee on Civil Rights to make recommendations about what should be done. In early 1948, armed with the committee's report (*To Secure These Rights*), Truman went to Congress and called for legislation that would establish "a permanent Commission on Civil Rights, a Joint Congressional Committee on Civil Rights, and a Civil Rights Division in the Department of Justice."[15] He also asked Congress to establish a Fair Employment Practice Commission and enact federal antilynching laws. And then five months later Truman issued Executive Order 9980 desegregating the civil service and Executive Order 9981 desegregating the armed forces. The impact of Truman's executive orders was far-reaching and, despite significant resistance, went a long way toward establishing a level of equality in federal jobs and the military. Truman's commitment to civil rights, however, nearly cost him the 1948 election when southern Democrats quit the convention, formed the States' Rights Party (dubbed by the press the "Dixiecrats"), and nominated the segregationist governor of South Carolina, Strom Thurmond, for president.

It was clear by the early 1950s that change was in the air regarding the issue of race and that change, when it came, would not be easy. The invention of television also had a profound impact on the emergence of the Civil Rights Movement. It meant that Americans, no matter where they lived in the United States, were exposed to escalating news coverage about racial matters—from Supreme Court decisions to lynchings and protests and boycotts in the South. Not only did television coverage of these events force Americans to form their own opinions about race, but also it embarrassingly revealed to the world at the height of the Cold War that American democracy was imperfect. This was especially discomforting to the American government because U.S. foreign policy focused on proving to the world, specifically the new independent nations of Africa, that the "American way" was superior to the Soviet system. In this way the emerging Civil Rights Movement had an impact on the propaganda war being waged between the United States and the Soviet Union for the hearts and minds of the Third World. And that ideological war had an impact on civil rights. If the United States was committed to containing communism and preventing the Soviet Union from extending its influence in the Third World, it was absolutely necessary that the federal government, no matter how reluctantly, respond to the demands of civil rights activists. The harsh realities of the Cold War struggle between democracy and totalitarianism turned civil rights into an issue of national security.

For decades NAACP lawyers had fought diligently to overturn the 1896 *Plessy v. Ferguson* "separate but equal" decision, which validated the Jim Crow laws, by taking case after case to the Supreme Court. Many of the cases were attempts to force poor southern school districts to abide by the *Plessy* decision, that is, to compel them to build separate schools for Black children in districts where the community could not afford to do so. This moderate form of protest by the NAACP actually did have some success in getting poor school districts to quietly open their existing schools to Blacks rather than to incur the expense of constructing another building. But the organization understood that it would take centuries to desegregate southern schools with this approach. By the 1940s the NAACP shifted its focus from enforcing the letter of the law to attacking head-on the doctrine of segregation itself. In two 1950 decisions the Court ruled that colleges in Oklahoma and Texas could not segregate students on the basis of race, and then the Court took on five separate cases dealing with segregation in public schools in Virginia,

Kansas, Delaware, South Carolina, and Washington, DC. On May 17, 1954, the Supreme Court unanimously overturned *Plessy v Ferguson*. After listening to testimony from legal authorities, psychologists, anthropologists, and educators, the Court ruled in *Brown v. Board of Education* that separating Black children "from others of similar age and qualifications solely because of their race generates a feeling of inferiority as to their status in the community that may affect their hearts and minds in a way unlikely ever to be undone." Even if Black children are placed in a superior school, the fact that they are set apart creates a feeling of inferiority and deeply affects their motivation to learn. "We conclude that, in the field of public education, the doctrine of 'separate but equal' has no place. Separate educational facilities are inherently unequal."[16]

Throughout the nation African Americans rejoiced. But the Supreme Court did little to enforce compliance with the decision other than urging that desegregation be carried out with "all deliberate speed." And when President Dwight D. Eisenhower commented that he did not think it wise to try to alter southern traditions overnight that had been in effect for generations, southern whites were emboldened to resist. What the president's reticence meant for African Americans was that more than a decade of activism, protest, and resistance lay ahead before the decision was fully implemented.

7

Civil Rights

The only weapon that we have in our hands this evening is
the weapon of protest. . . . And certainly, certainly, this is the
glory of America, with all of its faults. This is the glory of our
democracy. If we were incarcerated behind the iron curtains
of a Communistic nation, we couldn't do this. . . . But the great
glory of American democracy is the right to protest for right.
—Martin Luther King, Jr., address in Montgomery, Alabama,
December 5, 1955

In August 1955, fourteen-year-old Emmett Till of Chicago, visiting rela-
tives in Mississippi, was abducted by J. W. Milam and Roy Bryant, beaten,
shot, and dumped in the Tallahatchie River. His offense? He had "talked
fresh" to a white woman. When photographs of Till's brutalized, decom-
posed body were published in the African American press, the nation
was shocked. How could a fourteen-year-old be so savagely murdered for
such a minor infraction? The publicity surrounding the case generated
immense interest in the trial, and when it commenced at the end of September, hundreds of reporters descended on the courthouse in Sumner,
Mississippi. Although Moses Wright (Till's great-uncle) testified that he
had witnessed Milam and Bryant taking his nephew away, and though
it was clear that the two men were guilty of the crime, the all-white
jury deliberated for less than an hour before acquitting the defendants.
Around the world newspapers denounced the obvious miscarriage of justice. In West Germany a newspaper proclaimed that a Black person's life
in the United States was worth nothing. In Belgium a paper called it "a
judicial scandal." And France's Le Monde prophetically reported that perhaps the Till murder would serve to awaken America's consciousness.[1]

Two months later, on December 1, 1955, Rosa Parks refused to give up her seat on a Montgomery, Alabama, bus to a white man. Parks was a longtime community organizer and labor and civil rights activist. She was an active member of the Montgomery NAACP, and she had attended civil disobedience workshops at the Highlander Folk School in Tennessee. Her deliberate act of dissent motivated members of the African American community to stage a bus boycott. The one-day boycott was so successful that they formed the Montgomery Improvement Association (MIA) in order to coordinate a longer boycott. At a meeting at the Holt Street Baptist Church, a new minister in town, the twenty-six-year-old Martin Luther King, Jr., electrified the crowd with his stirring oratory. "We are not wrong in what we are doing," King proclaimed. "If we are wrong, the Supreme Court of this nation is wrong. If we are wrong, the Constitution of the United States is wrong. If we are wrong, God Almighty is wrong."[2]

The people mobilized quickly. King was elected to head the MIA, and with the hard work of Jo Ann Robinson, the association printed and distributed thousands of leaflets and organized carpools for workers who lived long distances from their jobs. The boycott continued month after month without any movement on the part of the city but with a great deal of harassment of the drivers running the carpools and the bombing of several civil rights leaders' homes. Still the boycott held. And still the protesters heeded King's call for nonviolence. Drawing on the ideas of Henry David Thoreau and Mahatma Gandhi, as well as the teachings of Jesus and the Social Gospel, King believed that nonviolence was the best tactic to defeat racism and segregation. Violence only begat more violence. Violence hardened attitudes on both sides of a dispute. Through nonviolence one could shame the system into seeing the injustice of racial discrimination; through nonviolence one could transform one's enemy into a friend.

The boycott continued. The Black citizens of Montgomery walked and walked and walked. Finally, in June 1956 the U.S. Supreme Court ruled that bus segregation was unconstitutional. After appeals, the ruling went into effect a year after the boycott began. On December 20, 1956, Blacks ended the campaign and resumed riding the buses—this time sitting in the front.

Early in 1957, King and a number of civil rights leaders founded the Southern Christian Leadership Conference (SCLC) as a grassroots organization to spearhead the Civil Rights Movement. Drawing its members from the South's African American churches, SCLC conducted educational programs and civil disobedience workshops throughout the region, coordinated protests and demonstrations, organized voter registration drives, and emphasized the moral element of the campaign against racism. By the 1960s, SCLC was one of the most important organizations fighting Jim Crow and putting pressure on the federal government to address racial injustice.

In 1957 a federal court ordered the Little Rock, Arkansas, school district to comply with the *Brown* decision and desegregate Little Rock Central High School. On September 4, Governor Orval Faubus defied the court order by ordering the Arkansas National Guard to prevent the admission of nine Black students. The standoff continued for two weeks until a federal court ordered the governor to remove the National Guard. On September 23 the students gained admittance to the school, but a white mob outside began breaking windows and beating up Black reporters who had come to Little Rock to cover the story. The police then stepped in and, in order to defuse the situation, removed the students from the school.

Though President Eisenhower had originally been critical of the *Brown* decision, it was his duty as president to uphold federal law. Fed up with Faubus's defiance, Eisenhower deployed the 101st Airborne Division to protect the students and restore order. And so, on September 24, the Little Rock Nine finally began taking classes at the high school. Throughout the country Americans could watch the daily scenes on television news of soldiers escorting the nine students up the steps and into the school. Despite the presence of the soldiers surrounding the school, each of the students endured hostility (punching, shoving, cursing, spitting) from the white students. After a few days of this each of the nine was assigned his or her own personal bodyguard—one of the soldiers—in order to minimize the harassment.

Like the Emmett Till lynching and the Montgomery bus boycott, the events in Little Rock focused the nation's attention on civil rights. What exactly *are* our rights? What is it exactly that the Constitution guarantees for American citizens? Americans believed that "all men are created equal." But what exactly did that mean? Why were African Americans in the South demonstrating to end state-mandated segregation, job discrimination, and voter suppression? Why were African Americans in the North demanding an end to housing segregation, non-legally-mandated segregation of schools and facilities, and endemic job discrimination? Why were African Americans fighting for empowerment and the opportunity to determine their own lives, culture, and communities? Newspaper accounts and televised broadcasts of the African American struggle to secure these rights underscored for most Americans the glaringly obvious fact that not all people were considered equal in the United States, that America was not living up to its own ideals. All of this served to broaden consciousness and to accelerate the dialogue. Americans who knew nothing about the African American experience were increasingly confronted with the evils of racism and segregation (de jure and de facto). And as time wore on, those who had no opinion about civil rights found that they were forced to develop an opinion, forced to choose sides.

Protests against segregation reached a new level on February 1, 1960, when four Black college students walked into the local Woolworth's in Greensboro, North Carolina, and sat down at the lunch counter. Even though African Americans were permitted to shop at the store, they were forbidden service at the lunch counter. As the four young men expected, they were not served. Over the ensuing days they returned, accompanied by ever-increasing numbers of their fellow students. Within a week the sit-ins spread to Nashville, Atlanta, Charlotte, and dozens of other cities throughout the South. As the sit-ins proliferated,

whites began a campaign of harassing the demonstrators—shouting racial slurs, punching them, pouring ketchup and mustard on their heads,
extinguishing cigarettes on the backs of their necks—until finally store
management called in the police. Instead of arresting the white thugs for
assault, the police arrested the protesters for disorderly conduct. Many
of the stores simply shut down their lunch counters. Since most of the
five-and-dime stores targeted were part of national chains, civil rights
activists launched a nationwide campaign to boycott all the stores, even
though the northern branches did not discriminate against Blacks. Thus,
around the nation, outside of Woolworth's and Kresge's and other stores,
demonstrators formed picket lines and carried signs urging shoppers
not to do business with chain stores that practiced segregation in the
South.

By summer, after thousands of arrests in dozens of cities throughout the South, the sit-ins bore fruit. Although some stores continued
to refuse service to African Americans for a number of years, most did
desegregate their lunch counters. Feeling the economic pinch, corporate
headquarters of national chains ordered their southern stores to serve
Blacks. In Nashville hundreds of protesters marched to city hall, where,
with the media recording the confrontation, they held a dialogue with
the mayor on the building's steps. When student activist Diane Nash
asked Mayor Ben West if he thought it was wrong to discriminate against
someone on the basis of race, he answered honestly that he *did* think
it was wrong. Nash followed up by asking him if he thought Nashville
stores should serve Blacks. West said "yes." Within a month Nashville
desegregated its lunch counters. It took six months in Greensboro, but
by July most stores began serving Blacks. Other cities, such as Atlanta,
took more than a year, but in the end desegregation came there, too.

* * *

Even though most of the nation's youth were more interested in
watching *American Bandstand* on television than civil rights demonstrations, they were aware of the news reports coming out of the South.

And many of them, as they entered college in the last years of the decade and the first years of the 1960s, perceived the African American struggle for civil rights as a just cause. Baby boomers had been taught that the United States was the greatest nation on earth, that the United States was superior to totalitarian Russia and China because in America everyone was free and equal. But the events in Montgomery and Little Rock and Greensboro contradicted that notion. The reality was that not everyone was free and equal. Unconsciously, and in many cases consciously, it occurred to young Americans that if they pointed out that there was some discrepancy between what is and what should be, then there was a chance that they could put things right so that the reality in America would more closely resemble the ideal. "We can change the world" became a rallying cry.

When John F. Kennedy was sworn in as president on January 20, 1961, he tapped into the idealism of the nation's youth. His entreaty to "ask not what your country can do for you, ask what you can do for your country" reinforced the belief that with enough energy and dedication, young people could indeed change the world. The idealism that JFK symbolized and promoted, along with the example of African American student activists, motivated white college students to participate in the struggle for civil rights.

And in May 1961 the next phase of the Civil Rights Movement commenced with the participation of larger numbers of whites than previously. The Congress of Racial Equality (CORE) sponsored a "Freedom Ride" in an effort to push the federal government to enforce the Supreme Court's 1960 *Boynton v. Virginia* decision, which outlawed segregation in interstate travel facilities: bus terminals, waiting rooms, restrooms. Although the ruling was already in effect, buses and bus terminals in the South remained segregated. The plan was for small groups of Black and white activists to travel on interstate buses from Washington, DC, to New Orleans. As the buses entered the South, white Freedom Riders would sit in the back of the bus and Black Freedom Riders in the front. At each rest stop along the way, the whites would use the Black restrooms and lunch counters, and the Blacks would use the white facilities. They reasoned that somewhere along the line they would meet with resistance and that an incident would trigger a federal response. On May 4, 1961, two buses left Washington, DC. In South Carolina two riders were beaten, another arrested. But the major confrontation took place shortly after the buses crossed from Georgia into Alabama. One of the buses was stopped and firebombed by Klansmen near Anniston, Alabama. The bus was destroyed, and the Freedom Riders suffered burns and smoke inhalation and were beaten—it was a miracle that no one was killed. The second bus made it all the way to Birmingham, where it was met by another mob of Klansmen. Again no one was killed, but several riders were beaten so severely that they were hospitalized. James Farmer, the national director of CORE, canceled the rest of the ride, and the riders abandoned the attempt.

The Student Nonviolent Coordinating Committee (SNCC)[3] now stepped into the fray. "We can't let them stop us with violence," proclaimed Diane Nash, one of the leaders of the Nashville sit-ins of the previous year. "If we do, the movement is dead."[4] She and other members of SNCC organized a second Freedom Ride, this time from Nashville to Birmingham. Before the bus arrived in Birmingham, however, state police stopped it and arrested the ten Freedom Riders. By this time the Kennedy administration, albeit reluctantly, was finally beginning to respond (President Kennedy, in the midst of escalating tensions with the Soviet Union, had asked his civil rights adviser, Harris Wofford, to tell the protesters to call off the Freedom Rides while the country was facing a showdown over Berlin). Attorney General Robert F. Kennedy worked out an agreement with the governor of Alabama that the state police would escort the bus from Birmingham to Montgomery. But when the bus arrived at Montgomery's city limits, the state police withdrew, leaving the riders unprotected. At the bus terminal the SNCC people were attacked by hundreds of stick- and pipe-wielding Klansmen and assaulted so brutally (one rider was set on fire) that several suffered permanent brain damage. Even Justice Department official John Seigenthaler was beaten unconscious. When the Montgomery police stepped in, they issued an injunction prohibiting the continuation of the Freedom Ride.

At this point Martin Luther King flew to Montgomery and held a mass meeting in support of the Freedom Riders at the First Baptist Church. "The federal government," King proclaimed, "must not stand idly by while bloodthirsty mobs beat nonviolent students with impunity."[5] But even as King addressed the rally, a violent mob surrounded the church shouting epithets and threats, overturned and set vehicles on fire, and threw bricks and tear-gas canisters through the church's windows. Federal marshals were barely holding the line against the enraged mob. With the congregation choking on smoke and tear gas and King describing the situation over the telephone to Robert Kennedy, the Alabama National Guard finally arrived on the scene. Even so, it took the rest of the night for the guardsmen and the marshals to disperse the mob and get the congregation safely home.

At the end of May, President Kennedy ordered the Interstate Commerce Commission (ICC) to establish a procedure to enforce the desegregation ruling, but nothing changed. And the Freedom Riders kept coming. Every week dozens of activists boarded buses in northern cities and rode into the Deep South. They never got farther than Alabama or Mississippi before they were arrested and thrown into prison. Mississippi's infamous Parchman Prison was overflowing with Freedom Riders. But the activists did not lose heart. Confined to their cells, they sang freedom songs—"We Shall Overcome," "If I Had a Hammer," "Oh Freedom," "We Shall Not Be Moved," "Ain't Gonna Let Nobody Turn Me Around"—even after guards removed their mattresses in an effort to silence them. Still, they kept singing. Finally, in September the ICC enforced the ban on segregated facilities and buses. Like the sit-in campaign of the previous year, direct action once again achieved a small victory.

The objective of the direct action campaigns was to force the federal government to acknowledge that African Americans were deprived of their basic citizenship rights and then to force Washington to intervene in the South to secure those rights. With a liberal Democrat in the White House, civil rights protesters had high hopes that Washington would respond to their demands, but Kennedy's reluctance to commit the administration (because he feared negative political fallout) frustrated and angered civil rights protesters. Kennedy continued to put pressure on the leaders of the movement to tone down the rhetoric and be less confrontational. But Martin Luther King, James Farmer, Diane Nash, John Lewis, and thousands of other dedicated protesters vowed to keep the pressure on until African Americans achieved the full rights of first-class citizenship.

* * *

The sit-ins and Freedom Rides inspired millions and spawned a host of demonstrations. In scores of cities and rural communities throughout the South activists marched, demonstrated, protested, and demanded the end of Jim Crow. Black students took the lead, but ordinary members of African American churches, elderly people, children, and even many whites also participated. And in every region of the country, Americans of all ethnicities and socioeconomic backgrounds were forced to think about civil rights and answer the question "which side are you on?"

When James Meredith was refused admittance to the University of Mississippi, he appealed to the Supreme Court that he had been rejected solely on the basis of his race. In September 1962 the Court ruled in Meredith's favor and ordered the all-white university to admit him. But when Meredith attempted to enroll, the governor of Mississippi, Ross Barnett, personally barred him from entering the registrar's office. Barnett's grandstanding was a calculated political ploy on his part to enhance his popularity as a defender of states' rights against the "despotic" federal government. He knew that if he blocked Meredith but was forced by the federal government to yield, he would be a hero in Mississippi. A few days later, federal marshals escorted Meredith as he enrolled at the university. A mob of two thousand angry students rioted and attacked the marshals, trying to get at Meredith. For more than twelve hours federal marshals fought a desperate battle through the night with the mob. By daybreak more than a hundred marshals had been wounded (twenty-eight with gunshot wounds), and two people were killed. In order to restore peace, President Kennedy finally sent in more federal marshals. The riot was quelled, and the University of Mississippi was at last integrated. But every day Meredith, whether in his dormitory room, walking across campus, or attending classes, faced constant harassment, threats, and intimidation.

At the urging of the Reverend Fred Shuttlesworth, Martin Luther King and SCLC organized a direct action campaign in Birmingham, Alabama. On April 6, 1963, as protesters began a march from the Sixteenth Street Baptist Church to city hall, the Birmingham police moved in and arrested dozens of demonstrators. At the next day's march more arrests were made when police chief Bull Connor sent in the fire department and a K-9 unit to confront the protesters. Around the country Americans were shocked at the photographs showing police dogs attacking peaceful demonstrators and firefighters using high-pressure fire hoses to knock people down. On Good Friday Martin Luther King was arrested. While King sat in solitary confinement, eight Alabama clergymen published an open letter in the *New York Times* in which they blamed King and the "outsiders" who had come to Birmingham for the violence provoked by the demonstrations. "We recognize the natural impatience of people," they wrote, "who feel that their hopes are slow in being realized. But we are convinced that these demonstrations are unwise and untimely."[6]

It was a critical moment for the Civil Rights Movement. King was acutely aware of this as he sat in his cell. Writing in the margins of the newspaper, King responded to the clergymen in one of the most seminal statements of dissent in American history. "I have yet to engage in a direct action campaign that was 'well timed,'" King writes, "in the view of those who have not suffered unduly from the disease of segregation." He understands the difficulty, he acknowledges, for whites to empathize with African Americans' impatience, but whites must try to understand that Blacks have waited for centuries for their rights. "The nations of

Asia and Africa are moving with jetlike speed toward the goal of political independence, but we still creep at horse-and-buggy pace toward the gaining of a cup of coffee at a lunch counter."[7]

Throughout the letter, King expounds the philosophy of nonviolence, defines civil disobedience, and lays out the aims of a direct action campaign. In response to the criticism that he has no respect for the law, King argues that he only breaks "unjust laws." Echoing Thoreau, King elaborates on the difference between "just laws" (laws that coincide with natural law or God's law and apply equally to everyone, such as laws against murder), which he honors, and "unjust laws" (those that do not coincide with natural law or God's law and that do not apply equally to all people, such as the Jim Crow laws).

To the charge that he is an "outsider," King replies, "I am in Birmingham because injustice is here. . . . I cannot sit idly by in Atlanta and not be concerned about what happens in Birmingham. Injustice anywhere is a threat to justice everywhere." And to the criticism that he is an "extremist," King simply responds, "was not Jesus an extremist for love?" In this context King positions himself as a reformer who stands "in the middle of two opposing forces in the Negro community": the conservative accommodationist and the radical revolutionary. He is not one of those who "have been so completely drained of self-respect and a sense of 'somebodiness' that they have adjusted to segregation." Nor is he a radical who is so filled with "bitterness and hatred" that he advocates violence. If whites do not embrace his nonviolent approach "millions of Negroes," he predicts, "out of frustration and despair, will seek solace and security in black-nationalist ideologies, a development that will lead inevitably to a frightening racial nightmare."[8] King in essence is warning white America, not so subtly, that he is the only reasonable alternative to Black militants.

Shortly after King's release the demonstrations intensified until Birmingham's business community, concerned about the loss of revenue, finally agreed to remove the segregation signs, integrate the stores, and hire more Black clerks. Thus the protests resulted in some modest progress, but more importantly they motivated President Kennedy to take a bold stand on civil rights. On June 11 he addressed the nation. "One hundred years of delay have passed," he said,

> since President Lincoln freed the slaves, yet their heirs, their grandsons, are not fully free. . . . And this Nation, for all its hopes and all its boasts, will not be fully free until all its citizens are free. We preach freedom around the world, and we mean it, and we cherish our freedom here at home, but are we to say to the world, and much more importantly, to each other that this is a land of the free except for the Negroes; that we have no second-class citizens except Negroes; that we have no class or caste system, no ghettoes, no master race except with respect to Negroes?

He announced that he was sending a civil rights bill to Congress that would abolish the Jim Crow laws and prohibit segregation in public housing, public accommodation, and workplaces. The time has come, he said, for every American to acknowledge that "race has no place in American life or law."[9]

But, as the administration expected, southern senators balked and began using every means at their disposal to prevent the bill from coming up for a vote. It seemed the bill was doomed. In order to put pressure on Congress to pass the bill, civil rights and union leaders coordinated a March on Washington for Jobs and Freedom to take place at the end of the summer. Kennedy was apprehensive that the march would turn violent or that it would be construed as critical of the president. But the event, on August 28, was peaceful as well as inspirational. Two hundred and fifty thousand people took part in the symbolic march from the Washington Monument to the Lincoln Memorial. There they listened to singers Mahalia Jackson, Peter, Paul, and Mary, Joan Baez, and Bob Dylan and speeches by A. Philip Randolph, James Farmer, John Lewis, and others. The highlight of the day was Martin Luther King's speech. "I still have a dream. It is a dream deeply rooted in the American dream that one day this nation will rise up and live out the true meaning of its

FIGURE 7.1. A twelve-year-old girl at the March on Washington for Jobs and Freedom, August 28, 1963. The original caption reads, "Photograph of a Young Woman at the Civil Rights March on Washington, DC, with a Banner, 08/28/1963."
Credit: Photographed by Rowland Scherman of the U.S. Information Agency. Courtesy of National Archives.

creed—'We hold these truths to be self-evident, that all men are created equal'"—King proclaimed. "I have a dream that my four little children will one day live in a nation where they will not be judged by the color of their skin but by the content of their character. I have a *dream* today!"[10]

Much of white America, at least outside the South, was impressed with the nonviolent crowd and the moving eloquence of Martin Luther King's oratory. The march won new converts to civil rights, and it elevated King to the status of undisputed leader of the movement. However, not all African Americans were in lockstep with King's message of nonviolence and hope, passive resistance and civil disobedience. Many felt that the government was responding far too slowly to the movement's demands and that the Black revolution needed to be more militant and not keep turning the other cheek. Malcolm X was one of the outspoken critics of King's nonviolent approach. The March on Washington, Malcolm X proclaimed later, "was a sellout." The Kennedy administration co-opted it and controlled it from beginning to end. "It lost its militancy. It ceased to be angry, it ceased to be hot, it ceased to be uncompromising."[11]

For several years Malcolm X had been the leading spokesman of the Nation of Islam, whose philosophy went against the grain of King's Christian Social Gospel message. Malcolm denounced whites as "blue-eyed devils" that would never treat Blacks equally. He called for African Americans to fight against white dominance and take charge of their own communities. He scorned integration for it implied that Black society was inferior to white society. Black society, he repeated over and over again, Black values, Black culture were *superior*. He called for "black nationalism," which meant that Blacks must have "complete

FIGURE 7.2. Bob Dylan and Joan Baez at the March on Washington, August 28, 1963. Photographer unknown.
Credit: Public domain; courtesy of National Archives.

control over the politics and the politicians of [their] own community":
"We should also gain economic control over the economy of our own
community, the businesses and the other things which create employment so that we can provide jobs for our own people instead of having
to picket and boycott and beg someone else for a job."[12] He argued for
self-defense. If a white man hits you, Malcolm X repeatedly advised, do
not turn the other cheek. Hit him back harder. And he will not hit you
again. In some ways it can be argued that many white Americans began
to embrace Martin Luther King and support the civil rights struggle
precisely because they were afraid of Malcolm X.

But even among King's most loyal followers there was a sense that his
tactics were too slow, that the movement was not accomplishing enough.
After all, the struggle had been going on for some time. Why does Congress not immediately pass the needed legislation? Why does the Justice
Department not provide adequate protection for civil rights activists?
Why does the federal government drag its heels? As if to underscore the
frustrations of those who sought a quicker end to racial injustice, less
than three weeks after the March on Washington, a bomb exploded at
the Sixteenth Street Baptist Church, in Birmingham. Fourteen children
attending Sunday school were injured. Four girls were killed. The euphoria and elevated hopes that the March on Washington had brought
to the movement vanished in the explosion. How could whites be filled
with so much hatred that they could kill four children in Sunday school?
It was a sobering moment as civil rights activists realized that there was
a long way to go.

The assassination of President Kennedy two months later was another important turning point. On one hand, the movement had lost
an ally who, although he had been slow to support civil rights, had finally thrown the weight of the Oval Office behind the movement. But
on the other hand, Kennedy's assassination was a boost for civil rights.
It prompted the new president, Lyndon B. Johnson, to take up the cause
more passionately than Kennedy had. "Let us continue," Johnson declared as he vowed his commitment to carrying on JFK's legacy in a

speech to Congress and the nation on November 27. Johnson used the occasion to boost the civil rights bill that was languishing in Congress. "No memorial oration or eulogy could more eloquently honor President Kennedy's memory than the earliest possible passage of the civil rights bill for which he fought so long."[13] Johnson used all of his power and persuasion over the next several months to cajole, convince, and coerce conservative Republicans and southern Democrats into supporting the bill. Had JFK lived, the bill would have died. But LBJ got it done. In July he signed into law the Civil Rights Act of 1964. The comprehensive bill did away with the Jim Crow laws and empowered the attorney general to enforce school desegregation. "All persons shall be entitled to the full and equal enjoyment of the goods, services, facilities, and privileges, advantages, and accommodations of any place of public accommodation . . . without discrimination or segregation on the ground of race, color, religion, or national origin." The act also outlawed discrimination "against any individual with respect to his compensation, terms, conditions, or privileges of employment, because of such individual's race, color, religion, sex, or national origin."[14]

Kennedy's assassination impacted the Civil Rights Movement in another way. Countless numbers of baby boomers had been inspired by Kennedy's appeal to their idealism, and many of them began to find ways to carry on his legacy. Kennedy might be gone, they reasoned, but we can take up the causes he fought for. Many volunteered for the Peace Corps, some enlisted in the military, others decided to get involved in politics, and untold thousands threw themselves into the Civil Rights Movement. In the spring of 1964 SNCC and CORE began organizing for "Freedom Summer." It was one thing, they reasoned, to gain access to a lunch counter to buy a cup of coffee or to be allowed to sit in the front of the bus. But none of these advances for Blacks did anything to enhance political power. Only through the ballot box could African Americans hope to gain some leverage in the American political system. And so Freedom Summer was conceived as a campaign to go into Mississippi in the summer of 1964, to set up "freedom schools" that would teach political awareness and encourage African Americans to take part in the political process, and to fan out through the state getting African Americans to register to vote. Blacks constituted about 50 percent of the population of Mississippi, but only 6.7 percent of them were registered. If African Americans voted, not only would they have a say in state politics and be able to elect members of their own community to political office, but even white politicians would have to address Black concerns if they hoped to win elections.

No sooner had the first cohort of volunteers arrived in Mississippi than three of them disappeared. On June 21, 1964, James Chaney, Andrew Goodman, and Michael Schwerner drove to the site of a burned-down Black church near Philadelphia, Mississippi. They were arrested for a traffic violation by the sheriff and held for some hours in the town jail. When they were released, members of the Klan picked them up, beat them, and shot them. Chaney was Black, Goodman and Schwerner white. For six weeks the FBI conducted a massive statewide manhunt for the three civil rights workers, but only after receiving a tip from a local resident did they find the bodies buried in an earthen dam. Instead of curtailing the number of civil rights workers descending on Mississippi during that summer, the disappearance and murder of the three men dominated headlines around the country, intensified interest in the struggle, and prompted more individuals to volunteer. The violence that southern whites perpetrated on civil rights activists was one of the most powerful forces galvanizing support for civil rights in the North. From Little Rock to Birmingham, from Freedom Summer to Selma, the beatings and killings of nonviolent civil rights activists invariably strengthened the movement.

One of the accomplishments of Freedom Summer was the creation of the Mississippi Freedom Democratic Party (MFDP). At the end of August the MFDP sent delegates to the Democratic National Convention in Atlantic City who they claimed were more representative of the state population than the all-white delegation of the regular Mississippi

Democratic Party. But the reality of power politics in the United States proved to be a bitter disappointment for the MFDP. President Johnson, wanting to avoid a controversy that threatened to divide the Democratic Party, insisted that the regular delegation be seated. When the credentials committee held a hearing about the conflicting demands of the two delegations and, as one of the MFDP delegates, Fannie Lou Hamer, launched into her compelling and emotional testimony, a fuming Johnson held a spur-of-the-moment (meaningless) press conference that preempted televised coverage of the hearing.

But Hamer's testimony was replayed again and again on newscasts. When she attempted to register to vote, she told the committee, she was arrested and thrown into a jail cell.

I was carried out of that cell into another cell where they had two Negro prisoners. The State Highway Patrolmen ordered the first Negro to take the blackjack. The first Negro prisoner ordered me, by orders from the State Highway Patrolman for me, to lay down on a bunk bed on my face, and I laid on my face. . . . The first Negro began to beat, and I was beat by the first Negro until he was exhausted. . . . [Then] the State Highway Patrolman ordered the second Negro to take the blackjack. . . .

All of this is on account of us wanting to register, to become first-class citizens, and if the Freedom Democratic Party is not seated now, I question America. Is this America, the land of the free and the home of the brave where we have to sleep with our telephones off of the hooks because our lives be threatened daily because we want to live as decent human beings, in America?[15]

Despite Hamer's powerful testimony, the credentials committee refused to seat the MFDP delegation. The delegates protested, sang freedom songs, and vowed that they would be heard, but to no avail. Disheartened African Americans, closely watching the drama unfold at the convention, grew bitterly skeptical about America's commitment to equality.

Many felt that the normative political process was not responsive to their demands and that more militant ways were going to be necessary in order to gain equal rights.

* * *

In September, Freedom Summer volunteers, overflowing with quasi-missionary fervor about their experiences in Mississippi, returned to college campuses around the nation. Many had been beaten by racists, hundreds had been arrested and harassed by the police, all of them felt they were risking their lives for the cause. And now as they told their stories, they urged others to make donations, join SNCC or CORE, or volunteer for the next direct-action campaign. At the University of California at Berkeley, school authorities told students that they could not set up their tables, hand out leaflets, solicit donations, or otherwise proselytize for a political cause on campus property. The students responded with shock and outrage. The university was telling them they could not discuss the most significant issue facing the nation! This was too much. Students from both the left and right protested the university's heavy-handed trampling on free speech. Thus was born the Berkeley Free Speech Movement—a direct offspring of Freedom Summer. And it quickly spread to other campuses. At first the primary issues that student protesters focused on were First Amendment rights, civil rights, and the policy of in loco parentis—the set of guidelines followed by most universities at the time that the institution acts in place of the parents as the moral and social guardian of its students. In loco parentis, students demanded, must be abolished. "We have an autocracy which runs this university," proclaimed Mario Savio in an impassioned speech to a crowd of thousands of protesters at Berkeley, which treats students as though they were mere "raw materials" and not human beings. "There is a time when the operation of the machine becomes so odious, makes you so sick at heart, that you can't take part; you can't even passively take part, and you've got to put your bodies upon the gears and upon the wheels, upon the levers, upon all the apparatus, and you've got to make it stop. And you've got to indicate to the people who run it, to the people who own it, that unless you're free, the machine will be prevented from working at all!"[16]

As the student movement was getting off the ground, Bernard Lafayette, John Lewis, C. T. Vivian, Martin Luther King, and others started a voter registration campaign in Selma, Alabama. During the early weeks of 1965, protesters conducted a series of demonstrations at the Selma courthouse, where they had been vainly attempting to register. Almost every day, reports of civil rights demonstrations were hitting the front pages of newspapers and were the top stories on radio and television. Whether it was the mainstream media or the African American press or publications such as the *Nation*, *I. F. Stone's Weekly*, *Time*, or *National Review*, civil rights was reported on, analyzed, criticized, lauded. It was not only news about the protests in Selma, especially after a protester, Jimmie Lee Jackson, was shot and killed by a state trooper; it was also Malcolm X's assassination in New York City in February. Was the Civil Rights Movement going to be able to continue working for change? Was nonviolence still possible? It was a question that went through many Americans' minds.

On Sunday, March 7, five hundred protesters, led by SNCC chairman John Lewis, set out from Selma for a planned march to Montgomery to demand that Governor George Wallace protect civil rights demonstrators. They had just crossed the Edmund Pettus Bridge when state troopers and the Selma police confronted them. Policemen attacked the marchers with billy clubs and tear gas. Mounted police trampled some of the demonstrators. Reporters and photographers captured it all, and that evening Americans watched newsreel footage of the brutal assault on the evening news. In many cities supporters took part in demonstrations of solidarity with the Selma marchers. Martin Luther King issued a call for Americans to come to Selma to take part in a second march on March 9. More than two thousand people responded to the call.

But a federal judge issued a restraining order prohibiting the march. King was in a quandary. As he had emphasized in "Letter from

Birmingham Jail," he made a distinction between just laws and unjust laws. Invariably the unjust laws that he transgressed, the laws upholding segregation, were state laws. King's strategy was to use the federal government to step in and force noncompliant state leaders to abide by federal law. King was reluctant to violate the federal restraining order. The standard SCLC course of action in cases like this was to get the injunction overturned in court. So, as the marchers set out from the Brown Chapel on March 9, this time more than twenty-five hundred strong, King settled on the idea of a "symbolic" march. He led the marchers across the bridge, where they were confronted by the police. King knelt and led the protesters in prayer, then turned everyone around and headed back to the chapel. Most of the marchers were confused. What was King doing? SNCC activists, especially, were angry that King turned the march around and did not continue toward Montgomery. Back at the chapel King promised the throng that SCLC lawyers would get the injunction overturned and that the march would take place later in the week.

That evening three white ministers who had come to Selma from Boston were assaulted by baseball-bat-wielding Klansmen. One of the ministers, James Reeb, was so severely beaten that he died two days later. The clergyman's death garnered a tremendous outpouring of public support for civil rights. President Johnson commented that the murder was "an American tragedy,"[17] and he called for Congress to begin work on a voting rights bill. But many African Americans, although they too mourned Reeb, were angry that the death of a white man engendered so much outrage, whereas Jimmie Jackson's death had hardly been noticed by white America.

On March 15 President Johnson went to Congress to introduce the voting rights bill. In perhaps the most eloquent speech of his career Johnson made it clear that he had listened to the demands of civil rights protesters and that he was committing himself and the nation to their cause. Calling racism an "American problem," LBJ spoke about what was happening in Selma. "There is no cause for pride in what has happened in Selma," Johnson said. "There is no cause for self-satisfaction in the long denial of equal rights of millions of Americans. But there is cause for hope and for faith in our Democracy in what is happening here tonight. For the cries of pain and the hymns and protests of oppressed people have summoned into convocation all the majesty of this great government." He went on to discuss the complexity of the issues surrounding civil rights. He spoke of the voting rights bill that he was submitting to Congress, and he urged the lawmakers to pass it swiftly. But it was not just a matter of law, he acknowledged; it was a matter of attitude, a matter of conscience, a matter of consciousness. "But even if we pass this bill the battle will not be over. What happened in Selma is part of a far larger movement which reaches into every section and state of America. It is the effort of American Negroes to secure for themselves the full blessings of American life. Their cause must be our cause too. Because it's not just Negroes, but really it's all of us, who must overcome the crippling legacy of bigotry and injustice." At this point the president paused, and then, looking directly into the camera, on national television, he said, "And we *shall* overcome."[18]

The speech electrified civil rights activists. They saw, for the first time clearly and unambiguously, that the man in the Oval Office was paying attention, that the purpose of the demonstrations—to persuade the people in power to exercise that power to guarantee fundamental rights to *all* Americans—was bearing fruit. Dissent was working.

Within a few days the federal judge in Selma rescinded the injunction, and on March 21 more than three thousand people from all walks of life, Black and white, young and old, ordinary citizens and celebrities, set out for the fifty-four-mile trek to Montgomery. This time when they crossed the Edmund Pettus Bridge, the heavily armed Alabama state troopers and Selma police officers allowed them to pass. Marchers linked arms and sang "We Shall Overcome" as they crossed over. Averaging about eleven miles a day, it took the marchers five days to arrive in the state capital. By the time they got to Montgomery, the number of protesters had swelled from three thousand to approximately twenty-five thousand.

They went to the statehouse with a petition. "We have come not only five days and 50 miles," the petition read, "but we have come from three centuries of suffering and hardship. We have come to you, the Governor of Alabama, to declare that we must have our freedom NOW. We must have the right to vote; we must have equal protection of the law, and an end to police brutality."[19] Governor George Wallace was conveniently not there, but Martin Luther King addressed the crowd. "We must come to see that the end we seek is a society at peace with itself, a society that can live with its conscience. That will be a day not of the white man, not of the black man. That will be the day of man as man." King acknowledged that the frustration of waiting for equal rights weighed heavily on those who had suffered and fought so long. "I know you are asking today, 'How long will it take?' I come to say to you this afternoon however difficult the moment, however frustrating the hour, it will not be long, because truth pressed to earth will rise again. How long? Not long, because no lie can live forever. How long? Not long, because you still reap what you sow. How long? Not long. Because the arc of the moral universe is long but it bends toward justice."[20]

Weary yet hopeful, the marchers began dispersing in carpools. One of the volunteers was Viola Liuzzo, a civil rights activist from Detroit, Michigan, who had come to Selma to assist with shuttling demonstrators to airports and bus stations after the march. As she was driving between Montgomery and Selma, a car pulled up alongside her vehicle, and three passengers started shooting. Liuzzo, a white mother of five children, was killed instantly. Once again television, radio, and newspaper headlines around the nation trumpeted the story of the murder of another civil rights worker.

* * *

Selma was the climax of the southern struggle against segregation. In the aftermath of Selma, President Johnson signed into law the Voting Rights Act, which did away with the most egregious discriminatory abuses such as the literacy tests that prevented Blacks from voting. By the end of the year 250,000 new Black voters had registered, and they became a powerful new voting bloc in the South. African Americans in the South were gaining, slowly but surely, political power. But Selma also signified a major turning point in the Civil Rights Movement for another reason—the movement was falling apart. Discontent, especially on the part of SNCC, with Martin Luther King's dominance of the movement and frustration that his tactics were not going fast enough and far enough, created a fissure in the movement. When Stokely Carmichael assumed the leadership of SNCC, he took up the Black separatism mantle of Malcolm X and other radical Black thinkers. "Black Power" became Carmichael's signature phrase as he went on a speaking tour of the nation's universities. Black Power meant that Blacks must seize equality for themselves, because whites will never grant it. Carmichael urged African Americans to unite "to recognize their heritage, to build a sense of community, . . . to define their own goals, to lead their own organizations." Furthermore, Blacks must do this for themselves, not with white help. "We cannot have white people working in the black community—on psychological grounds. The fact is that all black people question whether or not they are equal to whites, since every time they start to do something, white people are around showing them how to do it. If we are going to eliminate that for the generation that comes after us, then black people must be in positions of power, doing and articulating for themselves." Blacks, in short, must be self-reliant. Carmichael acknowledged that the phrase "Black Power" was intimidating for whites. "White people associate Black Power with violence because of their own inability to deal with blackness. If we had said 'Negro power' nobody would get scared. Everybody would support it."[21]

After Selma, with the split within the movement widening, civil rights moved north. And when it did, civil disobedience and demonstrations became less effective because the problems for African Americans in the North were more complex than those that could be solved by passing new laws. In northern inner cities the problems were economic. There were no Jim Crow laws, but Black neighborhoods in the North were just as rigidly segregated from white neighborhoods as they were in the South. And there seemed to be no easy solution for Black demands for economic justice. Martin Luther King observed that it had cost the federal government nothing to pass laws ensuring that African Americans had the right to have a cup of coffee at a lunch counter or to ride at the front of a bus, but it would cost millions of dollars for the government to do something about economic injustice and the crushing poverty of the ghetto.

Just days after President Johnson signed the Voting Rights Act, in August 1965 a routine traffic stop in the African American Watts neighborhood of south central Los Angeles escalated into an altercation between Black residents and the police officer. The situation got out of hand, more police were called in, a bystander was clubbed, and scores of African Americans gathered around, taunting and threatening the cops. Years of anger at police brutality and resentment about exploitive white landlords exploded. For five days Watts went up in flames. Hundreds of buildings and white-owned businesses were damaged or destroyed, thousands were arrested, hundreds were injured, twenty-five Blacks and nine whites were killed. The riot was only quelled after 16,000 National Guardsmen were deployed. But Watts was just the first of these inner-city rebellions. In 1966 there were riots in Cleveland and Chicago. In 1967 there were eight major uprisings. Those in Newark and Detroit eclipsed Watts. In Detroit five days of carnage left millions of dollars of property damage, 1,200 injured, and forty-three dead. In Newark, there were 725 injured and twenty-three dead and also millions of dollars of destruction. President Johnson had to send in army and National Guard troops to restore order.

Johnson, like most white Americans, was shaken by the uprisings and appointed a commission to investigate the causes and to propose a remedy. "White racism is essentially responsible," the Kerner Commission reported in 1968, "for the explosive mixture which has been accumulating in our cities since the end of World War II." Blacks living in the inner cities have been excluded from economic progress in the United

States. There is no opportunity for young people to escape. "What white Americans have never fully understood—but what the Negro can never forget—is that white society is deeply implicated in the ghetto. White institutions created it, white institutions maintain it, and white society condones it." The commission proposed numerous programs for federal, state, and local governments to initiate that would "expand opportunities for ghetto residents to participate in the formulation of public policy and the implementation of programs affecting them through improved political representation, creation of institutional channels for community action, expansion of legal services, and legislative hearings on ghetto problems."[22] Although Congress increased funding for welfare, the commission's recommendations were never implemented, and before the year was out, the white backlash against civil rights demonstrations and what was perceived as a government that was too accommodating to Black America gave Richard Nixon the victory in the presidential election.

Finding Martin Luther King's message of nonviolent resistance ineffective in dealing with the reality of the ghetto and fed up with the poverty, racial discrimination, and police brutality that African Americans faced every day, Huey Newton and Bobby Seale founded the Black Panther Party in Oakland, California. Adopting a more radical approach to dissent, they combined the philosophy of Black nationalism with Marxism. The Black Panthers believed that racism was essentially part of the global class struggle. And they believed in self-defense. African Americans have the right to protect themselves against racists. Armed Black Panthers wearing black leather jackets and black berets patrolled the streets of Oakland as a sort of town watch, looking to defuse volatile situations before they got out of hand. For example, if a Black man was stopped for a traffic infraction, Panthers would arrive on the scene and stand with rifles slung over their shoulders observing the interaction between the police officer and the detained person just to make sure that the officer did not use excessive force. White Americans were intimidated by the Panthers, but in reality the Panthers rarely engaged in any violence. They primarily concerned themselves with community action programs: they distributed food to schools and families in need, they fought for better employment and decent housing opportunities, they demanded equal opportunity for high-quality education, and they demanded an immediate end to police brutality. The Black Panther Party is a prime example of dissent taking a different form on the basis of a different set of convictions around the same issue. Whereas Martin Luther King's vision was to work within the system to reform race relations, Black Panthers moved in the direction of radically altering the system. Even so, the Black Panthers' reputation as extremists and revolutionaries has been wildly exaggerated by an antagonistic media and paranoid political officials. Their impact was more moderate. They raised new questions and offered new solutions to age-old problems and created a stronger sense of solidarity within the Black community. The FBI, however, treated the Panthers like a terrorist organization and, under Director J. Edgar Hoover, unleashed a relentless counteroffensive against the Panthers that eventually, by the early 1970s, destroyed the organization and killed most of its leaders. The most infamous episode of the FBI Counterintelligence Program (COINTELPRO) targeting Black Panthers was the raid on the Chicago Panther leader Fred Hampton's house in December 1969. Hampton and another Panther, Mark Clark, were killed in their beds at four a.m., although the FBI and the Chicago police insisted that they were shot resisting arrest. It was the beginning of the end for the Black Panther Party.

8

Counterculture

The young are in the forefront of those who live and fight for
Eros against Death, and against a civilization which strives
to shorten the "detour to death" while controlling the means
for lengthening the detour. . . . Today the fight for life, the
fight for Eros, is the *political* fight.
—Herbert Marcuse, 1966

Dissent exploded in the "long" 1960s. Starting with civil rights protests in the last years of the 1950s and not culminating until the end
of the Vietnam War in the mid-1970s the United States experienced an
outburst of dissent, demonstrations, disturbances, riots, and rebellion.
Everything was fair game. Everything was questioned—from race to
gender, from war to the environment, from consumerism to middle-
class values, indeed the American way of life itself. All was subject to
debate, dissection, analysis, criticism, reevaluation. Dissenters of all
varieties—reformers, reactionaries, revolutionaries—expressed their
grievances through civil disobedience, speeches, demonstrations, petitions, music, art, street theater, comedy, and even violence. By 1975 the
United States was transformed, and the fallout from that period is still
felt today.

* * *

JFK's appeal to youthful idealism and the bitter reality that sank in after
his assassination was a key factor that gave rise to the counterculture of
the 1960s. The suffocating conformity of suburbs and shopping malls
and McCarthyism, coupled with the iconoclastic attitude of the Beats
and rock and roll, also had a profound effect on making the 1960s what

they were. Most importantly it was the inspiring example of courageous African American college students confronting segregation with sit-ins and Freedom Rides and demonstrations that propelled a generation of white college students to rebel, to dissent, to question authority.

As the war in Vietnam began to escalate in mid-decade, dissent intensified at an exponential rate, not only in opposition to the war but also in questioning *everything* about American society. As more and more young radicals criticized the wisdom and motivation of U.S. involvement in Vietnam, their protests soon embraced all aspects of American policy and values. They recognized the demonization of communism and communists from Fidel Castro to Patrice Lumumba as pure propaganda, and they condemned Washington's inadequate and sluggish response to African Americans' century-long struggle for equal rights. If American government and society was suspect in these things, many young people reasoned, then American values themselves needed to be reevaluated.

At first many young men, answering JFK's call to pay any price and bear any burden in the struggle against communism, enlisted in the armed forces. But as the war escalated and the number of American troops in Vietnam swelled, so too did dissent against the war. In fact as Operation Rolling Thunder unleashing the bombing of North Vietnam began in March 1965, the first "teach-in" took place at the University of Michigan. This was an all-night event in which students and faculty participated in lectures and discussions examining the historical roots of the conflict and U.S. Cold War policy. For eleven hours they debated the arguments both for and against the war. A number of anti-teach-in protesters, believing the mere act of investigating U.S. policy was an act of treason, repeatedly challenged the speakers and in some cases heckled and disrupted them. But this only enhanced and deepened the intellectual analysis. All night long the presenters continued espousing the argument that the Vietnamese had been struggling for independence for centuries against the Chinese, the French, and the Japanese and that the United States was merely the latest nation seeking to control Vietnam. The war, they contended, was not about democracy versus communism; the war was about Vietnamese nationalism. When the teach-in ended, most (but by no means all) of the students agreed that the United States should pull out of Vietnam, and they endorsed a strong antiwar position. Over the next few weeks the teach-in phenomenon spread to other campuses from Berkeley to Columbia, from the University of Chicago to the University of Pennsylvania, as students and scholars debated the conflict in Vietnam. And then in May thousands, including some members of Congress, attended a National Teach-In in Washington, DC.

Events moved quickly. Thousands of protesters took part in an antiwar demonstration on the steps of the Capitol building in Washington, DC, in April, and then in June at the Pentagon. On November 2 Quaker pacifist Norman Morrison, calling for an immediate withdrawal of American troops, committed self-immolation below the window of Secretary of Defense Robert McNamara's Pentagon office. At the end of November the Committee for a Sane Nuclear Policy, with significant support from Students for a Democratic Society (SDS), Women Strike for Peace, and the National Coordinating Committee to End the War in Vietnam, organized the largest antiwar demonstration to that date. Thirty-five thousand antiwar protesters marched from the White House to the Washington Monument, where they listened to a speech by SDS president Carl Oglesby.

Students for a Democratic Society was an activist student organization founded in 1960 at the University of Michigan. Calling for "participatory democracy" SDS members sought to radicalize autoworkers in Michigan and also took part in the civil rights sit-ins, Freedom Rides, and Freedom Summer. Influenced by such left-wing political thinkers as Herbert Marcuse, C. Wright Mills, and Frantz Fanon, SDS was deeply critical of American capitalism. It denounced Cold War stereotypes and U.S. efforts to contain communism by supporting right-wing dictators who were guilty of flagrant human rights violations. According to SDS, America's demonization of communism was a smokescreen to mask U.S.

imperialism, and the escalating war in Vietnam was a prime example of this. Washington was not interested in democracy in Vietnam; it was simply interested in maintaining American economic dominance in Southeast Asia. SDS distanced itself from the Old Left's focus on organizing the working class to mobilizing students. Considering themselves the vanguard of the "New Left" they sought to change consciousness as well as the political system.

During his speech in the shadow of the Washington Monument the SDS president argued that the men who created the policy that led the United States into Vietnam were not monsters or right-wing ideologues but liberals, and their goal in Vietnam was not to stop the spread of communism but to preserve and expand the American corporate system. The National Liberation Front was fighting a revolution not unlike America's own revolution against Britain, Oglesby contended, but Americans were so caught up in opposing the Soviet Union and Communist China that it blinded us to the fact "that our proper human struggle is not with Communism or revolutionaries, but with the social desperation that drives good men to violence." Oglesby went on to summarize American foreign policy to prove his point that business interests were dictating that policy—oil in Iran, fruit in Guatemala, sugar in the Dominican Republic, and so on. The people behind the policy, Oglesby contended, were also "good men." But they were caught in the system and thus lost their compassion. "People become instruments. Generals do not hear the screams of the bombed; sugar executives do not see the misery of the cane cutters: for to do so is to be that much less the general, that much less the executive." We do not admit that our presence in Third World countries is based on such selfish grounds; we insist that we are pursuing loftier principles of liberty and freedom. This attitude allows us to depict "our presence in other lands not as a coercion, but a protection. It allows us even to say that the napalm in Vietnam is only another aspect of our humanitarian love—like those exorcisms in the Middle Ages that so often killed the patient. So we say to the Vietnamese peasant, the Cuban intellectual, the Peruvian worker: 'You are better

FIGURE 8.1. Vietnam War protesters in Washington, DC, October 21, 1967.
Credit: Public domain; courtesy of Lyndon B. Johnson Library.

dead than Red. If it hurts or if you don't understand why—sorry about that.'" Most of us, Oglesby concluded, are unaware of our personal responsibility for the war. It is not just the politicians and businessmen who are responsible but *all* of us. If we truly believe in America's human rights ideals, then each of us must accept our responsibility and do everything we can to change the status quo and bring about a "humanist reformation."[1]

Media coverage of the demonstrations was, for the most part, negative. From *Time*, *Newsweek*, the *Washington Post*, and the *New York Times* to ABC, CBS, and NBC, the mainstream media portrayed antiwar protesters as an unwashed, unruly mob of disloyal, procommunist radicals. Even the term "peacenik" that was applied to antiwar activists—an attempt to Russify them by evoking the image of disgruntled ne'er-do-wells who were really Soviet agents or at best sympathizers and dupes—indicted their loyalty. The truth is, however, that antiwar protesters came from a wide variety of backgrounds. Most of them were, like Oglesby, thoughtful, intellectual critics of American policy. And certainly the scholarly expertise of many antiwar dissenters from the academic community did bestow a level of respectability on the movement. Americans who took their patriotism seriously were aware that complex historical and political issues were at the crux of the Vietnam conflict. If one wished to develop an informed opinion one way or the other about the war, it was imperative to study history and examine these issues. And many did just that. In addition to academics and students, there were literally thousands of groups working locally and coming together several times a year for massive protests. As the war intensified, so too did the protests, and cogent antiwar arguments gained traction with millions and even tens of millions of Americans. Demonstrators were not, as the media liked to portray them, just hippies. Nuns, clergymen, politicians, housewives, Quakers, and groups such as Another Mother for Peace, Businessmen Against the War, and American Writers Against the Vietnam War were among those that participated in thousands of antiwar demonstrations.

Intellectual opposition to the war was only part of the picture. Many opposed the war because of the draft. For some it was purely a matter of self-preservation—they did not want to *be* killed. For others it was less self-interested than that—they did not want *to* kill. They questioned the morality of the war. As young men (many of whom had begun to question the validity of the war) received their draft notices, more and more of them began to actively oppose the war. Some joined demonstrations and protest marches, some refused to report for their physical examination, some were arrested, some fled to Canada. At demonstrations as early as 1965 antiwar protesters of draft age began publicly burning their draft cards—an act that could get them arrested. And hundreds were arrested. Antiwar protesters regularly held sit-ins at induction centers and Selective Service offices, attempting to block inductees and recruits from entering. Others engaged in more militant tactics. The Catholic priests Daniel and Philip Berrigan, leaders in the Catholic peace movement,[2] were arrested for breaking into draft offices in Baltimore and pouring blood on Selective Service files and in Catonsville, Maryland, where they destroyed draft documents with homemade napalm. Over the next few years there were break-ins in dozens of Selective Service offices around the country, during which an estimated five hundred antiwar activists stole or destroyed files. Before the war ended, more than one hundred thousand men refused induction into the U.S. Army, while more than half a million evaded the draft. More than twenty thousand men were put on trial, nine thousand were convicted, and four thousand served prison terms of up to five years. There is no accurate way of knowing how many men fled the country, but estimates are that between thirty thousand and fifty thousand draft-age American men left. Many of them never returned.

Each year the antiwar movement grew. By 1969 there were thousands of demonstrations annually, not only in large metropolitan areas but also in smaller cities and towns all over the nation. The demonstrations spread around the world to London, Rome, Berlin, Tokyo, Paris, and nearly every major metropolis in every country. Still, despite the

growing antiwar movement, most Americans were hawks who supported the president's policies and who believed in the legitimacy of
preventing a communist takeover of Vietnam. They accepted the common wisdom of the domino theory that postulated that if one country
fell to communism, then, like a row of dominoes, neighboring countries
would also fall. The hawks vilified the doves as being un-American. To
support the war, to support the troops, was patriotic. To question the
war was to be on the side of the enemy. Prowar Americans frequented
antiwar demonstrations, where they heckled the demonstrators, calling
them cowards and traitors and holding counterdemonstrations of their
own.

* * *

Concurrent with the New Left and the antiwar movement, many thousands of Americans, especially young people, began questioning the
prevalent assumptions of the social order. From the American way of
life to *all* bourgeois values, from the nature of patriotism to the sanctity of religious doctrine, from obeying authority to the legitimacy of
society's time-honored rules and regulations, everything was examined,
questioned, and challenged. And from this cauldron of reevaluation the
counterculture was born.

Hundreds of thousands of college students, inspired by JFK and the
Civil Rights Movement, still believed in the idealistic, somewhat naïve,
mantra that "we can change the world!" But it seemed increasingly clear
to them that the government was intentionally obfuscating, if not lying
about, the necessity for American military intervention in Vietnam.
If the authorities were not being entirely up-front with the American
people about Vietnam, many students believed, than perhaps the "Establishment" was not to be trusted about anything. Slowly at first but accelerating rapidly, large numbers of America's youth began questioning
all authority, all rules, all values, all morality.

Baby boomers had been brought up steeped in middle-class morality.
They were taught that the ideal life consisted of the nuclear churchgoing

family living in a comfortable house in suburbia far from the crime and grime (code for racial issues) of the city. Patriotism, religious faith, consumer products, and prosperity were the highest ideals. Those who did not exhibit such values were suspect, shady, un-American. Baby boomers had also been taught that sexual feelings and urges were basically sinful. Premarital sex was immoral. Sexual desire should be satisfied *only* in marriage, and homosexuality was particularly wicked. They were brought up in an environment of sharply delineated gender roles. Men were the breadwinners whose authority was not to be questioned, while women did the housework and cared for the children. Drugs too, especially marijuana, were classified as immoral. Only criminals and people living in the ghettoes of the nation's cities used drugs. But by the end of the 1960s, millions of baby boomers, in their politics, lifestyle, and relationships, defied *all* of these assumptions.

Dissent was expressed in a multitude of ways—music, art, comedy, theater, fashion, lifestyle, drugs, sex—and because of technological advances in television, radio, and recordings, the message that activists wished to disseminate reached a far wider audience in the 1960s and 1970s than in previous decades. Perhaps the most effective way of getting out the dissenting message was through song. By the end of the 1950s, the Civil Rights Movement and the popularity of the blacklisted folk group the Weavers brought about the folk music revival. Folk songs told stories. And many of the stories recounted the difficulties of the poor: miners owing their souls to the company store in "Sixteen Tons," workers dreaming of a better life in "I Dreamed I Saw Joe Hill Last Night," and above all, African Americans fighting for equal rights in "If You Miss Me at the Back of the Bus" and "We Shall Not Be Moved." Starting in 1958, the recordings of such popular performers as the Kingston Trio, the Brothers Four, Peter, Paul, and Mary, and Joan Baez increasingly invaded the pop charts and the consciousness of young people. Although the songs were easy enough for amateurs to play and the words and melodies were simple, many of the songs raised serious issues that stimulated critical thinking. Thousands of young people entering college were drawn to the reflective lyricism of the genre, and soon folk music (in an age before Facebook and Twitter and other forms of social media) linked Americans all over the country in a burgeoning culture of protest.

When Bob Dylan burst on the folk scene, protest music really took off. He recorded mostly traditional folk songs on his first album but then began recording his own songs, in which he dealt with personal as well as civil rights and antiwar themes. In "The Lonesome Death of Hattie Carroll" Dylan sings of the murder of a Black maid by a wealthy, white Baltimore socialite who gets off with a mere six-month sentence—a realistic depiction of the racial inequality in America. "Only a Pawn in Their Game" is a nuanced examination of the 1963 murder of Medgar Evers in which Dylan depicts the assassin as an ignorant white man who is "only a pawn" in southern racist politicians' "game." And in "Blowin' in the Wind" Dylan raises a litany of questions about the struggle for freedom that only the wind can answer. Such songs impelled listeners, even those who had never thought about civil rights or the plight of African Americans, to examine where they stood on the issue, to find the answers to the questions, and to form their own judgments. Dylan, obviously, was moved enough by the struggle for civil rights that it inspired him to write such songs. And these songs, in turn, wound up influencing Americans who had been apathetic about civil rights to reflect on these things and, in the end, to choose sides. Many joined the movement and as early as the 1963 March on Washington helped turn civil rights into an unstoppable force. Perhaps the lines in "Blowin' in the Wind" that resonated most with listeners were the ones in which Dylan wonders "how many ears must one man have / before he can hear people cry?" and "how many times must a man turn his head / pretending he just doesn't see?"[3] In essence Dylan is saying that you personally *must* get involved. The time for indifference is over. If you are not part of the solution, you are part of the problem. Soon civil rights protesters were singing "Blowin' in the Wind" along with "We Shall Overcome" in marches and demonstrations.

Dylan also tackled the issues of war, American militarism, and the potential consequences of the Cold War. In "With God on Our Side" Dylan ridicules the cliché that God is always on America's side in its military conflicts, and in "Masters of War" he excoriates the arms manufacturers who create the weapons for war and hide in their mansions "as young people's blood / flows out of their bodies / and is buried in the mud."[4] At the height of the Cold War, during the Cuban missile crisis, Dylan tapped into American angst in his apocalyptic vision of a post-nuclear future: "A Hard Rain's A-Gonna Fall."

Even after Dylan went electric at the Newport Folk Festival in 1965, abandoning his openly political lyrics for a more surrealistic commentary, moving from political dissent to countercultural dissent, his songs remained critical of the fake morals and superficiality of modern life. "Like a Rolling Stone" is a surrealistic critique of American culture, including underground culture. What is so significant about so many of Dylan's songs is that they imaginatively reflected the stresses and anxieties of contemporary life while at the same time pushed individuals to think for themselves and live a more thoughtful life. The songs encouraged active participation and being a part of one's own time. And Dylan was not alone. Hundreds of other musicians wrote politically- and socially-charged songs: Phil Ochs, Tom Paxton, Buffy Sainte-Marie, Paul Simon. Soon it seemed that the majority of the songs aired on the radio had some sort of sociopolitical message. And by mid-decade the example of Bob Dylan and other singer-songwriters wound up having a transformative influence on rock and roll. The Beatles led the way. With songs like "Eleanor Rigby" and "Nowhere Man" the Beatles opened up pop music to broader social issues than the hackneyed teenage lust that had dominated rock and roll since its inception. They understood that young people like themselves were not only interested in love and jealousy, holding hands and sexuality; they were also caught up in finding their own place in the world and living a meaningful life. When the band sang about a "Nowhere Man" who "doesn't have a point of view," it resonated with thousands of young people who were trying to find their way in life. By 1967 political rock permeated the airwaves. Whether it was the Mothers of Invention disparaging "plastic people! / oh, baby, now you're such a drag" or Jefferson Airplane observing that the pills "that mother gives you / don't do anything at all" or the Motown artist Edwin Starr shouting, "war, what's it good for?";[5] whether it was the Doors, the Grateful Dead, the MC5, Janis Joplin, Jimi Hendrix, or the Beatles and the Rolling Stones invading from England, rock and roll had become a critical commentary on modern-day life.[6]

One of the first things people think about when they think about the sixties is drugs. But drug use was not simply about self-indulgence or escaping from reality. Drugs, especially LSD and marijuana, were part of the 1960s search for authenticity. After psychology professor Timothy Leary was fired from Harvard for experimenting with lysergic acid diethylamide (LSD) with his students, he began touring college campuses around the country preaching the gospel of psychedelic drugs. Repeating his mantra of "Tune In, Turn On, and Drop Out," Leary urged listeners to tune in to their spiritual nature, turn on with LSD, and drop out of the bourgeois consumerist rat race. LSD, Leary proclaimed, was a mind-expanding drug that enabled the user to see into the true nature of things, to recognize the interconnectedness of all being, and as a result live a deeper, more fulfilling life. LSD led to *satori*, the enlightenment that Buddhist monks achieved after years of meditation. Leary struck a responsive chord with tens of thousands of young people who were already protesting against racism and the war in Vietnam, reevaluating middle-class values, and distrusting authority, especially when he advised them, "never trust anyone over thirty" (Leary was in his forties). By the late sixties untold numbers of young people had experimented with LSD and other psychedelic drugs, while the other popular drug, marijuana, was almost de rigueur for any person claiming to be hip and wishing to show his or her countercultural credentials. Although Leary encouraged widespread drug *use*, he warned against drug *abuse*. What many people missed was his injunction that drugs were not for everyone. Unless you were seriously interested in expanding your mind and deepening your awareness, you should abstain. "Acid is not for every brain," Leary wrote; "only the healthy, happy, wholesome, handsome, hopeful, humorous, high-velocity should seek these experiences."[7]

Left-wing political philosopher Herbert Marcuse also tapped into the rebellious impulses of the counterculture. In *Eros and Civilization* Marcuse combined Freud's ideas about sexual repression with Marx's critique of capitalism. Unlike totalitarian societies that control people through physical oppression, capitalist societies maintain control by restricting sexuality. In the United States, Marcuse argued, political, legal, and religious authorities have established a system in which there is excessive sexual repression—people are made to feel guilty for their sexual urges, premarital sex is taboo, homosexuality is forbidden. This "surplus repression" is manipulated by advertisers and manufacturers to fuel consumer capitalism. Individuals try to fill the inner void and find happiness through consumption—buying consumer goods, smoking, consuming alcoholic beverages, overeating, frequenting movies and sporting events, watching television (where they are exposed to even more consumer goods). If we become aware that we are sexually repressed, Marcuse contends, and if we develop a healthy, honest attitude about sex, then we will not only find erotic satisfaction, but we will be performing an act of revolution against consumer capitalism. Such ideas, coupled with the invention of the birth-control pill, became the basis for the sexual revolution of the 1960s. Young people everywhere rejected outmoded sexual morals and sought to establish a new model of sexual behavior. Like drugs, sex was perceived as a path to self-discovery and self-fulfillment—all part of the quest for authenticity. For many young Americans unrepressed sexuality was political. It was both an act of personal liberation and radical politics—the slogan "Make Love, Not War" became one of the catchphrases of the era.

Humor, too, was another form of dissent. From Mark Twain to H. L. Mencken societal critics employed humor as a way to express dissenting opinions. Lenny Bruce, a champion of the free expression guaranteed in the First Amendment, used every four-letter word in the book in his offensive, wry observations about American values. On Steve Allen's prime-time television show he admitted there were some words that offended even him: "Governor Faubus, segregation offend me; . . . the shows that exploit homosexuality, narcotics, and prostitution under the guise of helping these societal problems; . . . motion pictures that exploit race relations."[8] Other stand-up comedians, Dick Gregory, Richard Pryor, George Carlin, used their acerbic wit to challenge Americans to question the bourgeois, racist, classist, sexist ethos of the time.

Even the fashions of the 1960s were a manifestation of dissent. Because it was more important to be concerned with the serious issues of war and racism, to resist the forces of conformity, and to live an authentic life, young people everywhere rejected bourgeois notions of grooming and wearing such proper attire as suits and ties, modest skirts and blouses. There was little space for self-expression. And so young people playfully chose to wear bell-bottoms, old military-surplus shirts, tie-dye T-shirts, Indigenous-inspired shirts, miniskirts, and colorful earth-mother dresses. Men grew beards and let their hair grow long. Women stopped shaving their legs and armpits. And though many people belittled hippies as being just as conformist as the culture they were rejecting, the cultural rebels were *consciously* conforming to a new style, a new set of rules, a new set of values. Anyone encountering a hippie knew instantly where that person stood on civil rights, the war in Vietnam, drugs, and sexuality just by looking at him or her. And while not overtly political, the "hippie look" was a political statement. Sexual liberation, drugs, rock and roll, long hair—all of it was an individual expression of dissent and a refusal to go along with business as usual. By 1970 there was little to distinguish cultural and social dissent from political dissent. It was all part and parcel of the heartfelt determination to reject consumerism, conventional values, and political orthodoxy in favor of living an examined life honestly and fully.

As a means of broadcasting their defiance of mainstream culture, "Movement" activists published underground newspapers and magazines that offered an alternative New Left interpretation of the news and celebrated the provocative in-your-face lifestyle and morality of "hippie culture." For the most part the underground press's mission was to report the news that corporate media was not reporting and deride the daily newspapers and network news for doing nothing more than echo the official message of the military-industrial complex. Along with incisive left-wing analyses of American foreign policy and investigative reporting, many of the underground papers offered in-depth interviews with well-known countercultural figures like Timothy Leary and Abbie Hoffman, and rock musicians like John Lennon, Jerry Garcia, Joan Baez, Crosby, Stills, and Nash, and many others. Cartoonists drew mocking caricatures of political figures and critics reviewed rock albums and movies that expressed the concerns and attitudes of the counterculture. It was a form of grassroots journalism that anticipated social media. Some publications were outrageous, like *Ramparts Magazine* and *The Realist*, but many adhered (for the most part) to professional journalistic standards: *The East Village Other* in New York, *The Distant Drummer* in Philadelphia, *The Barb* in Berkeley, *The Paper* in East Lansing.

While these underground newspapers functioned on a localized basis, many were connected through nationally operating networks which aided distribution. Two examples of this were the Underground Press Syndicate (*The Barb*, *The East Village Other*, *The LA Free Press*, *The Paper*, and *The Fifth Estate* were all early members) and the Liberation News Service which distributed press packets containing radical reporting on U.S. and foreign politics and editorials on how the underground press itself should operate. These organizations helped facilitate the spread of local underground papers to other parts of the country and provided a model for how the press could adhere to New Left politics within the newsroom.

Probably the most famous of these publications was *Rolling Stone* magazine. The brainchild of Jann Wenner, *Rolling Stone* started out as an underground paper when it was first published in 1967 (long before it became a slick glossy), but it focused primarily on music and those musicians who influenced, and were influenced by, countercultural values. It also featured "gonzo" journalists, like Hunter S. Thompson, who became part of the story they were investigating. The scores of underground newspapers and magazines played a significant role in fortifying and disseminating the ideals of both the political and the cultural rebels of the 1960s.

* * *

The radical values of the 1960s were also expressed in paintings, posters, literature, and the performing arts. Art is always on the cutting edge of change. To be an artist is to question accepted norms. Perhaps no artist more exemplifies the sixties revolt against conventional standards than Andy Warhol. His celebrated paintings of Campbell's tomato soup cans, in which he challenges the viewer to look at the everyday images of modern society with new eyes, simply baffled most people. Warhol's "pop art" commented on the assembly-line nature of contemporary American life, in which all consumer products (including art) and the mundane experience of daily living were all repeated endlessly. Whether it was a Campbell's soup can, a Brillo box, or Marilyn Monroe, Mick Jagger, or Jacqueline Kennedy Onassis, Warhol's iconic images forced people to ponder, and presumably to question, the routine dreariness of their own lives. In a consumer society everything, even individuals, is mass-produced.[9]

Other visual artists were more explicit in their protests against the status quo. This was especially true in the realm of poster art. Hundreds of artists, both well-known and anonymous, produced posters that attacked the war in Vietnam, racism, and laws against drugs. One of the most famous posters was painted by Lorraine Schneider, a member of the antiwar group Another Mother for Peace. It was a simple drawing of a sunflower with the phrase "War is not healthy for children and other living things." Sister Mary Corita Kent, a nun in the Order of the Immaculate Heart, used her artistic talent to create antiwar silkscreen posters. Conservatives accused her of being subversive, but her art was primarily a conservative depiction of the golden rule. She advocated peace, love, and nonviolence. "I am not brave enough," she once said, "to not pay my income tax and risk going to jail. But I can say rather freely what I want to say with my art."[10] Graphic artists designed thousands of antiwar and antidraft posters. One was simply a photo of a young man burning his draft card, with the caption "FUCK THE DRAFT." Posters proliferated on walls, on telephone poles, on fences all over the country urging solidarity with the Chicago 8 during their trial, promoting the Black Panther Party, and demanding the legalization of marijuana, while others were psychedelic paintings proclaiming the virtues of getting high and taking acid trips or enjoining everyone to "Make Love, Not War."

Performance artists also employed their talents to protest the Vietnam War and to advocate alternative lifestyle choices. The experimental theater troupe the Living Theatre, founded by Judith Malina and Julian Beck, produced plays in which the theater itself became the medium to promote social and political change. In plays such as *Paradise Now*, *Mysteries and Smaller Pieces*, and *Frankenstein* they challenged audiences to reassess their ways of thinking and behaving. The antiwar activist Barbara Garson's *MacBird* was a droll retelling of Shakespeare's *Macbeth* satirizing President Johnson's rise to power. The surprise off-Broadway hit was a devastating and controversial critique of power that went so far as to accuse LBJ of murdering his predecessor. The Bread and Puppet Theatre performed regularly at antiwar marches and demonstrations. Using massive puppets ten to twenty feet tall, the performers translated political activism into street theater. The puppets, papier-mâché caricatures of Johnson, Nixon, Kissinger, Uncle Sam, and other political figures, invariably added a festive, humorous quality to the demonstrations. When the mischievous and subversive musical *Hair* moved to Broadway in 1967, the counterculture went mainstream. Although many theatergoers disapproved of *Hair*'s radical message—the joyous espousal of free love, marijuana, and the hippie lifestyle—they were nevertheless fascinated (and titillated) by the full-frontal nudity of the actors in the play's finale.

Dozens of films during the decade promoted an antimainstream point of view. Andy Warhol's experimental films, such as *Chelsea Girls* and *Blow Job*, were unapologetic critiques of middle-class morality. *Medium Cool*, set during the antiwar demonstrations in Chicago in 1968, was director Haskell Wexler's cinéma vérité take on the Marshall McLuhan thesis about the interplay between the media and cultural events—"the medium is the message." A number of provocative plays were also translated into cinema. *A Thousand Clowns* was a paean to nonconformity, and the film version of the Royal Shakespeare Company's *Marat/ Sade* was a riveting and profound view of the 1960s rebellion as seen through the prism of the French Revolution's Reign of Terror. Hollywood, too, got on the bandwagon with *The Graduate*, a humorous and poignant reflection on trying to be an individual in a conformist world; *Alice's Restaurant*, a film version of Arlo Guthrie's antidraft song; and *Easy Rider*, the story of two young men's disastrous motorcycle odyssey to free themselves from the constraints of conventional society. Millions of young Americans saw versions of themselves in these films.

* * *

In April 1967 Martin Luther King delivered a sermon at New York's Riverside Church in which he came out against the war in Vietnam. Civil rights activists feared that a public antiwar stance on King's part would lead to massive defections from the Civil Rights Movement. But King believed that he had to speak out because it was a question of morality just as important as civil rights. It is time, King said, "to break the silence." He spoke about his role as a civil rights leader and his commitment to the methods of nonviolence. But it is hard to convince people that the way to solve problems is through nonviolence when the United States is "using massive doses of violence to solve its problems, to bring about the changes it wanted": "the greatest purveyor of violence in the world today [is] my own government." After killing more than a million Vietnamese, we must take stock of ourselves and "admit that we have been wrong from the beginning of our adventure in Vietnam, that we have been detrimental to the life of the Vietnamese people."[11]

Around the nation millions of Americans denounced King as anti-American. President Johnson was furious. Even many of King's supporters felt he had gone too far, that he should not have taken up a cause that was viewed as outside his domain. But many others paused to reflect on his words and to reflect on whether they could continue to support America's actions in Vietnam. Senator Robert Kennedy also broke publicly with President Johnson over the war. He did not blame the war on Johnson, and he acknowledged that he himself had participated in decisions during his brother's presidency that led to deepening America's involvement in Vietnam. But what we were doing in Vietnam is immoral, and it was time to end the war.

At the end of October seventy thousand protesters marched on the Pentagon in one of the largest antiwar demonstrations in American history. Dr. Benjamin Spock, Noam Chomsky, Norman Mailer, and Abbie Hoffman were among the celebrated "peaceniks" participating in the march. Hoffman, vowing to exorcise the Pentagon, led a contingent of hippies in chanting "Om" in order to levitate the building and end the war in Vietnam. Meanwhile thousands of other demonstrators approached the main entrance of the building, where they were confronted by twenty-five hundred troops. Those who tried to break through the barrier were arrested. A famous photograph from the standoff depicts a young protester inserting a carnation into the barrel of a soldier's gun: flower power. A month later, on November 30, Senator Eugene McCarthy of Minnesota declared his candidacy for the Democratic presidential nomination in 1968 with the pledge that if elected president, he would end the war immediately. "I am hopeful that this challenge," McCarthy said, "may alleviate at least in some degree this sense of political helplessness and restore to many people a belief in the processes of American politics and of American government."[12]

* * *

The year 1968 was a watershed. At the beginning of the year more than 50 percent of Americans supported the Vietnam War; by December more than 50 percent opposed the war. The year began with the Tet Offensive, in which the Viet Cong launched a series of attacks throughout the length and breadth of Vietnam. They attacked American bases in every corner of the country. They even occupied the American embassy in Saigon for a few days. Up to this point most Americans believed the administration's reports that we were winning the war. But the disturbing images coming out of Vietnam contradicted the official reports and exposed a serious "credibility gap" between what the administration said about the progress of the war and what people saw on the evening news. U.S. Marines fighting their way back into the American embassy, children running down roads with napalm burns on their bodies, and the most searing image of all was the photograph of the South Vietnamese police chief Nguyễn Ngọc Loan summarily executing a Viet Cong guerrilla on a Saigon street. It certainly did not seem like the United States was winning the hearts and minds of the Vietnamese.

In March, while the Tet Offensive was still commanding headlines, Eugene McCarthy won 42 percent of the votes in the New Hampshire primary. The fact that an antiwar candidate had such an impressive showing against an incumbent president in a conservative state was a shock to the Democratic Party. Four days later Robert Kennedy entered the race. Kennedy had a vast following, not only antiwar radicals but also minority groups and civil rights activists, as well as the working class. It seemed that Kennedy had a legitimate chance to wrest the nomination away from Johnson.

On March 31 Johnson stunned the nation with his televised announcement that he would not seek the nomination for another term as president. The antiwar movement was elated. For four days a sense of euphoria swept through the ranks of antiwar activists. After all, it was clear that the demonstrations and protests had succeeded in forcing the abdication of Lyndon Baines Johnson. But on April 4, 1968, the euphoria vanished when Martin Luther King was assassinated. A sense of doom overwhelmed the left.

In April students at Columbia University, angered at the university's exploitive dealings with the African American residents of neighboring Harlem and furious with the university's connections with a weapons research thinktank that worked with the Pentagon, initiated a series of protests that led to their occupying the university's administrative offices. After several days the New York City police were called in and cleared the protesters out of the buildings. Most surrendered without resistance, but in some cases the police used excessive force to remove them. Hundreds were arrested, 148 protesters and bystanders were injured.

The protests at Columbia continued in May and helped inspire students at the Sorbonne in Paris to carry out their own protests against the university's repressive rules and regulations. Soon the Paris uprising turned violent. Property destruction was widespread as student demonstrators set up barricades in the streets, and when the working class joined the students (an alliance that did not take place in any of the protests in the United States), President Charles de Gaulle was forced to call for a general election. For the next several months protests spread to Berlin, London, Tokyo, Mexico City, Prague, and many other cities as the spirit of dissent swept around the world. It seemed that forces had been unleashed that no one could control or even fully understand. Rebellion was contagious.

On June 5, just moments after winning the Democratic primary in California, Robert Kennedy was gunned down by an assassin. The hopes of activists for a quick end to the war in Vietnam died with Kennedy. For the next two months some clung to the flimsy chance that against-all-odds McCarthy would get the Democratic nomination or that antiwar delegates would at least be able to insert a peace plank into the platform. But this was not to be. Party professionals were able to secure the nomination for Vice President Hubert Humphrey at the convention in Chicago and fend off the peace-plank effort. With thousands of militants protesting the war on the streets and with the Chicago police beating, tear-gassing, and arresting the demonstrators, a bizarre scene played out on the convention floor. Antiwar Democrats from New York, California, Wisconsin, and other states joined in with the spirit of dissent when they began singing "We Shall Overcome." On national television, before the eyes of millions of viewers, the Democratic Party was disintegrating in a wave of frustration and anger.

In November, Richard Nixon was elected president of the United States.

* * *

Despite the assassinations and the violence and the crushed hopes of those who so desperately desired change, the protests continued. In fact they mushroomed. Some of the largest demonstrations against the war took place in 1969, 1970, and 1971. Even so, many young people turned from trying to change the world to working on changing their relationship to the world. Some established utopian communes. They took up meditation, yoga, and macrobiotic diets. They read books about Zen Buddhism and holistic medicine and used *The Whole Earth Catalog* as a resource for innovative, alternative living. In San Francisco the Diggers experimented with a community free of money by preparing and distributing free food and organizing free parties, free concerts, and free theatrical performances.

Others took a different route. Since they could not end the war through the political process or nonviolent protest, it was time to embrace revolutionary violence. Claiming that the only way to change the system was through destruction, a splinter group of SDS formed the Weathermen (later the Weather Underground). Their slogan, "bringing the war home," meant overthrowing the power structure that was waging the war. Pulling the troops out of Vietnam was not enough. Bringing down imperialism was the goal. In early October 1969 Weathermen set out on their "Days of Rage" campaign in Chicago. It started when Bill Ayers and Terry Robbins blew up the statue in Haymarket Square memorializing the policemen who had died there in the infamous 1886 confrontation with labor organizers, and it continued with several hundred Weathermen stormed through Chicago's Gold Coast smashing car and store windows. For a total of three days they clashed with police and National Guardsmen (who outnumbered the Weathermen approximately three thousand to six hundred) in a series of separate incidents. Nearly three hundred Weathermen were arrested, scores injured, and several shot. Americans were outraged at the Days of Rage, and the Weather Underground's action did not win any new converts to the antiwar cause; nor was it supported by even the most radical members of SDS. Most antiwar dissenters viewed the Days of Rage as senseless. The reaction of a socialist newspaper in New York was typical of leftist opinion: "the most significant aspect of the surrealistic contretemps created by the Weatherman microfaction of SDS last week was that the rest of the movement had the revolutionary sense to stay away."[13]

Just a week after the Weather Underground's Days of Rage fiasco in Chicago, the Vietnam Moratorium Committee organized a "Moratorium" against the war—a day of coordinated protest marches in Washington, DC, New York City, San Francisco, and most major cities in the country. More than two million people took part in the demonstrations. A month later a coalition of antiwar groups formed the New Mobilization Committee to End the War in Vietnam and organized a "March Against Death" that would, like the October Moratorium, be a day of coordinated protests around the country. The March Against Death was a massive event. Millions of people, not only in the United States but at American embassies in London,[14] West Berlin, and Paris, participated in the demonstrations. For hours solemn demonstrators marched past the White House in Washington and the American embassies reading out the names of American soldiers killed in Vietnam and placing a card with each individual soldier's name in a coffin. It took two days to read all the names.

The Moratorium and the March Against Death were sandwiched between two significant countercultural events that revealed both a buoyant festive side of the counterculture and a destructive side. Woodstock and Altamont gave thousands of young people the opportunity to do their own thing and flaunt conservative, traditional values. In August hippies, college students, and high school kids descended on Bethel, New York, to participate in a huge rock festival. Jimi Hendrix, Janis Joplin, the Grateful Dead, Jefferson Airplane, Santana, and dozens of other performers celebrated the birth of a new lifestyle, of a new America, of "Woodstock Nation." Pot and LSD and sex and jubilation filled the air, and inhibition fell by the wayside as festivalgoers greeted what they thought was the dawn of a new age. Everyone could be free. But in December at Altamont, California, all inhibitions collapsed, and a dark side appeared. Too many people got wasted. Too many people equated freedom with license. Too many people lost control. And the festival turned truly ugly when a contingent of Hell's Angels assaulted and killed a young man in front of horrified onlookers. The incident seemed to confirm middle-class Americans' worst fears—that the counterculture would destroy all values, all sense of decency. Newspapers, pundits, commentators, and politicians had a field day pronouncing, with a noticeable trace of schadenfreude, the demise of the counterculture.

* * *

On April 30, 1970, President Nixon acknowledged that the United States had been secretly bombing Cambodia and revealed that he had authorized U.S. forces to invade that country. Nixon called it an "incursion" and stressed that we were *not* "invading" Cambodia. Nevertheless, hundreds of thousands of protesters took to the streets denouncing the widening of the war. At Kent State University in Ohio, student protesters set fire to the ROTC building on May 2, and the governor sent in the National Guard to quell the disturbance. Two days later guardsmen fired into a crowd of two thousand protesters. Nine were wounded, four were killed. The reaction around the country was overwhelming. On nearly every campus students held protests and vigils. Polls showed that close to 90 percent of students had serious misgivings about the government and believed that the administration was lying to the American people. But other Americans, especially working-class Americans and those whom President Nixon called the "silent majority," just as loudly and passionately proclaimed that the student protesters got exactly what they deserved. In New York City a group of protesters spontaneously marched to city hall and lowered the flag to half-staff. Shortly thereafter a group of hard-hat construction workers assaulted the demonstrators and raised the flag back up to full staff. In the end, the Kent State shootings revealed the depth of how far the nation had become polarized.

In early 1971 eight activists, consumed by the nagging conviction that antiwar groups were being infiltrated and undermined by the FBI, broke into an FBI field office in Media, Pennsylvania. Not knowing what they were looking for, or even whether proof of FBI subversion could be found, they stole *all* the files. After sifting through the files, two weeks later, they began distributing documents to the *Washington Post* and the *New York Times* that uncovered the FBI's Counterintelligence Program (COINTELPRO) and its shadow campaign to crush antiwar and civil rights organizations. The documents eventually led the U.S. Senate to establish the Senate Select Committee to Study Governmental Operations that investigated a plethora of intelligence abuses committed by the FBI, the CIA, and other federal agencies. Despite one of the most massive manhunts in FBI history, the eight burglars were never caught.[15]

A month after the burglary, in April 1971, hundreds of Vietnam veterans marched on Washington to protest the war. For several days they demonstrated at Arlington National Cemetery, the Pentagon, the Capitol building, and the steps of the Supreme Court. At the Supreme Court the veterans demanded to know why the Court had not ruled on the constitutionality of the war. At the Pentagon fifty vets attempted to turn themselves in to the bewildered guard as war criminals. And at the Capitol building nearly one thousand veterans denounced the war, voiced their sense of guilt at having taken part in it, and in a gesture of disgust threw their medals and ribbons onto the Capitol steps.

During the week that Vietnam Veterans Against the War (VVAW) protested in the nation's capital, one of them, John Kerry, the future senator, presidential candidate, and secretary of state, gave two hours of emotional testimony to the Senate Foreign Relations Committee. Kerry said that he was not just speaking for himself but for the hundreds of "winter soldiers" (as they called themselves) who had come to Washington to protest the war. The United States should never have involved itself militarily in Vietnam, Kerry testified. What was happening in Vietnam was a civil war that posed no threat whatsoever to the United States. The Vietnamese only sought independence. Most of them "didn't even know the difference between communism and democracy. They only wanted to work in rice paddies without helicopters strafing them and bombs with napalm burning their villages and tearing their country apart." What the United States had done, Kerry maintained, was the height of hypocrisy and immorality. "We rationalized destroying villages in order to save them. We saw America lose her sense of morality as she accepted very coolly a My Lai and refused to give up the image of American soldiers who hand out chocolate bars and chewing gum." We must look into our hearts and question our motivations, and we must immediately pull our soldiers out of Vietnam. "We are asking Americans to think about that because how do you ask a man to be the last man to die in Vietnam? How do you ask a man to be the last man to die for a mistake?"[16]

The impact of Kerry's testimony, and even more so the sight of veterans throwing their Purple Hearts, Silver Stars, Bronze Stars, and Service Crosses onto the Capitol's steps, unnerved many Americans who had enthusiastically supported the war. World War II and Korean War veterans who cherished their own medals and ribbons were especially troubled by the Vietnam vets' demonstration. For the first time, many of these older vets began seriously questioning American involvement in Vietnam. In one week the VVAW protests convinced more mainstream Americans to question the war than six years of student protests had done.

* * *

FIGURE 8.2. "The War is Over!" celebration. A group of antiwar activists celebrates the end of the Vietnam War in New York's Central Park, May 1975.
Credit: Image © Leif Skoogfors; courtesy of Leif Skoogfors, Corbis.

It was another four years before the war finally came to an end. Many pro-testers despaired that their demonstrations, their petitions, their speeches, and their rallies had virtually no impact on changing policy. But there is little doubt that the massed power of the antiwar movement put signifi-cant pressure on the government and that it did hasten the end of the war (although not fast enough for antiwar activists). Dissent mobilized tens of millions against the war and eventually persuaded enough members of Congress to pull the plug on financing the war. One victory of dis-sent was the eventual elimination of the draft, and to this day it does not seem feasible that any politician would suggest reinstating it, especially for a limited conflict somewhere in the world that does not obviously and immediately threaten national security. The impact of the antiwar move-ment also influenced American foreign policy for the rest of the twentieth century. "No more Vietnams!" became the mantra for policy makers when considering intervention in Latin America or the Middle East.

The counterculture's criticism of middle-class values changed America. Social and cultural critics forced Americans to reevaluate their basic assumptions about race, gender, relationships, and indeed, even dissent. In the decades following the 1960s Americans developed more open relationships (marriage was no longer considered the only option for people who wanted to live together); fashion and style became less constricting and more eclectic and expressive; life became more open; and increasing numbers of Americans, some for purely selfish purposes, others for more spiritual reasons, engaged in self-help and self-improvement programs. And because dissent had toppled the Jim Crow laws, expanded rights for Black Americans, and helped end the Vietnam War, Americans clearly saw dissent as an effective instrument for change. Witnessing the impact of dissent on the big issues of civil rights and the war in Vietnam, Americans abandoned whatever reticence they may have harbored about protesting and became willing participants in dissent movements for the causes they believed in: feminism, Chicano rights, Native American rights, gay rights, environmentalism. The 1960s spawned a mobilization of minorities of every imaginable stripe as dissent took center stage. If civil rights activists could end segregation and antiwar activists could hasten the end of the war, then surely women and gays and Chicanos and American Indians and all the other marginalized American groups could make their voices heard too.

9

Mobilization and Backlash

Feminism is the radical notion that women are people.
—Marie Shear, 1986

When did you ever see a fag fight back? . . . Now, times are
a-changin'. Tuesday night was the last night for bullshit. . . .
Predominantly, the theme [w]as, "this shit has got to stop!"
—anonymous participant in the Stonewall riot, 1969

The 1960s produced irreversible change in the United States. The Civil
Rights Movement sent currents of inspiration so deeply throughout
the land that there was no going back to the days when any American
would settle for less than full constitutional rights. But still, during the
1970s and 1980s, even as American society continued to evolve, as more
and more people from every conceivable ethnic and racial background
demanded their rights, there was a powerful backlash against what many
conservatives viewed as the excesses of the immoral, licentious sixties.
Dissenting values of the 1960s set off another chapter in the culture wars.

The most significant movement to come out of this period was
second-wave feminism. Winning the right to vote in 1920 was a political
victory for women, but women's social position did not change much.
Forty years later women were still experiencing second-class status and
what Betty Friedan called "the problem that has no name." Friedan was
interviewing her classmates from Smith College fifteen years after grad-
uation when it became apparent to her that even though most of the
women were living successful lives, married to successful men, raising
successful children, they themselves felt inexplicably unfulfilled. They
were victims of the "feminine mystique," the belief that women's source

of satisfaction came from being homemakers. Women needed an out-
let for their creative energies, a way of experiencing their full potential.
And the only remedy for that was to overthrow the outmoded male-
dominated ways of thinking. Friedan called for a reevaluation of gender
assumptions and demanded equal educational and career opportunities for women as well as equal pay for equal work. The publication of
her book *The Feminine Mystique* in 1963 inaugurated a new era in the
struggle for women's rights. "The problem lay buried," Friedan wrote,
"unspoken, for many years in the minds of American women. . . . As
she made the beds, shopped for groceries, matched slipcover material,
ate peanut butter sandwiches with her children, chauffeured Cub Scouts
and Brownies, lay beside her husband at night—she was afraid to ask
even of herself the silent question—'Is this all?'"[1]

In 1966 Friedan, along with Congresswoman Shirley Chisholm,
the Reverend Pauli Murray, and twenty-five other women and men,
founded the National Organization for Women (NOW) in order "to
take action to bring women into full participation in the mainstream
of American society now, exercising all the privileges and responsi-
bilities thereof in truly equal partnership with men." NOW issued a
"Statement of Purpose" delineating its goals: "We believe the time has
come . . . to confront, with concrete action, the conditions that now
prevent women from enjoying the equality of opportunity and freedom of choice which is their right, as individual Americans, and as
human beings." Women, the statement read, were "first and foremost"
human beings and thus deserved exactly the same opportunities available for men.[2]

NOW pushed for enforcement of equal pay for equal work and demanded that the Equal Opportunity Employment Commission enforce
Title VII of the 1964 Civil Rights Act, which prohibited discrimination
in the workplace on account of sex. It pressured colleges and universities to open up professional programs to women and to include women's
studies courses in their curriculum. It pushed the government and private business to provide day-care centers for children. And perhaps most

importantly, certainly most controversially, NOW lobbied vigorously for women's reproductive rights and the decriminalization of abortion.

Many members of NOW were professional women with connections, looking for equality and self-determination. Others, influenced by the general milieu of 1960s dissent, were housewives who were frustrated by the constraints of the 1950s and looking to gain greater opportunity and possibilities in a world that was not structured by rigid gender lines and subordination to men/husbands. A third faction consisted of radical women looking to rethink the meaning and practice of gender and gender relations. Involvement in the Civil Rights Movement, antiwar protests, and the counterculture had deepened these women's political consciousness, made them keenly aware of the limitations placed on them in the social structure, and radicalized them. They studied the works of radical political philosophers from Marx and Lenin to Marcuse and Fanon and consequently began examining their own lives through the prism of leftist analysis. More and more they argued for the restructuring of gender relationships in postcapitalist society. But paradoxically their radicalization was also brought about because they discovered that even within the New Left sexism ran rampant. At the national SDS convention in 1965 women staged a walkout to protest the expectation that after an evening of intellectual discourse they were expected to make coffee and sandwiches, to clean up, and to be available for sex. Radical men, it seems, were just as chauvinistic as the rest of American men. The gender attitudes of New Left males, as much as dialectical materialism, radicalized the women's movement.

The most important phase of the radicalization process took place in the women's caucuses that developed in response to sexism. These were consciousness-raising sessions in which women discussed such taboo subjects as sexuality, lesbianism, masturbation, unwanted pregnancy, and illegal abortions. They encouraged each other to see through and cast aside the artificial existence and role-playing imposed on them by a male-dominated society. The sense of solidarity, of sisterhood, that these sessions generated strengthened the women's movement and gave women the daring to become more militant.

Feminist groups promoted these consciousness-raising workshops and urged their members to participate. One of them was Redstockings, which was founded in New York City by Shulamith Firestone and Ellen Willis in early 1969. "Women are an oppressed class," the Redstockings Manifesto declared. "Our oppression is total, affecting every facet of our lives. We are exploited as sex objects, breeders, domestic servants, and cheap labor. We are considered inferior beings, whose only purpose is to enhance men's lives. Our humanity is denied." Arguing that relationships between men and women are class relationships, Redstockings identifies "the agents of [women's] oppression as men. Male supremacy is the oldest, most basic form of domination. All other forms of exploitation and oppression (racism, capitalism, imperialism, etc.) are extensions of male supremacy; men dominate women, a few men dominate the rest." Relationships between "men and women are political conflicts that can only be solved collectively." The sooner women recognize this, the sooner they will be liberated.[3]

By the end of the 1960s radical feminist groups were proliferating, and their members were eager to experiment with all sorts of in-your-face tactics. On September 7, 1968 hundreds of women protested the Miss America Pageant in Atlantic City. They dressed a sheep in a bikini and "Miss America" sash and paraded her on the boardwalk, announcing that she was a prime piece of American meat. Demonstrators carried signs that read "Welcome to the Miss America Cattle Auction," while inside the convention hall activists unfurled a huge banner from the balcony proclaiming, "Women's Liberation." With dozens of male hecklers surrounding them, they threw their bras, girdles, curlers, high-heel shoes, makeup, and other symbols of male oppression into a "Freedom Trash Can."

A month later, on Halloween night, another widely covered piece of radical feminist street theater took place: a Witches' Dance in front of the New York Stock Exchange. Women from W.I.T.C.H. (Women's

International Terrorist Conspiracy from Hell) dressed up as witches, danced on Wall Street and put a hex on the stock market. Later in the year they protested the House Committee on Un-American Activities, and in 1969, wearing black veils, they held another guerrilla-style protest at a Bridal Fair at Madison Square Garden. As the women's liberation movement grew and became more threatening to conservatives, such radical actions, although they were obviously humorous, tongue-in-cheek attempts to raise consciousness, only served to provoke a powerful antifeminist backlash. Antifeminists portrayed feminists as male-bashing, antisexual, humorless shrews. The word *feminist* became, in their lexicon, a pejorative term, a joke even, and for many Americans this association has endured despite numerous gains that feminists have won for women.

Still, the essential arguments put forth by feminists resonated—with men as well as women—and set in motion a growing impulse to reconsider age-old labels and stereotypes. What does it mean to be a man or a woman in a society that imposes strict roles on individuals on the basis of gender? Women's liberation sought to free women from oppressive stereotyping that denied their individuality and hindered them from pursuing their full creative potential. What many men began to realize was that women's liberation also freed men from the roles and expectations that constricted their own individuality. "'Women's liberation,'" as Gloria Steinem wrote in a *Washington Post* op-ed piece in 1970, "aims to free men, too." The movement is not really a "feminist" movement; it is a "humanist" movement. "The first problem for all of us, men and women, is not to learn, but to unlearn." We must examine and question the antiquated assumptions that dominate our thinking. "Patriotism means obedience, age means wisdom, woman means submission, black means inferior: these are preconceptions imbedded so deeply in our thinking that we honestly may not know that they are there." If we can recognize these erroneous assumptions and get beyond them, we will all be free to experience *who* we are in our unique individuality. Men will not have to prove their masculinity, women will not have to prove their submissiveness, men will be

FIGURE 9.1. Feminist protest during the bicentennial in Philadelphia, Pennsylvania, July 4, 1976.
Credit: Image © Leif Skoogfors; courtesy of Leif Skoogfors, Corbis.

permitted to give their feminine side free rein, and women, their masculine side, for in truth we are all yin and yang, black and white, masculine and feminine. Denying one side of ourselves limits us. There are enough limitations in life; why impose artificial limitations on ourselves? Women's liberation frees everyone. "No more alimony. Fewer boring wives. Fewer childlike wives. No more so-called 'Jewish mothers,' who are simply normally ambitious human beings with all their ambitiousness confined to the house. No more wives who fall apart with the first wrinkle because they've been taught that their total identity depends on their outsides. No more responsibility for another adult human being who has never been told she is responsible for her own life." What both women and men need is a revolution in consciousness.[4]

The most controversial accomplishment of the movement was the successful campaign for reproductive rights. After years of debate and lobbying, organizations such as NOW and NARAL (the National Association for the Repeal of Abortion Laws) stepped up the pressure by coordinating demonstrations and rallies demanding the decriminalization of abortion. Redstockings organized a series of "abortion speak-outs" in New York and other cities, giving women a public platform to openly discuss the illegal and risky abortions that so many of them had undergone. Finally, a case on abortion rights made it to the Supreme Court, and on January 22, 1973, the justices, in a 7–2 decision, decriminalized abortion. The broader question of "women's rights" was not an issue in *Roe v. Wade*; the Court was more concerned with physicians' rights to perform abortions legally and with women's privacy rights. Regardless of the rationale behind the decision, women rejoiced that they were freed from governmental interference in a difficult and emotional personal decision. Women's reproductive rights were recognized and affirmed by the federal government.[5]

* * *

The Civil Rights Movement inspired other minorities to organize and to demand their rights. In California, Mexican American (Chicano) migrant workers banded together to protest against the fruit and vegetable growers that routinely exploited them by paying far less than minimum wage for long hours of backbreaking work. One of these workers, César Chávez, organized the National Farm Workers Association (later the United Farm Workers) to stand up to the growers. From 1965 to 1970 the UFW coordinated a grape strike that focused national attention on the plight of California migrant workers. Throughout the strike (*La Huelga*) Chávez adopted the nonviolent tactics of Martin Luther King and even took a page out of Gandhi's book by carrying out a twenty-five-day hunger strike in 1968 that garnered much-needed publicity for the workers' cause. By 1970 the nationwide grape boycott pressured growers to recognize and negotiate with the union. The UFW's success inspired other Latinos around the country to fight against discrimination. In 1969 activists formed La Raza Unida to engage in political battles on a local level with the goal of organizing Latinos as a bloc to elect state and national representatives committed to passing legislation to end discrimination. La Raza Unida and Chávez's UFW formed the basis of what evolved into a growing and significant movement to apply pressure on federal, state, and local governments to guarantee equal rights for Spanish-speaking Americans.

After enduring centuries of injustice, prejudice, brutality, and outright murder, American Indians too were propelled to action by the radical currents of the times. By 1968 thousands of Native Americans adopted 1960s-style militancy and protest as the means to fight for equality and the basic civil rights they had been denied. Using the phrase "Red Power" as their rallying cry, Indigenous activists formed the American Indian Movement (AIM) in 1968 and organized protests and acts of civil disobedience to force the federal government to redress their grievances. Dennis Banks, Russell Means, and Leonard Peltier emerged as three of AIM's most prominent militants, and they became national figures in the struggle for Native American rights. In November 1969 AIM and about six hundred American Indians from fifty tribes occupied Alcatraz Island in San Francisco Bay. They demanded that they be allowed to keep the island where they hoped to set up an American Indian university, museum, and cultural center. "We are a proud people!" they proclaimed. "We have observed and rejected much of what so-called civilization offers. We are Indians! We will preserve our traditions and ways of life by educating our own children. We are Indians! We will join hands in a unity never before put into practice. We are Indians! Our Earth Mother awaits our voices. . . . WE HOLD THE ROCK!"[6] Though the occupation created publicity for the deplorable conditions American Indians were subjected to, it ended in June 1971 without their demands being met when President Nixon ordered federal marshals and the FBI to retake the island and evict the protesters. Undaunted, AIM and members of other American Indian organizations organized a march on Washington in 1972. Calling it the "Trail of Broken Treaties," hundreds of activists drove in a caravan to the nation's capital. When members of Congress refused to meet with them, they occupied the Bureau of Indian Affairs and issued a proclamation demanding that the United States honor all the treaties it has broken, that those that have not been ratified be submitted to the Senate, that Congress "relinquish their control over Indian Affairs," that 110 million acres be restored to the American Indians, that Indigenous civil rights be restored, and that all crimes against Native Americans be treated as federal crimes.[7] In 1973 some members of AIM seized the Wounded Knee battlefield site calling on the United States to honor the Fort Laramie Treaty of 1868 guaranteeing the Black Hills to the Lakota in perpetuity. The Wounded Knee siege led to a seventy-one-day confrontation between AIM and federal marshals, during which a federal officer and two Lakota were killed. In the end, however, as with the Alcatraz standoff, the protesters were removed, and their demands went unmet.

Even groups with the least power of all, prison inmates, were motivated by the radical activism of the time to rise up in rebellion. Prisoners in New Jersey, California, Massachusetts, and most notoriously Attica Prison in New York mutinied against the inhumane conditions to which they were subjected. Employing the rhetoric of Marx, the Black

Panthers, and other revolutionary groups, they issued a series of political demands.[8] But inmates' rebellions were invariably crushed. Indeed, although the uprisings called attention to their legitimate grievances and although there was some governmental response at least to evaluate and study their grievances, the inmates achieved only limited success. Still, public consciousness was expanding. Americans were realizing that there were problems that needed to be addressed.

* * *

In June 1969, the police raided the Stonewall Inn, a well-known gay bar in New York's Greenwich Village. This was not an unusual occurrence. Gay bars were habitually raided, with patrons apprehended and then released. It was an attempt to intimidate and humiliate gay men, who for the most part lived secret lives, fearful for their jobs, parental disapproval, and societal condemnation. Some bars, such as the Stonewall Inn, were operated by the Mafia; the owners paid off the police and served watered-down, overpriced drinks to people seeking a welcoming place where they could meet, dance, hook up, and be openly themselves. There were organizations in the 1950s, such as the Mattachine Society and the Daughters of Bilitis, that created a supportive community for gays and lesbians. And over the years there were protests and demonstrations and even a riot (in 1966) when police tried to arrest several drag queens and transvestites at a cafeteria in San Francisco, but for the most part the gay and lesbian world stayed below the radar. By 1969 the social and political unrest of the times, the example of civil rights and antiwar protesters, and the do-your-own-thing values of the counterculture emboldened homosexuals. On that June night in 1969 when the police raided the Stonewall Inn, the clientele fought back. Some refused to leave, and they forced six officers back into the bar as hundreds of gay men in the neighborhood gathered on Christopher Street outside the bar. For several days protesters and police clashed in the streets, while activists distributed flyers urging others to join the demonstrations and occupy the streets of Greenwich Village. "Get the mafia and the cops out of gay bars," demanded one of the flyers. "The nights of Friday, June 27, 1969 and Saturday, June 28, 1969," it went on to explain to the public, "will go down in history as the first time that thousands of Homosexual men and women went out into the streets to protest the intolerable situation which has existed in New York City for many years—namely, the Mafia (or syndicate) control of this city's Gay bars in collusion with certain elements in the Police Dept. of the City of New York." Calling themselves HYMN (the Homophile Youth Movement) and taking a page from the philosophy of the Black Power movement, the writers of the flyer made clear that "the only way this monopoly can be broken is through the action of Homosexual men and women themselves." They demanded the boycotting of Mafia-owned establishments and that "Gay businessmen step forward and open Gay bars that will be run legally with competitive pricing and a healthy social atmosphere." And they also appealed to Mayor John Lindsay to open "a thorough investigation and effective action to correct this intolerable situation."[9]

The Stonewall Riots lasted for only six days, but the movement was gaining momentum. In July gay activists called for strategy meetings and more demonstrations. "Do you think homosexuals are revolting?" one widely distributed placard asked. "You bet your sweet ass we are. We're going to make a place for ourselves in the revolutionary movement. We challenge the myths that are screwing up this society." And they announced a planning meeting for July 24, 1969. Another handout from the summer of '69 that was pasted on walls, nailed to trees, and slipped under parked cars' windshield wipers read,

Homosexuals Are Coming Together at Last
To examine how we are oppressed and how we oppress ourselves. To
fight for gay control of gay businesses. To publish our own newspaper.
To these and other radical ends.[10]

In the ensuing months several gay rights organizations were founded, among them the Gay Liberation Front (equating itself with the

Vietnamese National Liberation Front) and the Gay Activists Alliance. And this was only the start. From these beginnings scores of organizations were formed throughout the 1970s and 1980s (and indeed in the 1990s and 2000s) that increasingly demanded equal rights for gays, lesbians, bisexuals, and transgender persons. As the movement grew, people's attitudes and public policy slowly began to evolve. In cities with large gay populations, such as New York, Philadelphia, and San Francisco, politicians gradually began endorsing proposals and passing statutes that modestly improved the standing of gays. For example, in California, State Assemblyman George Moscone openly supported gay rights and was instrumental in pushing the legislature to repeal the state's sodomy law. Later, when he was mayor of San Francisco, he continued his support for gay rights and backed candidate Harvey Milk for election to the San Francisco Board of Supervisors. Milk, a vocal leader of San Francisco's gay community, had run for political office several times in the past, but his election as a supervisor in 1977 was his first victory. It was the first time that an openly gay man was elected to political office in the United States. Milk was hoping to make a difference through the conventional political process, and his major achievement was a civil rights bill that banned discrimination against anyone for sexual orientation. However, after only eleven months in office Milk (along with Mayor Moscone) was assassinated. His assassination and the enormous outpouring of grief by the citizens (gay and straight) of San Francisco focused attention on the gay rights movement at a critical moment and went a long way toward expanding Americans' consciousness in the same way that violence against Freedom Riders did for the Civil Rights Movement.

During the 1980s and 1990s gay rights activists kept increasing pressure on lawmakers to end antigay discrimination. When the federal government essentially ignored the AIDS crisis that exploded in the 1980s, gays founded the AIDS Coalition to Unleash Power (ACT UP) and organized a series of protests demanding that Washington authorize funds for AIDS research and that the Food and Drug Administration approve and release new experimental AIDS drugs. By the turn of the century gay activism was gaining considerable visibility, and with increased visibility came increased success.

* * *

As early as the nineteenth century environmentalists such as John Muir and John Burroughs toiled to raise awareness of the fragility of the environment. Muir was especially influential during Theodore Roosevelt's presidency when he urged TR to establish more National Parks and National Forests in order to keep pristine lands out of the hands of developers. By the 1960s, large numbers of Americans, concerned about water and air pollution and the rapid destruction of natural resources, began organizing to "save the planet." Implementing the slogan "think globally, act locally," environmentalists argued that doing something in their own neighborhoods, their own cities, to reverse the negative human impact on the environment was the best way to find a solution for a global problem. The longtime dissenter and folk singer Pete Seeger, who had been involved in the struggle for workers' rights as well as the civil rights and antiwar movements, began a campaign in 1968 to clean up the Hudson River. He raised money to build a replica of a nineteenth-century sloop, and then he and his crew sailed the sloop *Clearwater* up and down the river, performing concerts at towns along the way, raising political awareness about the devastating effects of the PCBs and other pollutants dumped into the river by such companies as General Electric. By 1978 the concerts had evolved into an annual two-day folk festival that continued for more than forty years and was a major factor in cleaning up the Hudson River. In fact the efforts to decontaminate the river were so successful that sturgeon reappeared in the Hudson after an absence of a century.

In 1970, environmentalists organized the first "Earth Day," which has become an annual environmental awareness rally in cities around the nation. And in the early 1970s Greenpeace was founded with the mission of confronting companies and countries that endanger the Earth's ecology.

Greenpeace has interfered with Japanese and Norwegian whaling ships, American military tests, and French vessels carrying nuclear waste. But nonviolent efforts, civil disobedience, or even disruptive tactics to purify the atmosphere, rivers, and oceans; to protect endangered species; and to fight against the proliferation of nuclear power is a very slow process. It might take years, if not decades, before the hard work pays off. In an age of the increasingly devastating effects of climate change and dwindling resources, environmentalists fight on with intensifying urgency.

* * *

By the end of the 1970s a full-fledged backlash exploded against the radical 1960s. Frightened by the radicalism of, and angry at the attention paid to, African Americans, women, Hispanics and gays, many whites, especially those of modest income, felt victimized. They resented a government that ignored their struggles while giving preferential treatment to minorities; they felt Congress was giving handouts to people who did not deserve it; they felt cheated. And they hated the challenges posed to traditional American mores, religion, and ethical values. And they began to revolt. This conservative backlash against 1960s radicalism fostered new dissent movements that sought to overturn the gains made by African Americans, women, gays, and radicals.

One of the most conspicuous manifestations of this backlash was the "pro-life" movement. As soon as *Roe v. Wade* established a new norm expanding women's reproductive rights, a new dissent movement—the antiabortion movement—was born. Hundreds of thousands of Americans formed organizations and political action groups with the specific goal of overturning *Roe*. One of the leading organizations spearheading the backlash was the National Right to Life Committee, which argued on moral grounds that a fetus's right to life trumps a woman's right to choose. Antiabortion activists lobbied politicians and held demonstrations on a regular basis, they picketed Planned Parenthood clinics and the offices of physicians who perform abortions, they organized demonstrations on college campuses, and every year on the anniversary of the *Roe* decision, they held a protest rally at the Supreme Court. The movement quickly gained the backing of fundamentalists, the Roman Catholic Church, and after the 1980s, the Republican Party. In fact, since the 1980s, pro-life has become so central to Republican ideology that it is regarded as a litmus test for would-be Republican political candidates. And to be nominated for the presidency Republicans had to pledge to appoint Supreme Court justices who would overturn *Roe*. What feminists regarded as a personal issue became a public political issue. As pro-life rallies and demonstrations mounted in the 1980s and 1990s, NOW and other feminist groups fought against the backlash by organizing pro-choice rallies supporting *Roe* and reproductive rights.

By the 1990s, protests at Planned Parenthood clinics and other women's health facilities escalated to the point that several abortion-provider physicians and clinical workers were murdered by zealots who justified such acts as necessary to save the lives of the innocent, the unborn. The majority of pro-life advocates deplored such murderous deeds, but the killings underscored the raw emotions that were unleashed on both sides of the issue. The issue, of course, is far more complicated than the reductive terms of "pro-life" and "pro-choice," which give the false impression that there are two, mutually exclusive points of view. Nevertheless, the forces arrayed against reproductive rights were formidable and kept up the pressure through demonstrations and litigation for the next forty-nine years. They were finally victorious in 2022, when the Supreme Court, in *Dobbs v. Jackson Women's Health Organization*, disregarded the doctrine of *stare decisis* and overturned *Roe v. Wade*, to the great shock and consternation of millions of pro-choice women and men. Thus underscoring a major truism about dissent—rights gained, like democracy itself, need constant vigilance to be maintained.

Conservatives targeted other progressive accomplishments of the 1960s. After the Supreme Court upheld busing as a tool to integrate de facto segregated school districts (busing African American students to school districts where most of the students were white, and vice versa), a number of cities experimented with the policy. The hope was that

214 | MOBILIZATION AND BACKLASH

mixing students from diverse ethnic and racial backgrounds would reduce prejudice and racial strife and produce more equal education opportunities. However, this busing mandate produced intense backlash,
when enraged white working- and lower-middle-class Americans who
could not afford to send their children to private schools, fearing social displacement (and backed by conservative politicians), took to the
streets in massive protests. Boston was not the only city that witnessed
such protests, but it became the most notorious with the publication of
a Pulitzer Prize–winning photograph of a white protester attempting
to impale an African American lawyer on the pole of the American
flag he was wielding. This image of unrestrained rage being expressed
in the streets of the city that ignited the American Revolution, became
a major hub of the abolitionist movement, and raised the first African
American regiment (the 54th Massachusetts) in the Civil War, left an
unforgettable and paradoxical impression on Americans' minds.

Supreme Court decisions strengthening separation of church and state
by banning prayer in public schools also angered many conservatives,
particularly evangelical Christians. The ban, they believed, endangered
religious freedom and so they protested. If they could get the ban overturned, if they could soften the impenetrable barrier separating church
and state that had existed from the nation's founding, they believed it
would help prevent the country's slide into immorality. Emerging from
such religiously motivated protests, the Christian Right was born. Jerry
Falwell founded the Moral Majority in 1979 as a pro-evangelical Christian
lobby group that would back candidates who were pro-family, pro-life,
pro-prayer, pro-Israel, and staunchly anticommunist. The Moral Majority threw its support behind Reagan in the 1980 presidential campaign. A
second powerful lobbying group was the Christian Coalition, headed by
another evangelical minister, Pat Robertson. Robertson also founded the
Christian Broadcasting Network, which became a means to disseminate
his sermons and political diatribes. Planned Parenthood, he warned, "is
teaching kids to fornicate, teaching people to have adultery, every kind of
bestiality, homosexuality, lesbianism—everything the Bible condemns."[11]

This sentence succinctly enunciates the Christian Coalition's position and its goal of electing politicians who would put an end to such offenses.

At the height of dissent in the 1960s and 1970s the United States also embarked on a War on Crime that was in no small part a backlash to the Civil Rights Movement. Equating antiwar and civil rights protests with disorder and crime allowed first President Johnson and then President Nixon to police African American, Latino, and poor neighborhoods much more aggressively. With President Reagan's war on drugs in the 1980s more aggressive policing was augmented by new laws as well as much harsher sentencing policies, which in turn led to a critical incarceration crisis in this country. By 2000 the United States had more people incarcerated than any other country in the world, and those people were overwhelmingly and disproportionately African American, Latino, and poor.

With Reagan in the White House, the conservative backlash swelled dramatically. The Christian Right acquired formidable power and prestige, right-wing talk-show hosts gained enormous followings on radio and television, and Democrats—not just moderate Democrats—for the most part went along with the backpedaling on social programs. Academics, pundits, and media personalities, such as Paul Weyrich, Phyllis Schlafly, Irving Kristol, and Rush Limbaugh, won considerable followings by vilifying countercultural morals. They promoted family values, pro-life militancy, antifeminism, homophobia, religion in the public sphere, the sanctity of marriage, and other conservative values, while smearing 1960s radicals, such as Timothy Leary, Abbie Hoffman, Jane Fonda, and H. Rap Brown, as disloyal, as un-American, as traitors.

* * *

Nixon's election in 1968 was an early sign of a rising conservative backlash. Nixon won not because the left was split (although that did help the Republicans) but mostly because the white middle class, the "silent majority," was fed up with radicalism, disorder, and the defiance of American values. The election was a sign of the potency of a white backlash against the Civil Rights Movement. It was a sign of middle-class abhorrence (and fear) of the radical challenge to the affluent consumerist society, to Christian values, to the American way of life. Indeed, when one adds the votes cast for the racist third-party candidate George Wallace to Nixon's totals, the conservative vote was a landslide against liberalism. The backlash was immediately evident with the National Guard shooting of unarmed demonstrators at Kent State and with the brutal no-holds-barred suppression of the Attica Prison rebellion. It was visible in the forceful retaking of Alcatraz and Wounded Knee from American Indian protesters. By the 1980s the long-term white backlash set in: the gutting of welfare programs, the defunding of the Justice Department's Civil Rights Division, the acceleration of mass incarceration. In some ways this was comparable to the backlash against the abolition of slavery during Reconstruction. In the immediate aftermath of the Civil War the Ku Klux Klan and other organizations used violence and terrorism to maintain white supremacy; then, with the end of Reconstruction, long-term backlash set in through legal and political means, with the Republican Party's abandonment of its focus on freedpeople and redemptionist southern state legislatures' instituting Jim Crow laws, literacy tests, and poll taxes and redefining crime and incarceration in such a way that increased the African American prison population. Some historians have labeled the Civil Rights Movement and the Civil Rights and Voting Rights Acts of the 1960s a "Second Reconstruction," drawing a parallel between the backlash against these progressive gains with the white supremacist "Redemption" following the abandonment of the first Reconstruction in 1877.[12]

By the time Reagan became president in 1981, it was clear that the majority of Americans *had* turned their backs on the sixties. Still, dissent continued. There were demonstrations and protests in the 1980s, although not on the scale of those of the 1960s and 1970s, against the Reagan Doctrine of backing and aiding brutal regimes, most notably in El Salvador, where death squads roamed at will exterminating peasants and leftists who opposed the CIA-supported right-wing dictatorship. When the United States armed and trained the Contras in Nicaragua, thousands of Americans protested. And left-wing activists initiated a series of annual demonstrations at Fort Benning, Georgia, where the Department of Defense's School of the Americas, now renamed the Western Hemisphere Institute for Security Cooperation, trained (still trains) Latin American dictators and their security forces in the finer points of suppression and torture to eliminate political dissidents.

When the Cold War ended with the fall of the Soviet Union in 1991, the United States was the last superpower standing. Americans, cheering that "we won the Cold War," were filled with optimism that a new era of peace was about to dawn. But such hopes were chimerical, and it soon became clear that American policy was partly to blame for the evaporation of prospects of a peaceful new world order.

10

Dissent in a New Age

It is my belief that the writer, the free-lance author, should be
and must be a critic of the society in which he lives. . . . The
moral duty of the free writer is to begin his work at home:
to be a critic of his own community, his own country, his
own culture. If the writer is unwilling to fill this part, then
the writer should abandon pretense and find another line of
work: become a shoe repairman, a brain surgeon, a janitor, a
cowboy, a nuclear physicist, a bus driver.
—Edward Abbey, 1988

When President George H. W. Bush launched Operation Desert Storm
with the backing of the UN Security Council to oust Saddam Hussein
from Kuwait in 1991, another (albeit small) antiwar movement was
born. But the Gulf War was too brief for a full-fledged antiwar movement to emerge. If it had gone on longer, there is little doubt that more
Americans, still unnerved by the bitter experience of the Vietnam War,
would have protested the war. There were however, a couple of instances
of rather unconventional dissent in the 1990s. Julia Butterfly Hill, for
example, garnered media attention when she climbed into a thousand-
year-old giant redwood that the Pacific Lumber Company was about to
cut down and vowed not to return to earth until the company agreed to
spare the tree. She lived in the branches of the redwood, 180 feet from
the ground, for 738 days. Finally, after more than two years of negative
publicity, the Pacific Lumber Company acquiesced in Hill's demands
and pledged not to cut down the tree. Theodore Kaczynski, aka the Unabomber, was a sort of twentieth-century Luddite who decided to protest
against technological progress by mailing letter bombs to scientists at

research and development laboratories. Kaczynski's goal was to start a revolution against technology, which he believed was destroying human life. "The Industrial Revolution and its consequences," he proclaimed in his Manifesto, "have been a disaster for the human race." They have "destabilized society, have made life unfulfilling, have subjected human beings to indignities, have led to widespread psychological suffering . . . and have inflicted severe damage on the natural world." Therefore, he argued, there must be "a revolution against the industrial system . . . to overthrow . . . the economic and technological basis of the present society."[1]

Julia Butterfly Hill and the Unabomber were solo acts, but there were environmental organizations, notably the Earth Liberation Front (ELF) and Earth First! that made headlines with their actions. Both organizations, like Greenpeace, used civil disobedience, but they went beyond protests and disruptive direct action campaigns such as tree sitting and road blockages. They also engaged in sabotage (which they called "ecotage"). Destroying ski lodges, pouring sugar into the gas tanks of Hummers parked in automobile-dealership lots, pouring chemicals on golf-course greens. The Earth Liberation Front, the more radical of the two organizations, has been designated a domestic terrorist organization by the FBI. ELF has taken credit for torching a ski lodge in Vail, Colorado (because the lodge was expanding into a forest that endangered the habitat of the Canada lynx), and attempting to burn down the U.S. Forestry Service facility in Irvine, Pennsylvania. One of the spokespersons for ELF, Craig Rosebraugh, testified at a congressional hearing investigating both foreign and domestic terrorism. The history of the United States, Rosebraugh said in his statement, shows that social change only comes about through civil disobedience. "Perhaps the most obvious . . . historical example," he said, "of this notion supporting the importance of illegal activity as a tool for positive, lasting change, came just prior to our war for independence. Our educational systems in the United States glorify the Boston Tea Party while simultaneously failing to recognize and admit that the dumping of tea was perhaps one of the most famous early examples of politically motivated property destruction." We do not label our founding fathers as terrorists, but this is what the similar actions of the Earth Liberation Front are labeled by the federal government: ecoterrorism.[2]

Along with the radicalization of environmentalism a burgeoning anti-government movement got a lot of press coverage in the 1990s. Believing that individual liberty and the Constitution must be protected from an intrusive federal government, right-wing paramilitary militias in Michigan and Montana attracted many discontented supporters. They were anti-tax, anti-government, and pro–Second Amendment. They armed themselves in order to prepare for the day when governmental restrictions on liberty would become intolerable. Just as the minutemen at Lexington and Concord stood up to unjust taxes and a despotic Parliament, so too must Americans stand up to the tyranny in Washington. The government must not interfere in their lives. They yearned for the supposedly good old days of the nineteenth-century pioneers who built this country through their rugged individualism. However, these modern-day minutemen overlooked the fact that it was the federal government that subsidized the railroads and irrigation projects that made it possible for settlers and homesteaders to move into the West and farm the land. When the FBI had shoot-outs with the Freemen of Montana at Ruby Ridge, Idaho, in 1992, killing two people, and with the Branch Davidians (a religious cult) at their compound in Waco, Texas, in 1993, which resulted in the deaths of seventy-six men, women, and children, membership in right-wing militias soared. These heavy-handed attacks by federal agencies were proof to many people of a vast government conspiracy to stamp out personal liberty.

On the second anniversary of the Waco raid, Timothy McVeigh (who was associated with, but not a member of, the Michigan Militia) staged a horrific protest against the U.S. government by blowing up the Alfred P. Murrah Federal Building in Oklahoma City. 168 people, including nineteen children in a daycare center, were killed, hundreds wounded. This act of violent dissent sickened Americans. For days the nation was in shock. McVeigh and his accomplices were quickly apprehended, tried, and convicted. (McVeigh was executed in June 2001; his accomplices received prison sentences.) Though McVeigh was not actually a member of any of the right-wing militias, the bombing and the trials discredited much of the anti-government militia ideology. Still, these militias continue to gain members as they prepare to defend themselves against all enemies, foreign or domestic.

* * *

The issue that provoked the most dissent at the turn of the century was globalization. With bipartisan support President Bill Clinton signed the North American Free Trade Agreement (NAFTA), creating a free-trade zone linking the United States with Canada and Mexico, and the General Agreement on Tariffs and Trade (GATT), establishing the World Trade Organization. "Antiglobalists" denounced these measures as corporate power rolling over workers, merely a dressed-up version of imperialism. When the World Trade Organization met in Seattle in November 1999, more than forty thousand protesters, representing dozens of disparate groups that normally do not see eye-to-eye with each other, descended on the city. Environmentalists concerned that environmental standards were nonexistent in the Third World countries where the WTO was sponsoring free trade, thus exacerbating climate change, labor unions worried about the loss of American jobs, and human rights activists denouncing sweatshops that exploited children and the poor got together for several days of massive demonstrations.

The most famous proponent of antiglobalization was consumer advocate Ralph Nader. He warned Americans that *both* the Democrats and the Republicans were owned by corporate interests, and they were not at all responsive to the needs of the people. Democracy was endangered because NAFTA and GATT concentrated too much power and wealth in the hands of multinational corporations. Americans, Nader pointed out, have a moral objection to those who need a handout from the federal government. But the small amount of money that welfare recipients receive, Nader insisted, is nothing compared to the welfare the government doles out to corporations in the form of subsidies and tax breaks. "By any yardstick," Nader said, there is "far more welfare disbursement . . . in the corporate world than in the impoverished street arena." Americans need to wake up. "We're supposed to have a government of, by and for the people. Instead we have a government of the Exxons, by the General Motors and for the DuPonts. We have a government that recognizes the rights and liabilities and privileges of corporations, which are artificial entities created by state charters, against the rights and privileges of ordinary people."[3]

* * *

Millions of Americans believed that the world changed on September 11, 2001. But the world did not change. What did change was that Americans suddenly had to come to grips with the fact that the world viewed us differently than we viewed ourselves. For several weeks, as Americans rallied around the president and proudly flew flags from their cars and houses, they tried to understand why "they hate us." Was it because the Arab world hated our freedom? Our way of life? Was it because our policies had the effect of denying those rights to the people of the Middle East while enriching the autocratic regimes that ruled them?

While Americans pondered these imponderables, Washington retaliated. With a 90 percent approval rating President George W. Bush sent American forces into Afghanistan to hunt down Osama Bin Laden and to destroy Al-Qaeda and the Taliban. But as the war on terror escalated, as more and more troops were sent to Afghanistan, as Bin Laden proved too elusive, and as the United States geared up for a war with Iraq, dissent intensified. Some argued that the United States should not be going to war but should be reevaluating the policies that provoked the attacks. Some felt that the attacks were a product of what the CIA calls "blowback"— unanticipated consequences of CIA activity. Some protested against the PATRIOT Act. Within weeks of the attacks Congress had passed this act, which expanded the definition of terrorism and eased restrictions on

the government's ability to wiretap telephones, monitor financial trans-
actions and Internet use, engage in secret background checks and surveillance of citizens and noncitizens suspected of terrorist sympathies,
increase border security, and hold aliens for questioning. Although most
Americans were sufficiently concerned about security to support these
measures, many, both on the right and on the left, were infuriated at this
misguided move to restrict individual liberty. They feared that in our
quest for security we were fatally eroding the constitutional principles
that were the foundation of American democracy.

In the weeks immediately following the attacks there was an extraordinary show of unity in the United States. Pundits, regardless of political leanings, were calling for the destruction of Afghanistan. "Bomb
them back to the Stone Age" was one of the sentiments expressed. But
there were also those who questioned the wisdom of retaliatory attacks
that would likely kill far more innocent civilians than Al-Qaeda terrorists or their Taliban allies. Some argued that what the United States
needed to do was to revise its foreign policy. In October 2001 singer/
songwriter Ani DiFranco penned "self evident," a poem about "the day
that america / fell to its knees / after strutting around for a century /
without saying thank you / or please" that struck a chord with those who
were critical of U.S. foreign policy. In the poem she catalogs decades
of American imperialism in Latin America and the Middle East that
she believes prompted the terrorist attacks.[4] Of course, many Americans
were deeply offended by DiFranco's leftist critique, calling her unpatriotic, a traitor, even a terrorist. But anyone who dissented against the
government's response to 9/11 in those first weeks after the attacks found
themselves labeled un-American or traitors—or worse. Every point of
view, every thought, every action seemed black or white; there were no
shades of gray in people's thinking.

But there were hundreds of thousands of dissenters even in the midst
of this almost jingoist, knee-jerk reaction on the part of so many Americans. Those who did not go along with the herd mentality questioned
the bombing of Afghanistan and U.S. Middle East policy in general,

but they were also severely critical of the PATRIOT Act and the blanket arrests of noncitizens. Amnesty International was one of the organizations leading the way. It released a report in March 2002 that exposed the extent of the sweeps. More than twelve hundred aliens, mostly of South Asian or Arab ethnicity, were incarcerated during the first two months after the attacks, and hundreds, without having formal charges levied against them, were still in custody six months later. "A significant number of detainees," the report stated, "continue to be deprived of certain basic rights guaranteed under international law. These include the right to humane treatment, as well as rights which are essential to protection from arbitrary detention, such as the right of anyone deprived of their liberty to be informed of the reasons for the detention; to be able to challenge the lawfulness of the detention; to have prompt access to and assistance from a lawyer; and to the presumption of innocence." While granting that Washington needs to protect national security, Amnesty International is nevertheless "concerned that the government has used its expanded powers to detain non-nationals in the wake of September 11 without the necessary safeguards under international law. . . . The secrecy surrounding the detention process has, further, created a serious lack of public accountability." The organization then spells out the ways the government could protect basic civil liberties.[5]

The American Civil Liberties Union, as would be expected, condemned the attempts to stifle dissent. In 2003, the ACLU published *Freedom under Fire: Dissent in Post-9/11 America*, in which it claimed that the administration was making a determined effort to question the patriotism of its critics. And it was not just the administration but also the media and other members of the power structure that were engaged in the policy of intimidation. "White House spokesman Ari Fleischer," the report declared, "also warned Americans to 'watch what they say.' Conservative commentators like Bill O'Reilly suggested prosecuting war protesters as 'enemies of the state.' Since 2001, hundreds have been arrested for exercising their constitutionally protected freedoms, and some have lost their jobs or been suspended from school." Clearly, Americans "need to stop and consider the direction in which we are going, for we are in danger of allowing ourselves to be governed by our fears rather than our values. We are not the first generation to face this challenge."[6] The rest of the document recapitulated the history of past attempts to stifle dissent, from John Adams and the Alien and Sedition Acts to Lincoln's suspension of the writ of habeas corpus to the Sedition Act of World War I to the incarceration of Japanese Americans during World War II. Although the administration continued its campaign of labeling critics unpatriotic, the ACLU and other organizations championing free speech kept the issue in people's consciousness.

All through 2002 the Bush administration made an unrelenting (if knowingly inflated) case for invading Iraq. Saddam Hussein, key officials insisted, had weapons of mass destruction (WMD). They claimed the CIA had irrefutable evidence that Iraq had a stockpile of chemical and biological weapons and was nearing completion of an atomic bomb. They claimed that we must invade Iraq and topple Saddam Hussein before it is too late. "The problem here," National Security Adviser Condoleezza Rice said, in a metaphor that was to be repeated countless times by other members of the administration, "is that there will always be some uncertainty about how quickly he can acquire nuclear weapons. But we don't want the smoking gun to be a mushroom cloud."[7] Such scare tactics worked. In October 2002 Congress passed a resolution granting the president the necessary powers to go to war with Iraq without a formal declaration of war.

But as the inexorable buildup for war escalated, so too did antiwar dissent—not only in the United States but also worldwide. On February 15, 2003, coordinated protests took place in hundreds of cities around the globe. Millions demonstrated in Rome, London, Dublin, Paris, Berlin, Athens, New York, Philadelphia, Chicago, San Francisco, Los Angeles, Seattle, and other cities, demanding that the United States not embark on this war, not invade Iraq. Protesters insisted that there was literally no proof that Iraq had weapons of mass destruction, nor was there any evidence whatsoever that Iraq was involved with or supported the terrorists who were responsible for 9/11. The outpouring of public sentiment at these demonstrations was extraordinary. It seemed that more Americans opposed the war with Iraq *before* it started then opposed the Vietnam War even four years into that ill-advised conflict.

But the demonstrations and marches had no influence on the administration. Bush dismissed the protesters as a "focus group" and went ahead with the invasion on March 19. Still, antiwar activists, though disheartened, continued to organize protests, demonstrations, vigils, acts of civil disobedience, and teach-ins. On April 9–10, 2003, the American Historical Association's "Historians Against the War" coordinated a nationwide teach-in that took place on scores of college campuses around the country. From UCLA to NYU, from Stanford to Rutgers, from the University of Montana to the University of South Carolina, hundreds of students and faculty attended teach-ins. At Temple University in Philadelphia more than a hundred students attended a seven-hour teach-in analyzing the policy behind the war—a war that at that time was less than a month old. And on many campuses teach-ins continued on a regular basis.

Vietnam Veterans Against War as well as veterans of the Gulf War also leapt into the fray. They issued a joint "Call to Conscience from Veterans to Active Duty Troops and Reservists," in which they urged troops to resist the war. "We are veterans of the United States armed forces," they began. "We stand with the majority of humanity, including millions in our own country, in opposition to the United States' all-out war on Iraq. We span many wars and eras, have many political views and we all agree that this war is wrong."[8] David Wiggins, a West Point graduate, posted an online statement to the troops about to be deployed in which he urged them to look deeply into the ethical ramifications of what they were about to do and, ultimately, to follow their conscience. "With all due respect, I want you to know that if you participate in this conflict, you are not serving me, and I don't support you." If you participate in the war, you "will be damaging my reputation as an American, and further endangering me and my children by creating hatred that will someday be returned to us—perhaps someday soon. Your actions will not lead to a safer world, but a more dangerous world of pre-emption and unilateral decisions to commit mayhem. I don't support that."[9]

With each passing month, with each passing year, as American troops got bogged down in a poorly conceived occupation and casualties kept mounting, antiwar dissent grew. MoveOn.org, a liberal political action committee, urged Americans to get active in the antiwar movement. It produced a documentary film, *Uncovered: The Whole Truth about the Iraq War*, which persuasively argued that the Bush administration "cherry picked" intelligence reports about the so-called weapons of mass destruction that Saddam Hussein was stockpiling, and thus the rationale for going to war was a lie.

Recording artists, inspired by the antiwar songs from times past, protested against the Iraq War with their music. (Some musicians even recorded new versions of earlier antiwar songs, such as Pearl Jam's cover of Dylan's "Masters of War," which the band performed on the *Late Night with David Letterman* television show.) One of the most powerful indictments of American foreign policy, the war in Iraq, and the cheerleading role of the media was the hip-hop artist Immortal Technique's 2003 song "The 4th Branch." It is a compelling and unwavering in-your-face denunciation of American foreign policy. "You really think this country, never sponsored terrorism? / Human rights violations, we continue the saga / El Salvador and the contras in Nicaragua / And on top of that, you still wanna take me to prison / Just cause I won't trade humanity for patriotism." In the end, he orders listeners to "turn off the news and read . . . ! Read . . . read . . . read."[10] Countless artists recorded songs protesting against the war, against President Bush, and against American policy: Eminem's "Mosh," OutKast's "War," Pearl Jam's "World Wide Suicide," Billy Bragg's "The Price of Oil," and Steve Earle's "Rich Man's War." The latter song is a particularly poignant reflection on the impact of war on ordinary individuals caught up in fighting, not for their own dreams or interests but for the benefit of global corporations and politicians. For those facing the guns, whether a working-class U.S. soldier or a desperate Palestinian suicide bomber, there are no winners. Earle gives a twenty-first-century take on an age-old antiwar sentiment: "Just another poor boy off to fight a rich man's war."[11] Although protest music and the recording industry has changed considerably since its heyday in the 1960s and 1970s, music still has the power to raise important questions and shape the conversation about controversial issues. It can still transform apathy into commitment.

* * *

Despite the historic election of Barack Obama, the ending of the Iraq War, and the elimination of Osama Bin Laden, dissent was still commonplace in the second decade of the twenty-first century. Pundits, talking heads, and comedians still denounced and mocked the people in power. Right-wing political commentators such as Glenn Beck and Sean Hannity, as well as left-wing commentators such as Rachel Maddow and Chris Matthews, have many devoted fans, although it is doubtful that their critiques changed any minds since they were preaching to their respective choirs. More effective were comedians like Stephen Colbert and Jon Stewart, who were truly subversive in their use of humor to ridicule the power structure. Like H. L. Mencken before them, they induced people to look with new eyes at the underlying absurdity of the things corporate executives and political leaders say and do.

Ever since the New Deal, conservative Americans opposed what they saw as an out-of-control Big Brother–style government. They wanted less government, less regulation, less taxes, less intrusion into their lives. It was not just the Democratic Party that was anathema to them; the Republican Party under George W. Bush too was just as guilty of expanding a vast, bloated, inefficient federal bureaucracy. Conservative organizations such as Americans for Prosperity and FreedomWorks, founded by the ultraconservative billionaires David and Charles Koch, promote political action to resist big government and support ultraconservative politicians. The passage of the Troubled Asset Relief Program (signed by George W. Bush to address the economic crash of 2008), the election of the nation's first African American president, the implementation of the Homeowners Affordability and Stability Plan, and the passage of healthcare reform in 2010 inflamed conservatives. During 2009 and 2010 a new organization, the Tea Party, held hundreds of demonstrations and rallies around the country. Many activists dressed in eighteenth-century costumes, wigs, and tricornered hats carried signs and shouted slogans paraphrasing the rallying cries of 1776. They compared Obama, variously, to George III, Adolf Hitler, and Joseph Stalin. They portrayed the government in Washington as the archenemy of liberty and Christian values. However, it soon became clear that the Tea Party was not a grassroots protest movement. It was sponsored by corporate insiders who cultivated the anger and confusion over change (and the accompanying declining power of whiteness) that many Americans felt. Rightwing billionaires, among them the Koch Brothers, financially backed the movement in order to secure their political ends and protect their economic agenda. The Tea Party also benefited from extensive favorable promotion by the conservative media and rapidly gained supporters in every state.[12]

Many on the left ridiculed the Tea Party, but they stopped laughing when the 2010 midterm election resulted in a thorough repudiation of Obama and the Democratic Party. Republicans gained in just about every state legislative and gubernatorial election in the country, they gained seats in the Senate, and they won an overwhelming majority in the House of Representatives. The new legislators were passionately devoted to principle; they vowed to overturn "Obamacare" and the other measures that had been passed to deal with the economy, and they vowed to lower taxes. The Tea Party had tapped into a deep vein of populist anger and developed a massive following.

Within a year of the Tea Party's successes protesters from the left, outraged at the economic inequality that was (and still is) growing out of control in the United States, launched the Occupy Movement. The demonstrations started on September 17, 2011, when protesters converged on the statue of the Wall Street bull in New York City. Within a few days hundreds had descended on lower Manhattan and began camping out

FIGURE 10.1. Tea Party protesters in Washington, DC, September 12, 2009, venting their anger at what they perceive as an intrusive federal government. This march was sponsored in part by an organization named 9.12dc.org, which was founded by Fox Television's Glenn Beck. Photograph by David King.
Credit: CC BY 2.0; courtesy of dbking on Flickr.

in Zuccotti Park, renamed Liberty Park. "We are the 99 percent!" they proclaimed, referring to the fact that 42 percent of the nation's wealth is possessed by the elite 1 percent, while 99 percent share the rest. Within weeks Occupy Wall Street spread to other cities: Philadelphia, Boston, Los Angeles, Oakland, Seattle, Denver, Atlanta. Even small towns had versions of the Occupy movement. Soon it reached London, Rome, Athens, Frankfurt, and other international cities. Something was happening around the world: a deep, unfathomable discontent with the harsh economic realities that most people face on a daily basis. In the United States so many Americans, most of them middle class, were feeling that the American Dream was slipping through their fingers, that no matter how hard they tried, they would only take baby steps in getting ahead, whereas the 1 percent kept accumulating more and more wealth at the expense of the 99 percent. Indeed the government bailout of the banks and industries that were "too big to fail" mostly profited the 1 percent. The Occupy protesters had a plethora of grievances—unemployment, mortgage defaults, loss of savings and pensions, overwhelming student debt—but they were united in demanding that the government in Washington, the president, the Senate, and the House of Representatives, listen to them.

Shortly after the occupation began, the protesters issued a declaration. "As one people, united, we acknowledge the reality: that the future of the human race requires the cooperation of its members; that our system must protect our rights, and upon corruption of that system, it is up to the individuals to protect their own rights, and those of their neighbors; that a democratic government derives its just power from the people, but corporations do not seek consent to extract wealth from the people and the Earth; and that no true democracy is attainable when the process is determined by economic power." They went on to denounce the corporations that "place profit over people, self-interest over justice, and oppression over equality, [that] run our governments." Emulating the Declaration of Independence, they listed numerous specific grievances that they demanded must be addressed.[13]

Occupy Wall Street was not particularly radical in that most of the demonstrators called for the reform, not the destruction, of capitalism. In some ways they were more akin to the Progressives of the early twentieth century than to the IWW or the radical socialists and anarchists who sought to smash capitalism. But by year's end most of the occupations around the country were dislodged by law enforcement officials, and the movement lost its momentum. The problem that Occupy Wall Street faced was that linking a protest with a specific space is an

FIGURE 10.2. Occupy Wall Street, November 15, 2011. Photograph by David Shankbone. Credit: CC BY 3.0; courtesy of David Shankbone on Wikimedia Commons.

existential problem. It is one thing to stage a civil disobedience action for a day or two, occupying a space or blocking traffic, but it is quite another to attempt an indefinite occupation without an end date. If the protest and the space are separated, if the protesters are removed, it ends the demonstration. The Bonus Army experienced this in 1932. Columbia student radicals experienced it in 1968. Occupy Wall Street experienced it in 2011. Still, in all those cases the ending of a specific dramatic action did not silence the protesting voices. The fight continued.

Superficially there were some similarities between the Tea Party and Occupy Wall Street. Both movements hated the vast amounts of taxpayer money that bailed out the financial industry. But after that their views diverged. Whereas Occupy Wall Street saw government as part of the solution, the Tea Party saw it as *the* problem. Furthermore, the Occupy movement was truly a "grassroots" movement whereas the Tea Party was a manufactured movement. An "Astroturf" movement. The Tea Party had the financial resources to be successful in the voting booth, but one thing Occupy Wall Street accomplished was to change the focus of the political discussion. Before Occupy everyone was talking about the deficit. By the time Occupy was evicted, economic inequality was the focal point. Everyone, even the Republican leadership, who of course had vastly different ideas than Occupy about how to address the problem, was talking about the 99 percent.

11

Dissent, Lies, and Insurrection

From the streets of Cairo and the Arab Spring, to Occupy
Wall Street, . . . social media was not only sharing the news
but driving it.
—Dan Rather

If we really are to be partisans of democracy, the rule of law,
human rights, and basic decency, then this is a painful truth.
Policy has its limits. Negotiations must be grounded in not
only good faith but reality, and not lies or myths.

The demands of extremists are meant to be impossible to
fulfill:. . . . the election must be overturned and Mike Pence
hanged. People issuing such demands are not interested in
discussion or compromise; indeed, they'd be disappointed
if they got what they wanted, because their anger sustains
them and gives meaning to their lives.
—Tom Nichols, 2022

After the election of Barack Obama in 2008, political discourse took
on a nastier (although not necessarily new) tone of bitterness and par-
tisanship. The rise of the Tea Party and its irreconcilable stance against
big government and taxation, angry protests against health-care reform,
vilification of "illegal aliens," and relentless questioning of the religion
and even the nationality of the nation's first Black president reflected a
deep-seated fear on the part of some people (reminiscent of the 1920s
clash between modernism and traditionalism) that the United States
was moving too rapidly into an unknown, frightening future. A vari-
ation of this fear was a motivating force for the Occupy Wall Street

movement—the fear that the United States had abandoned the principles of the founding fathers and that democracy of the people, by the people, and for the people had truly perished under the onslaught of corporate power.

There were also protests during the Obama years demanding that Congress fix broken immigration laws and provide a way for undocumented immigrants to become American citizens. Thousands of Americans protested against fracking, against mountaintop-removal coal mining, against gun violence, against attempts to restrict voting rights with voter ID laws, against the exploitation of migrant workers, against racially motivated police shootings of young unarmed Black men, and, in the light of whistleblower Edward Snowden's revelations, against the National Security Agency's violation of the Fourth Amendment. The protests to stop the construction of the Keystone XL Pipeline finally ended in triumph for the activists in 2021. Members of the LGBTQ+ movement also saw success, after years of protest, when the Supreme Court's rulings in *United States v. Windsor* (2013) guaranteed marriage equality and in *Obergefell v. Hodges* (2015) validated same-sex marriage.

Technology played an extremely important and significant role for all dissent movements, whether of the left or the right. Viral videos on YouTube had the impact of reaching massive audiences and raising public awareness of an injustice, or a perceived injustice. Postings on Twitter and Facebook spread the word to protesters of the time and place of the next rally or demonstration or civil disobedience action or spontaneous "flash protest." Individuals backing a specific cause have used the Internet to obtain millions of signatures on petitions that are then sent to government officials or corporations, demanding they change a law or policy. The possibilities are endless for activists to utilize these tools to spread the word, educate people, and increase participation in their movement. And clearly, both the Tea Party and Occupy Wall Street, as well as the Occupy movements in Europe and the Arab Spring in the Middle East, successfully used social media and the Internet to expand their message and mobilize supporters. There has been, however, a significant downside to electronic media. It can misrepresent a cause, distort a message, paint a false picture of what actually happened at a protest march, or even sabotage legitimate protests. So, users, beware. Furthermore, unlike the antiwar and civil rights protests of the 1960s, which called for a real commitment on the part of activists to go to a public space and participate in a demonstration, the use of electronic media has produced the phenomenon of what has been called "slacktivism" or "clicktivism." By clicking "like" on a group's social media page or signing an online petition, individuals have the tendency to feel that they have done their part, that they have participated, that they have fought the good fight, without actually doing so, without actually making a physical commitment. Still, while passive advocacy is no replacement for activism, it is clear that social media is one of the most powerful tools to fan the fires of dissent.

* * *

In 2016 protest took an unexpected turn during an extremely contentious and unprecedented presidential election campaign. The entire campaign itself can be viewed as a profound expression of dissent as Americans in droves rejected politics-as-usual. On the left huge numbers of voters were fed up with the Democratic Party believing it was no longer the party of the working class, but just as beholden to the moneyed interests as the Republican Party.[1] And so millions turned from the establishment candidate Hillary Clinton and flocked to the progressive banner of democratic socialist Bernie Sanders. And on the right there were those who rejected all fifteen of the mainstream Republican candidates and supported political outsider Donald Trump.[2] Millions of middle-class Americans, mired in the inescapable consequences of intensifying economic inequality and pessimistic about their future in a country where the political establishment ignores their plight, voted enthusiastically for a billionaire political novice who promised to make America great again. Their vote was not only a protest vote against the acute economic anxiety they were suffering, but also a protest against social displacement. Financial insecurity combined with the social changes produced by such dissent movements as civil rights, feminism, the counterculture, and LGBTQ+ activism had produced a fierce backlash against progressivism.

With the presidency of Donald Trump, Americans experienced a new era in which dissent took on an entirely different shape. It reflected more deeply than ever the no-holds-barred rancor of the fractious nature of politics. Trump did not originate this, but he certainly fanned the flames and used it to his advantage. His racist, bigoted rhetoric emboldened those who shared his attitudes, giving them permission to express their views openly. Those who had been seething for years against "political correctness" now opened their mouths to voice their true views and fears about the "other": that the expansion of democracy to minority groups meant American democracy no longer had meaning for them, that American democracy itself was suspect, that American democracy was undemocratic for favoring people of color and abandoning middle- and working-class whites.

The unrestrained reactionary dissent that surfaced in some ways was a natural product of two trends: long-term Republican efforts, starting with Nixon's "Southern Strategy," to gain political dominance by playing, subtly, to the lowest common denominator instead of Lincoln's "better angels of our nature,"[3] along with the centuries-long tradition of anti-intellectualism that runs through American history that the distinguished historian Richard Hofstadter analyzed so astutely.[4] It also reveals one of the truisms about dissent: once a dissent movement gains traction it inevitably creates its own dissenters. As progressive policies dominated during the Obama years, conservatives were roused to form their own dissent groups to organize resistance against those policies.

This white backlash against the Obama presidency that Trump rode into the White House was clearly a reaction to a "Third Reconstruction." Three times during the history of the United States African Americans experienced significant progress in their status and each time there was a powerful backlash. After the abolition of slavery and the end of

Reconstruction in 1877 the backlash expressed itself in the Jim Crow Laws, literacy tests, poll taxes, Ku Klux Klan terrorism, an explosion of lynching, and the glorification of the "Lost Cause" with the erection of thousands of public monuments honoring Confederate heroes. When the Civil Rights Movement succeeded in pressuring the federal government to pass the Civil Rights Act of 1964 and the Voting Rights Act of 1965, a second backlash came swiftly when President Lyndon B. Johnson signed legislation instituting the War on Crime, which eventually led to mass incarceration, the violent suppression of the Attica prison revolt, and the racist tactics employed in the policing of Black neighborhoods. The Third Reconstruction spawned the racially reactionary times of President Donald Trump.[5] Some white Americans were deeply afraid that society had become a zero-sum game in which their way of life was about to be extinguished by the elevation to full citizenship of people of color. A small but significant number of them formed highly-visible, well-armed white supremacy groups to combat multiculturalism and return the country to a mythical all-white past. They very successfully used social media to manipulate facts, spread disinformation, promulgate conspiracy theories, to convince untold numbers of unwary readers that multiculturalism was un-American.

* * *

The Trump presidency also ignited a wave of progressive dissent, demonstrations, and protests that had not been seen on such a level since the 1960s. On the day following his inauguration a coordinated series of "Women's Marches" took place around the country (and indeed the world) attracting millions of people protesting the rise to power of Mr. Trump. In Washington, New York, Philadelphia, San Francisco, London, Paris, Tokyo, millions of people joined massive protest marches. The majority of protesters feared that this racist, xenophobic, sexist, narcissistic individual, who played to the most sordid instincts and prejudices of the electorate, was a threat to American democracy. Progressives around the country organized political engagement groups to oppose the new administration and the Republican-majority congress. Operation 45, #KnockEveryDoor, Swing Left, Run for Something, Movement 2017, the Pussy Hat Project, Millennials for Revolution joined with more established organizations like the American Civil Liberties Union, MoveOn.org, and the Southern Poverty Law Center to resist the Trump administration's policies. One of the new organizations, Indivisible, had more than 5000 chapters by the end of 2017 and adopted the right-wing Tea Party's successful tactics against Obama policies as a means to thwart the Trump political agenda. Specifically, Indivisible convened weekly meetings and sent out daily action alerts on social media platforms like Twitter, Slack, and Facebook to inform members of specific actions they could take on any particular day. For example: attend town hall meetings of their members of congress (MoC) and demand that they answer their constituents' questions; circulate telephone numbers, email addresses, and websites of their MoCs; deluge congressional offices with coordinated phone calls, letters, postcards, and emails demanding that congress investigate the administration's conflict-of-interest issues; post lists of vulnerable Republican office holders; organize groups to visit MoC's district offices; instruct members how to reach out to the media; organize and participate in rallies to protect the Affordable Care Act and Planned Parenthood; protest against executive orders restricting refugees and immigrants from Muslim countries by flocking to international airports chanting "Let them in, let them in!"

* * *

By the end of the 2010s the Black Lives Matter (BLM) movement had grown into the largest, most potent protest movement in the nation. In 2012 an African American teenager, Trayvon Martin, was murdered by George Zimmerman, a zealous town watch volunteer in a Florida community. Zimmerman's highly-publicized trial was closely watched and when he was acquitted, three African American activists, Alicia Garza, Patrisse Cullors, and Ayọ Tometi (at the time named Opal Tometi), founded #BlackLivesMatter (BLM). Their purpose was to highlight the entrenched racism, discrimination, and racial and economic inequality at the core of American society as well as expose the excessive use of force by the police in everyday encounters with African Americans. BLM closely monitored police violence and expertly used social media to spread the word and organize major protests whenever an unarmed African American was killed by law enforcement.

The organization expanded after Michael Brown, another unarmed Black teenager, was killed by a police officer in Ferguson, Missouri, in 2014. Organizers began using the #BlackLivesMatter hashtag to coordinate protests in Ferguson as well as other cities. Subsequently Garza, Cullors, Tometi, and others organized BLM chapters in eighteen cities around the country. And during the next few years, as other African Americans were killed by the police—Tamir Rice, Eric Garner, Freddie Gray, Tanisha Anderson, Philando Castile, Sandra Bland, Breonna Taylor were just a few of them—Black Lives Matter supporters took to the streets in huge numbers. "Black Lives Matter," Garza, Cullors, and Tometi posted on their website, "is an ideological and political intervention in a world where Black lives are systematically and intentionally targeted for demise. It is an affirmation of Black folks' humanity, our contributions to this society, and our resilience in the face of deadly oppression."[6] After the protests in Ferguson "people were hungry to galvanize their communities to end state-sanctioned violence against Black people, the way Ferguson organizers and allies were doing." BLM established an infrastructure for a decentralized global network "to support the development of new Black leaders, as well as create a network where Black people feel empowered to determine our destinies in our communities."[7]

Between 2014 and 2020 Black Lives Matter became a global initiative with a mission "to eradicate white supremacy and build local power to intervene in violence inflicted on Black communities by the state and vigilantes. By combating and countering acts of violence, creating space for Black imagination and innovation, and centering Black joy, we are winning immediate improvements in our lives." Unlike earlier civil rights organizations from the 1960s, BLM also "affirm[s] the lives of Black queer and trans folks, disabled folks, undocumented folks, folks with records, women, and all Black lives along the gender spectrum. Our network centers those who have been marginalized within Black liberation movements."[8]

The movement achieved critical mass in May 2020 after the murder of George Floyd during an arrest in Minneapolis. Officer Derek Chauvin, supposedly in an effort to subdue Floyd, pinned him down on the ground with his knee on his neck. Despite the handcuffed Floyd's pleas that he could not breathe, Chauvin continued the chokehold for more than eight minutes, the last three of which were *after* Floyd became unresponsive.[9] Bystanders with smartphones photographed and videoed the entire incident, many of whom implored the officer to release the chokehold. Chauvin finally did so when an ambulance arrived, but by that time Floyd was dead. Within hours protests erupted in Minneapolis. And in the following days and weeks hundreds of thousands of outraged citizens throughout the country protested this blatant example of state-sanctioned murder. Protests took place in all fifty states and in scores of countries around the world. In big cities like Chicago and Houston, and small towns like Lambertville, New Jersey and Burns, Oregon. People from all walks of life, ages, races, and ethnicities were united in their condemnation of police brutality. People chanted "I can't breathe," and "Black Lives Matter," and the call-and-response, "say their names" followed by George Floyd, or Breonna Taylor, or Freddie Gray, or Eric Garner, or any of the other names on the list of Black victims of police violence. After more than three years BLM protests still continue because there were always new names to add to that tragic list.

Many police forces were restrained in their response to these demonstrations, but in numerous cities around the country police engaged in aggressive tactics to contain the protests. In more than 100 cities, according to a *New York Times* report, the police used tear gas on peaceful demonstrators. "Thousands and thousands of utterly ordinary people who thought they were going to an ordinary protest event are finding

FIGURE 11.1. George Floyd Protests, Miami, Florida, June 6, 2020, in the days and weeks after the police killing of George Floyd, hundreds of thousands of people protested throughout the country. Photograph by Mike Shaheen.
Credit: CC BY 2.0; courtesy of Mike Shaheen on Wikimedia Commons.

themselves receiving a really aggressive police response. . . . That itself is a bit horrifying. The police have actually succeeded in making people more angry."[10] The vast majority of the protests were nonviolent, respectful, and civil,[11] but a small percentage did turn violent as the frustration and despair of some protesters about the persistence of overt and systemic racism spilled over into property destruction. In some cases opportunists and troublemakers infiltrated demonstrations not to protest but to take advantage of the opportunity to engage in looting and arson. During the first weeks after George Floyd's death the National Guard was mobilized in twenty-one states to prevent looting. In Minneapolis protesters torched a police station and several stores. Even though property destruction only occurred in roughly 5 percent of the demonstrations, the media and right-wing talk show hosts exaggerated these instances and demanded a robust law enforcement response. President

Trump was so incensed that he delivered an ultimatum threatening to send in the military to quell the protests. "When the looting starts," he said, "the shooting starts."[12]

Non-state actors also committed acts of violence against peaceful protesters. There were dozens of car-ramming incidents in which anti-BLM individuals drove into crowds, injuring demonstrators and numerous instances of armed members of right-wing paramilitary groups showing up with the purported purpose to "keep the peace." And in Kenosha, Wisconsin, a teenager armed with an assault rifle walked past police officers and opened fire on demonstrators, killing two and wounding one.[13]

To put Black Lives Matter in historical context, we must reflect on the fact that the killing of young, unarmed Black men and women is nothing new. Think of the civil rights activists in the 1960s like James Chaney or Jimmie Lee Jackson who were killed by local sheriffs, or the countless killings of Blacks since then in confrontations with law enforcement during the war on drugs and those imprisoned by the present-day carceral state. Think of Attica in 1971. Think of MOVE in 1985. Or reflect on the thousands of lynchings from the end of the Civil War to the 1960s. The reason the Black Lives Matter protests have attracted so many millions of outraged participants is because witnesses to these killings have recorded them on their smartphones and posted the videos on social media sites like YouTube. The reality of actually witnessing, through a video recording, the murder of an unarmed, non-resisting person leaves the viewer with no alternative but to be horrified at the injustice of such an act.

There are many BLM activists, like writer Shaun King, who continue to monitor and publicize police brutality directed at African Americans as well as call out those whites who report Blacks to law enforcement officials because they are "acting suspicious." Notifying the police unnecessarily has often led to the person reported on, being unlawfully detained, or harassed, or, in some cases, killed by police officers solely on the basis of a white person's suspicions. Were the suspicions the result of genuine fear? Or racism? There are times when white racism, whether explicit or implicit bias, has led to instances of vigilante "justice" or public lynching. For example, when Ahmaud Arbery, a twenty-five-year-old African American was jogging one night in 2020 near his home in Brunswick, Georgia, he was chased, tracked down, and murdered by three white men.

Clearly, social media is the driving force behind the expansion of Black Lives Matter. The adroit use of the Internet galvanized millions of white Americans (shocked and infuriated when they saw the video recordings of police violence) to take part in the marches and demonstrations in numbers far larger than had participated in the 1960s Civil Rights Movement. When all white Americans become just as outraged as African Americans at the systemic racism and the storm-trooper tactics of the police, then, and only then, will the United States start to live up to the democratic ideals it embraced at its creation. This has given BLM significant momentum. But it has also unleashed a powerful white supremacy backlash.

* * *

While Black Lives Matter was the most momentous and far-reaching movement of the 2010s and early 2020s, other groundbreaking protest movements emerged that provoked considerable debate and reflection. #MeToo was founded in 2006 by community organizer and New York activist Tarana Burke as a support network for women in the Bronx who were victims of sexual violence. For its first decade it "brought resources, support, and pathways to healing" for women who had been victims of sexual assault, and then, in 2017, "the #metoo hashtag went viral and woke up the world to the magnitude of the problem of sexual violence. What had begun as local grassroots work had now become a global movement—seemingly overnight. Within a six-month span, our message reached a global community of survivors. Suddenly there were millions of people from all walks of life saying 'me too.' And they needed our help."[14]

It was the Harvey Weinstein scandal that exploded on the scene in 2017 that sent the hashtag viral. Immediately, hundreds of thousands of women became part of a dramatic, unstoppable movement using the #MeToo hashtag on social media. Weinstein was a formidable movie and television producer who wielded great power in Hollywood. He was in a position to make or break careers, and he used this threat to force actresses and other women working in the film industry to provide him with sexual favors. Scores of actresses, and aspiring actresses whose careers were terminated by Weinstein, came forward to tell their stories to investigative journalists: Alyssa Milano, Rosanna Arquette, Annabella Sciorra, among others. As the scandal widened over the next few years, more and more accusations were brought against famous, powerful men in major corporations, the entertainment industry, and politics who were sexually harassing, abusing, and assaulting women (and sometimes men) over whom they had some control: Charlie Rose, Garrison Keillor, Roger Ailes, Kevin Spacey, Al Franken, are just a few of the hundreds of prominent men whose careers were derailed by accusations of sexual harassment and/ or assault. And with each new revelation, #MeToo, through social media, expanded into a global movement—from North America to Asia, South America to Europe. Fed up with the power dynamic that subjected them to sexual abuse by men who had authority over them, women demanded accountability and government action to create a safe working environment.

The movement has had a profound impact on gender relations. Men who thought they knew how to act around women, especially those who had grown up in an era when young men were expected to compliment women on their appearance and trained in the etiquette of opening doors and pulling out chairs for women now suddenly found themselves uncertain as to how to act, or what behavior was acceptable and where the boundaries were that must not be crossed. Many reflected on their own past interactions with women and reassessed how comments they made, or actions they committed, were offensive.

This has influenced many men to readjust their attitudes about gender roles and to be more mindful of their behavior. Also in response to the #MeToo movement, most corporations, government agencies, and educational institutions have set up sexual harassment training workshops and clinics, and created guidelines that are strictly enforced to ensure safety in the workplace for all employees. Still, it is clear from the massive response of women all around the world, that this is a problem that has deep historical roots and that is far from being resolved.

In 2018 the "March for Our Lives" movement was founded by students from Marjory Stoneman Douglas High School in Florida after a mass shooting that took the lives of seventeen students and teachers. What happened at the school was by no means an isolated incident. School shootings have been happening, with increasing frequency, for decades. At Columbine High School in 1999: twelve students, one teacher. Sandy Hook Elementary School in 2012: twenty children (between six and seven years old), six staff. But not only schools. Churches. Walmarts. Country music festivals. Theaters. Bars. Grocery stores. Almost any place where large numbers of people can gather is a potential target. The National Rifle Association, gun manufacturers and dealers, as well as Second Amendment devotees have enormous political power over lawmakers, and they make sure that any legislation to control access to guns is immediately tabled. It is a matter of fear (mostly irrational) that many Americans have that any sensible legislation to reduce gun violence will lead eventually to the government confiscating their guns. But mostly it's a matter of profits for gun manufacturers. Just days after the murders at Marjory Stoneham Douglas High School students founded the March for Our Lives movement with the goal of forcing and shaming politicians to finally address these tragedies with legislation rather than their vapid "thoughts and prayers." Through civic engagement and protest marches they demanded that politicians do something to end the epidemic of gun violence. "We cannot allow," their mission statement declares, "one more person to be killed by senseless gun violence. We cannot allow one more person to experience the pain of losing a loved one. We cannot allow the normalization of gun violence to continue. We must create a safe and compassionate nation for all of us."[15]

A little over a month after the tragedy these students led a massive march on Washington of 200,000 people and coordinated simultaneous demonstrations at 763 other locations that were attended by close to two million people.[16] March for Our Lives continues to organize marches and protests to put pressure on local, state, and federal lawmakers to enact legislation to reduce gun violence. It is a hard fight, the opposition is formidable with unlimited financial resources, but the students are wise enough to know that if they get out the youth vote, if they can inspire the generation of eighteen- to thirty-year-olds to become politically engaged, then there is the opportunity to replace those politicians who are in the pocket of the NRA and the gun industry with those who *will* enact gun control legislation.

Another contemporary dissent movement that has strengthened in the last few years is the coming together of many people protesting the inaction of Washington to address climate change. Some progressive politicians have proposed a "Green New Deal," but are unable to find any bipartisan support for its recommendations, while many grassroots organizations initiated campaigns to push the United States to rejoin the Paris Agreement and make a commitment to pass laws regulating carbon emissions and addressing climate change. Many young people have followed the lead of Greta Thunberg, the teenage Swedish environmental activist who has galvanized youth around the world to demand that their countries' leaders pass legislation that will assure them that there will still be a habitable earth for them when they reach the age of sixty. Thunberg initiated the #FridaysForFuture movement in 2018 when she began a three-week strike for climate change at the entrance of the Swedish Parliament in Stockholm. The movement quickly became global as young people in other countries organized sit-ins and strikes at government buildings to force lawmakers to tackle climate change. Specifically, they demanded standards to prevent the global temperature from rising more than 1.5 degrees Celsius and to "ensure climate justice and equity, listen to the best united science currently available, [and] follow the Paris Agreement." The #FridaysForFuture website gives advice on how to organize strikes, sign petitions, and schedule days of action. "We are fighting for our future and our lives because they are directly threatened by the climate crisis and the ecological breakdown. We are taking action because we want to protect the beauty of the earth, the diversity of species and the lives of all beings. Our goal is to overcome the climate crisis and to create a society that lives in harmony with its fellow beings and its environment."[17]

Climate scientists and environmental organizations are unanimous that climate change is happening,[18] it's a serious crisis, it's too late to reverse it, but there are ways, if we act now, to mitigate its negative impact. But, in the United States, and many of the industrialized countries, most politicians seem to be so beholden to Big Oil that it seems impossible to get them to frame legislation that would at least minimize the irreversible impact of climate change.

It is not only students, young people, and environmental activists who have participated in protests demanding government action on climate change, but also scientists. In April 2022, more than 1,000 scientists took part in protests in Washington and more than two dozen countries in the "Scientist Rebellion," after the release of the Intergovernmental Panel on Climate Change's *Report* that verified "'rapid and deep' cuts to greenhouse gas emissions are needed to stay at or below the targeted 1.5 degrees Celsius of global warming. Without strengthening climate policies, greenhouse gas emissions are projected to lead to a median global warming of about 3.2 degrees Celsius by 2100."[19] And this would have devastating consequences. The scientists who took part in the protests, like so many of the younger activists, were distraught at the inaction and unwillingness by governments to adequately address this impending catastrophe. Essentially they were saying the time to act is now.

This movement is young, and it has a long way to go to get the powers-that-be to commit to a united front in order to deal with the problem, but it has clearly become impossible for people, no matter where they live, to ignore climate change. The mounting frequency and intensity of hurricanes, tornadoes, heatwaves, flashfloods, mudslides, and wildfires occurring on every continent, and in places that have never before experienced such dramatic climate disasters, are sobering to reflect on and certainly underscore the fact that climate change is a reality every country needs to confront. And yet there are climate change deniers who believe it's all a hoax. Even if one disputes the scientific conclusion that climate change is a phenomenon caused by human activity, it does not negate the fact that it is in our power to moderate the worst effects. And environmental activists and other concerned, informed citizens insist that it is our duty to do so.

Some environmental groups, like the Sunrise Movement, Just Stop Oil, and the Extinction Rebellion, have gone beyond peaceful demonstrations and strikes and have engaged in disruptive civil disobedience. In 2019, Extinction Rebellion, a group that has chapters in several countries as well as the United States, initiated protests that created massive traffic jams in Washington, DC. They also disrupted traffic in Los Angeles, New York, and London to stress the urgency for needed action to address climate change. In 2022, volunteers from Just Stop Oil (a London-based organization) glued themselves to masterpieces in art museums, smeared a Van Gogh painting at the National Gallery with tomato soup, and chained themselves to goal posts at soccer matches, much to the irritation of the public. Members of these organizations are grateful that their actions are being supported by the Climate Emergency Fund and the Equation Campaign. Both of these groups donate significant funds to support the activists' campaigns, provide money to cover the legal expenses of those who are arrested while protesting, and also pay for salaries and living expenses for organizers and dedicated volunteers. The *New York Times* reported recently that the Climate Emergency Fund and the Equation Campaign are themselves financed by wealthy heirs of two of the major fossil fuel companies: Getty Oil and Standard Oil. Aileen Getty, whose grandfather established Getty Oil, was a cofounder of the Climate Emergency Fund, and "the Equation Campaign [was] started in

2020 with a $30 million pledge . . . from two members of the Rockefeller family, Rebecca Rockefeller Lambert and Peter Gill Case." Case explained that he felt "a moral obligation to do my part."[20]

After years of pressure by activists, and total resistance by Republicans, the Democratic Congress finally passed with the narrowest of majorities, a bill that addressed climate change. The modest bill, that President Joseph Biden signed into law on August 12, 2022, is viewed by young activists as an absolutely necessary first step that does not go nearly far enough to mitigate the deleterious effects of climate change. It's merely a down payment. One of the founders of the Sunrise Movement observed that the "bill is not the bill that my generation deserves and needs to fully avert climate catastrophe, but it is the one that we can pass, given how much power we have at this moment." The bill provides subsidies for companies to invest in solar, wind, and other sustainable energy sources to reduce dependence on fossil fuels and thus, hopefully, lower carbon emissions. "But scientists say the United States needs to do more. It must stop adding carbon dioxide to the atmosphere by 2050. . . . Beyond that threshold, the likelihood increases significantly of catastrophic droughts, floods, wildfires and heat waves." Still, it is a step, and it is a modest victory for climate activists to at least get the government moving in a direction that could eventually be built on. Historically, most dissent victories do tend to be incremental and are usually achingly slow for dedicated advocates of a cause.[21]

* * *

Understanding dissent during the Trump years is complicated. Some of it was genuine dissent by conservatives who felt that political correctness, the emphasis on woke culture, social dislocation, and economic uncertainty were jeopardizing their future. Some of it was genuine dissent on the part of progressives who feared that the gains they fought so long for would be reversed under the onslaught of a powerful conservative backlash. But many of the protests defy any definition of dissent because they were not based on actual grievances, but on falsifications, fear, conspiracy theories, and outright lies that had no authentic basis in reality. Disinformation and misinformation have always been factors propelling events throughout history but have become particularly problematic since the widespread accessibility of the Internet and social media. Unlike the cardinal rule for journalists that all stories have to be based on verifiable evidence, when it comes to the Internet, anyone can post anything without authenticating it. It could be an unconventional opinion, or it could be the most outlandish conspiracy theory. And the more outlandish it is, the faster it goes "viral," spreading to millions of credulous people who don't question the legitimacy of the source because it coincides with their preconceived notions and biases. One of the most important skills in this Internet age, when millions of people are able to spread information about everything from protests to conspiracy theories to extremist political ideologies, is information literacy. Especially when the domain is .com. It is essential for individuals to learn how to discriminate between fact and fiction; to always question the source of the information (or disinformation) in order to analyze the reliability of that information. What are the credentials of the source? Are they an expert in the field? Whom are they speaking to? What is the basis for their claim? Who benefits from spreading the information? What is the agenda? Compare the information with other sources. And, above all, become informed by reading widely and examine all points of view, especially those that challenge one's own perspective.

Since 2017, partly based on fears of social and racial displacement, and frequently connected with fringe conspiracy theories, there has been an alarming rise in extreme right-wing dissent and a proliferation of white supremacist groups. White supremacy is not a new phenomenon, it has existed from our earliest history, but the recent wave has expanded rapidly in response to the Black Lives Matter movement as well as the national campaign to remove the Confederate monuments that have dominated public spaces in southern states for the past century. Many Americans object that statues celebrating the military and political leaders of the Confederacy who sought to destroy the Union are celebrating treason, and, as a consequence, they have demanded that they be removed. In September 2017, thousands of white supremacists from the KKK, the American Nazi Party, and other groups descended on Charlottesville, Virginia for a "Unite the Right" rally to denounce the planned removal of a Robert E. Lee statue. With chants of "You will not replace us!" they staged a torchlight parade through the city, with Nazi salutes, swastikas, and Confederate battle flags. When activists from BLM and Antifa (an anti-racist, anti-fascist group that aggressively confronts right-wing militants) assembled to protest white supremacy, one of the neo-Nazis drove his car through the crowd of protesters, injuring dozens and killing 32-year-old Heather Heyer.

Some people view white supremacist rallies as merely another form of dissent. But white supremacy has been embedded in American society from the beginning, and it is one of the most intransigent forces that dissenters have been protesting since the birth of the republic. While there is a long tradition of American dissent, there is also a long tradition of American violence. The violent maintenance of boundaries, of violently suppressing the rights of others, whether they be African Americans, Hispanics, Chinese Americans, undocumented immigrants, gay men, or American Indians is, as SNCC leader H. Rap Brown famously declared more than fifty years ago, as American as cherry pie. Slavery, the Trail of Tears, the overthrow of Reconstruction as former Confederates reclaimed political power in the South, the anti-Chinese rampages during the Gilded Age, the attacks on African Americans during the Great Migration, the resurgence of the KKK in the 1920s and again in the 1960s, are all part of this violent tradition.

Present-day white supremacy is terrorist ideology and cannot be viewed through the same lens as the dissenters who are protesting against injustice.[22] Dissenters are willing to reason with and convince the powers-that-be that their cause is just. Terrorists, however, see only one course of action—the annihilation of the "other." They have given up on democracy and orderly dissent in favor of insurrectionary, anti-democratic violence. There have been many instances in recent years when white supremacists have targeted minorities and people of color. In 2015 a white supremacist killed nine African Americans in the Emmanuel African Methodist Episcopal Church in Charleston, South Carolina; in 2018 a white supremacist killed eleven worshippers in the Tree of Life Synagogue in Pittsburgh, Pennsylvania; in 2019 a white supremacist killed twenty-one people (mostly Latinos) in an El Paso, Texas, Walmart. This is not dissent. This is terrorism.

* * *

Since the 2020 election the deep political schisms in the country have given rise to groups protesting not against injustice or discrimination, but against ideology. In 2019, a year marking the four hundredth anniversary of the establishment of American slavery, the *New York Times Magazine* inaugurated an initiative called the 1619 Project. The aim of the project is "to reframe the country's history by placing the consequences of slavery and the contributions of black Americans at the very center of our national narrative."[23] It is an interactive project that regularly posts written and photo essays and analyses and podcasts by historians, journalists, and artists describing the brutal facts about slavery and countering the traditional narrative of American history that has always emphasized the importance of the Anglo-Saxon settlers and founding fathers while diminishing or ignoring that of African slaves in building, first the colonies, and then the United States. For much of the nineteenth and twentieth centuries slavery was taught as a benign institution portraying the enslaved as somewhat contented with their plight. Even before the Civil Rights Movement became a force to be reckoned with in the 1950s, this "Gone with the Wind" interpretation of slavery was discredited by historians. The 1619 Project has currently been adopted by many school districts around the country as a basis for educators to teach a more accurate description of slavery and the experiences of the enslaved, as well as explaining the indispensable role played by African Americans in the making of the United States. This enables students to develop a deeper understanding of the ramifications of racism and how deeply embedded it is in our society.[24]

Critical race theory (CRT) is an intellectual theory that legal scholars, historians, sociologists, political scientists, and other academics have been developing for the past forty-plus years. It is fundamentally a postmodernist theory that argues that racism has evolved and continues to fester not just because of racist attitudes, but because it is entrenched, both consciously and unconsciously, in just about all aspects of law and society. "The core idea is that race is a social construct, and that racism is not merely the product of individual bias or prejudice, but also something embedded in legal systems and policies."[25] Academics, from a variety of disciplines, studying redlining, criminal justice, mass incarceration, economics, and other subjects have contributed to a significant body of research and literature on CRT for decades. And CRT has shown why there continues to be structural and systemic racism in the United States despite the gains of the Civil Rights Movement and legislation to ensure fair housing, lending policies, and affirmative action. Recently school districts around the nation have begun using some of this research to educate students about how to think critically about race, policy, and racial prejudice.

The importance of the 1619 Project and critical race theory for the American educational system has led, unsurprisingly, to rancorous protests. Conservative pundits have disparaged the project and CRT from their bully pulpits in the media and online, and groups like Moms for Liberty, Inc. (an Astroturf organization funded by right-wing money)[26] have begun a campaign attacking school boards and inciting hundreds of conservative parents to flock to school board meetings to vociferously denounce educators and administrators who support these new programs. Indeed, school board meetings and elections have increasingly become the front lines of political conflict. Conservative activists argue, without evidence, that critical race theory teaches white children to feel guilty about their white privilege, which in turn demoralizes them and damages their feelings of self-worth. That, in effect, CRT is reverse racism. But these arguments reveal that those objecting to CRT do not grasp what it is. In essence what they are really protesting is the culturally relevant teaching (that public schools have engaged in since the 1990s) that highlights diversity and multiculturalism. These education battles between parents who feel they, and not professional educators, should have the final say in what their children are taught is often expressed in raucous shouting matches at school board meetings as well as online harassment of teachers and administrators (an example of how electronic media has been used—in this case misused—as a means to express dissenting opinions). In addition to targeting the 1619 Project and critical race theory, many parents have also condemned the way school districts approach sex education and gender studies fearing that their children will be exposed to sexuality and LGBTQ+ classmates in ways that are anathema to them. In order to prevent educators from advancing the new standards that many states have adopted they have forced some school districts to ban and remove books from the curriculum that advance acceptance of sexual and gender diversity, critical race theory, and the 1619 Project. During the 2022 midterm elections this controversy became such a major political issue that politicians, on both sides of the debate, used it as a campaign tool to bludgeon the opposition.

This attempt to prohibit educators from teaching controversial subjects is a threat to democracy. "In our increasingly diverse nation," education scholars Heather C. McGhee and Victor Ray wrote in an opinion piece at the height of this conflict, "insulating students from lessons about racism will create a generation ill equipped to participate in a multiracial democracy. When partisan politicians ban the teaching of our country's full history, children are purposely made ignorant of how American society works. And the costs of this ignorance to American democracy will be borne by us all." Furthermore, they conclude, "contemporary attacks on teaching true history are authoritarian attempts to impose a sanitized curriculum. America's book banners and anti-critical race theory zealots are following a path well worn by authoritarian regimes in Russia and Hungary, which have issued laws targeting the teaching of L.G.B.T.Q. issues."[27]

* * *

On the other side of the political spectrum, progressive activists have also engaged in ardent protests against momentous ideological transformations that they believe are unacceptable. In the summer of 2022 the Supreme Court ruled on several major cases that convinced liberals and progressives that the Court had abdicated its traditional constitutional role as an apolitical branch of government and become a highly effective partisan institution. In a series of decisions the Court overturned, in some cases contrary to long-established precedent, much of the progressive agenda on climate change (*West Virginia v. Environmental Protection Agency*), gun regulation (*New York State Rifle & Pistol Association v. Bruen*), separation of church and state (*Kennedy v. Bremerton School District*), and reproductive rights (*Dobbs v. Jackson Women's Health Organization*). Within minutes of the release of each of these decisions, thousands of liberals and progressives picketed and marched and demonstrated in front of the Court's "Marble Palace," and in cities around the country, decrying the politicization of the Supreme Court. Despite the fact that all Supreme Court justices throughout the nation's history had political convictions and those convictions, even when they strove to rise above them, inevitably influenced their judicial decisions, many Americans believed that this particular court was more politically biased than previous courts. What protesters considered most disturbing is that the Court is moving in a direction of taking away long-established rights rather than expanding rights. Thousands have called for the impeachment of conservative justices, or congressional legislation to set time limits for justices' tenure, or empower the president to appoint additional justices. Still, it is clear that it is the Senate, during its hyper-politicized hearings interrogating Supreme Court nominees, that has damaged the credibility of the Supreme Court, and not the justices themselves. Nevertheless, many vowed that they would not rest until the Court's power was checked.

* * *

There are many levels of dissent and many ways that people express that dissent. Most dissent in American history has been nonviolent. Demonstrations, marches, vigils, moratoriums, boycotts, and civil disobedience are all, even when they are disruptive, nonviolent. Sometimes dissenters go beyond nonviolence and commit acts of property destruction such as the 1773 Boston Tea Party or the burning down of a Vail, Colorado, ski resort by the Earth Liberation Front in 1998, but it is still dissent. But there are profound differences between dissent and protest, rioting and insurrection, terrorism and revolution. When individuals' lives are threatened, or when they are physically assaulted and murdered, it is no longer dissent. It has reached the threshold of terrorism, insurrection, rebellion. Dissenters are seeking to reform society from within the system; terrorists and revolutionaries are trying to smash the system. Often without any clear idea about the details of setting up a new system to replace the old.

Dissenters have legitimate grievances against the dominant power structure. True dissent is based upon expressing truth and exposing injustice. But what happened on January 6, 2021 was not legitimate at all. The actions of the mob were based on falsehoods that were skillfully disseminated through spurious websites. This has nothing to do with dissent. Many of these people were ordinary Americans, swept along with a mob of extremists who were acting in the long American tradition of violence, spurred on by highly-organized members of the Proud Boys, the Oath Keepers, and the Three Percenters who stormed the Capitol because they chose to believe President Donald Trump's relentless lie that the 2020 election was stolen.[28] Though many of the people who briefly occupied the Capitol building do have authentic reasons for their anger, they could not see the root of their discontent and for that reason their "anger and . . . disillusionment, is easily manipulated," as former labor secretary Robert Reich observed.[29] They were pawns of a charismatic demagogue who were short-circuited by conspiracy theories and disinformation, who had a distorted, mythic view of American history. They were susceptible to Trump's lies because he reinforced their bigoted insular world view. They were protesting a chimera. And it made them susceptible to the seditious plotting by extremist groups for a takeover of the Capitol and "forcibly oppose the transfer of power" from Donald Trump to Joseph Biden. This is not dissent.[30]

The January 6 insurrectionists' distorted, mythic view of American history is a considerable challenge for historians. It is incumbent on historians and educators to teach the accurate, unvarnished and, yes, often uncomfortable, truths about the origins and complicated evolution of American democracy so that "we the people" understand that democracy is a fragile aspiration and will always be a work in progress. If we understand the historical context of such contemporary problems as racism, poverty, and inequality, then that understanding will guide us in the attempt to address those problems. That is America's existential challenge in the politically troubled times of the twenty-first century.

Conclusion

The Arc of Dissent

The more of the 99 percent that begin to see themselves as sharing needs, the more the guards and the prisoners see their common interest, the more the Establishment becomes isolated, ineffectual.
—Howard Zinn

May we never confuse honest dissent with disloyal subversion.
—Dwight D. Eisenhower

On January 21, 2017 I was in Philadelphia where I witnessed one of the hundreds of demonstrations that were being held nationwide in conjunction with the Women's March on Washington. As I observed the countless angry, alarmed, clever, and often humorous signs that people had fashioned, I was struck again by the essential truth that democracy in America didn't just happen; it was fought for. And it doesn't just happen to endure; it has been fought for continually ever since 1776: in the abolitionist movement, the Civil War, the women's suffrage movement, the fight for workers' rights, the fight for economic justice, the Civil Rights Movement, the LGBTQ+ movement, Chicano rights, environmentalism, Black Lives Matter . . . The list goes on. Clearly the fight is a constant battle.

It has become painfully apparent in this time of "alternative facts" and fake news, conspiracy theories, election denial, and an attempted coup, that huge numbers of Americans have at best a superficial understanding of the rich, complex history of this country. This is a problem that needs to be addressed because the key to a functioning, flourishing democracy is an informed electorate. It is the duty of all of us to study the past, to learn how to separate myth from reality, and acquire a deeper understanding of the nuances and complexities of our history, to think historically and cultivate the insight that we are the sum total of the agonies and ecstasies, the failures and triumphs of the past. How else can we understand the present? Or have a vision for the future?

When the Constitutional Convention adjourned in September 1787, a woman approached Benjamin Franklin and asked him what kind of government the convention finally established. "A republic," he purportedly replied, "if you can keep it." Franklin of course was highlighting the obvious fact that because the people created the republic, the people were ultimately responsible for preserving this experiment in democracy.

There have been many marches on Washington throughout this nation's history. In 1894 Jacob Coxey led a march of a few hundred men to Washington, demanding that the federal government take action to create jobs for the legions of unemployed during the recession that gripped the nation at that time. In 1913, on the day before Woodrow Wilson's inauguration as president, thousands of women marched in a massive demonstration in the nation's capital, demanding that the new president push Congress to pass the women's suffrage amendment. And throughout the twentieth century, marches on Washington became a regular occurrence as protesters increasingly realized it was an effective way to publicize their various causes. Whether they demanded equal rights or the safeguarding of rights that were imperiled, whether protesting against unjust laws and policies that threatened democratic rule or calling for new programs to expand rights, whether protesting against World War I or the Vietnam War or the wars in Iraq and Afghanistan, dissenters repeatedly marched on Washington in shows of force and solidarity in an effort to convince lawmakers and their fellow citizens that their cause was for the greater good of the country. Protesters simply wanted the United States to live up to its promise, to *be* the United States. Protest is the highest form of patriotism.

In its founding documents, the United States expressed the lofty ideals that all men are created equal and that we all have basic natural rights. In a sense, the Declaration of Independence together with the Constitution was a contract between the government and the people. This contract stipulated that we empower the government and agree to be governed while the government recognizes that we have rights, including the right to dissent. It is imperative, if we value these rights, that we push the government, nay, force the government to live up to its part of the contract.

* * *

Dissent is the fuel for the engine of progress. But "progress," like "dissent" itself, is a disputed concept. For some, progress is creating a more just society in which all Americans enjoy the rights set forth in the Declaration of Independence and the Constitution. For some, the progress that dissenters seek is an unmitigated disaster, a drastic deviation from the ideals of the founders that will bring the country to ruin. Throughout the country's tumultuous history, the long tradition of skepticism and questioning authority has moved the United States, somewhat erratically in fits and starts, generally in the direction of "all men are created equal." Whether it is progress or not, whether it is evolution or devolution, is in the eye of the beholder.

And in the eyes of this beholder dissenters need to push people to a broader, more inclusive consciousness, to open their minds to see beyond their own narrow self-interests, to realize that what is good for everyone is good for them and ultimately coincides with their own self-interest. And we need to understand too that, in the end, the arc of dissent, to paraphrase Martin Luther King, Jr., in a different context, bends toward justice.

But at this moment in our history it seems that Martin Luther King's arc of justice has been stretched to the breaking point. For nearly 250 years the pivotal episodes of American dissent have focused on the expansion of democratic rights—the abolition of slavery, women's suffrage,

Black suffrage, the expansion of the electorate through lowering the voting age, the extension of legal rights to nonnormative individuals. But as we approach the United States' Semiquincentennial too many Americans are stuck in their own ideological echo chambers and are deaf to other voices. Dialogue seems no longer to be a thing that is valued. Cable news is thoroughly partisan. Objective newspapers and nonpartisan national news are becoming less important to more people. Every educational setting from kindergarten to our colleges and universities are becoming the battlegrounds of our culture wars, and Americans no longer communicate with those not living in their ideological silos. More and more people are gravitating towards the ideologically and theologically familiar in order to make their lives more perfect, less complicated. Recently conservatives from California have moved to conservative communities in Texas, while progressives in Texas have moved to progressive communities in California. If we cannot live together we cannot learn from each other and learn to compromise with one another and thereby foster the space for democratic dialogue that makes dissent possible within the framework of a representative democracy.

At a time when election denial and its institutionalization within the American political system, in the wake of two failed impeachment efforts and accompanying resurgence of energy on the right to limit voting access, the threat to American democracy is indeed alarming. Election denial and restriction of access to the electoral system for some voters are part and parcel of the same strategy, which is not a kind of dissent designed to make democracy more representative, but less so. Indeed, election denial and "voting integrity" are among the most popular refuges for people who do not care about democracy; who only care about maintaining their own political and social power.

At a time when so many Americans uncritically consume news reports and preposterous conspiracy theories they find posted on the Internet, while others claim they get a more accurate perspective of the events happening in the world from Comedy Central shows hosted by Trevor Noah and John Oliver than they do from "real" network evening news or political punditry, it is clear that it is our duty, if we value American democracy, to be informed citizens and to listen to one another. And we need to demand more responsible journalism, we need to demand politicians who are beholden to the people and not to those who bankroll them, we need to question authority, we need to speak out, we need to make sure that "We the People" really means something. We need to dissent.

ACKNOWLEDGMENTS

American Patriots: A Short History of Dissent is my analysis of the decisive importance dissent played in the creation and shaping of the United States. Although the interpretation is mine many colleagues and students have contributed to broadening my insights and sharpening my thinking. Bryant Simon, David Farber, and Heather Ann Thompson volunteered their time to read several chapters and offer valuable suggestions that have improved this book. David Wrobel, Krystof Kozak, and Vlad Zubok were also helpful with their critical comments. This book is better because of their insights. Any errors are solely mine.

Teaching "Dissent in America" and leading the weekly teach-ins at Temple University since 2002 has been the most amazing experience of my professional career. This book, like my previous books on dissent in America is the product of the course, the teach-ins, and the extraordinary discussions with students and colleagues. I especially want to thank former students Tom Mosher, Brianne Murphy, Sierra Gladfelter, Evan Hoffman, Armond James, Julia Foley, Adam Brock, Jessica Churchman, and Zeinah Latefa for their insights and inspiration as well as colleagues Richard Immerman, Arthur Schmidt, Lila Corwin Berman, Petra Goedde, Mónica Ricketts, Phil Evanson, Howard Spodek, Mohammad Kiani, Robin Kolodny, Mark Pollack, Rebecca Alpert, Laura Levitt, Ruth Ost, Terry Halbert, and Lynne Andersson, who have supported and participated in the teach-ins.

I wish also to thank the Fulbright Specialist Program for the grant to teach my "Dissent in America" seminar at Università Degli Studi Roma Tre in Rome, and the American Embassy in Prague for supporting the seminars at Univerzita Karlova. Thanks also to Alison Young, Kerry Sautner, and Michael Gerhardt at the National Constitution Center for bringing me in for talks and workshops on dissent and the Constitution, and Matt Ewalt and Michael Hill for inviting me to deliver the Keynote Address on "The Ethics of Dissent" at the historic Chautauqua Institution.

Two well-known American dissenters inspired me to write this book. I met Pete Seeger in 1969 and over the years spoke with him on several occasions at the Philadelphia Folk Festival and the Clearwater Hudson River Revival. He was always accessible, always willing to talk about his latest cause (and there were many). In February 1980 I spent a day and evening in lively conversation with Allen Ginsberg and continued a correspondence with him for the next eight years. These two American dissenters had a profound influence on me and the way I perceive the joys and the sorrows and the complexities of this planet we all share.

Others have had a more personal impact on me. I want to thank Daniel Wood for teaching me to fall in love with words, Leif Skoogfors for showing me how to look at the world through an artist's eyes, Don Fries for those scintillating discussions that inspired and influenced me more than he knew, Chris Davies for teaching me that the only wrong decision is indecision, Rafe Stefanini for his Italian joie-de-vivre, Ellen Gibson, Cyndy Jahn, and Kathy Franklin for their always lively opinions, Peter Hiler for his knack for unearthing the most hard-to-find books, Robert E. Wall, Jr., for having unbounded confidence in me and pointing me in the right direction, my sister Millie Isaksen for her deep faith and love and for demonstrating the meaning of perseverance, Cara and Sean for letting me in, my late parents Ralph Eric Young and Emily Mildred Young for making sure I did not become part of the military-industrial complex, and my wife Pat for her intellectual curiosity, inspiration, strength, compassion, and love.

NOTES

INTRODUCTION

1 Eric Foner, *The Story of American Freedom* (New York: Norton, 1998), xiv.

1. DISSENT AND THE SHAPING OF A NATION

1 Roger Williams, *The Bloudy Tenent of Persecution* (London, 1644), ed. Samuel L. Caldwell (Providence, RI: Narragansett Club, 1867), 138–139, 248–249.

2 John Peter Zenger, editorial, *New York Weekly Journal*, November 19, 1733.

3 Quoted in Livingston Rutherfurd, *John Peter Zenger, His Press, His Trial, and a Bibliography of Zenger Imprints* (New York: Dodd, Mead, 1904), 116.

4 Abigail Adams to John Adams, March 31, 1776, in *Adams Family Correspondence*, vol. 1, *December 1761–May 1776*, ed. L. H. Butterfield (Cambridge: Harvard University Press, 1963), 370.

5 Ralph Waldo Emerson, *The Essay on Self-Reliance* (East Aurora, NY: Roycroft, 1908), 9, 11, 14.

6 Ibid., 19–20, 23.

7 Henry David Thoreau, *Walden* (New York: Thomas Y. Crowell, 1910), 8, 427, 430.

8 Margaret Fuller, *Woman in the Nineteenth Century* (New York: Greeley and McElrath, 1845), 103, 107.

9 Henry David Thoreau, *Walden; and Resistance to Civil Government*, 3rd ed., ed. William Rossi (New York: Norton, 2008), 230.

10 Ibid., 234.

11 Ibid., 236.

12 See Douglas A. Blackmon, *Slavery by Another Name: The Re-enslavement of Black Americans from the Civil War to World War II* (New York: Random House, 2008), for a detailed account of the intricate procedure through which southern states reenslaved African Americans.

13 Ida B. Wells-Barnett, *Lynch Law in Georgia: A Six-Weeks' Record in the Center of Southern Civilization, as Faithfully Chronicled by the "Atlanta Journal" and the "Atlanta Constitution"* (Chicago: Chicago Colored Citizens, 1899), 7, 10.

14 Ida B. Wells-Barnett, "Lynch Law in America," 1900, available online at www .digitalhistory.uh.edu (accessed December 27, 2022).

15 Emily Cochrane, "Congress Gives Final Approval to Make Lynching a Hate Crime," *New York Times*, March 7, 2022, www.nytimes.com (accessed October 14, 2022). The House of Representatives passed the bill in February and the Senate

(unanimously) in March. For the full text of the Act, see H.R.55—Emmett Till Antilynching Act, www.congress.gov (accessed October 14, 2022).

16 Susan B. Anthony, "Remarks by SBA in the Circuit Court of the United States for the Northern District of New York," June 19, 1873, in *The Selected Papers of Elizabeth Cady Stanton and Susan B. Anthony*, vol. 2, *Against an Aristocracy of Sex, 1866–1873*, ed. Ann D. Gordon (New Brunswick: Rutgers University Press, 2000), 613.

17 Susan B. Anthony, "Is It a Crime for a U.S. Citizen to Vote?," January 16, 1873, in ibid., 556.

18 Carl Schurz, "The Issue of Imperialism," January 4, 1899, in *Speeches, Correspondence, and Political Papers of Carl Schurz*, vol. 6, *January 1, 1899–April 8, 1906*, ed. Frederic Bancroft (New York: Putnam, 1913), 11, 28, 29.

19 William Jennings Bryan, "Notification Speech," August 8, 1900, in *Life and Speeches of Hon. Wm. Jennings Bryan* (Baltimore: R. H. Woodward, 1900), 394–396.

2. PROGRESSIVES, REFORMERS, RADICALS

1 Richard Hofstadter, *The Age of Reform: From Bryan to FDR* (New York: Knopf, 1955).

2 Lester Frank Ward, "Mind as a Social Factor," *Mind* 9, no. 36 (1884): 563–573.

3 The right to vote, of course, was not fully realized for African American women (and men) until the passage of the Voting Rights Act in 1965.

4 Jane Addams, *Twenty Years at Hull House* (New York: Macmillan, 1910), 100.

5 Quoted in Herbert Asbury, *Carry Nation* (New York: Knopf, 1929), 87.

6 Booker T. Washington was the founder of the Tuskegee Institute.

7 "Niagara's Declaration of Principles, 1905," Yale MacMillan Center, available online at https://glc.yale.edu (accessed February 14, 2023).

8 Charles Sheldon, *In His Steps: "What Would Jesus Do?"* (Chicago: Advance Publishing Company, 1898).

9 Sinclair's comment was originally published in *Cosmopolitan* (October 1906), quoted in John Milton Cooper, *Pivotal Decades: The United States, 1900–1920* (New York: Norton, 1990), 86.

10 Mary Harris Jones, "The March of the Mill Children," chap. 10 in *The Autobiography of Mother Jones*, ed. Mary Field Parton (Chicago: Charles H. Kerr, 1925), 71–72.

11 Ibid., 74, 75.

12 Ibid., 76–77, 79.

13 Ibid., 83.

14 Quoted in Neil A. Hamilton, *American Social Leaders and Activists* (New York: Infobase, 2002), 197.

15 Quoted in Chaim M. Rosenberg, *Child Labor in America: A History* (Jefferson, NC: McFarland, 2013), 175.

16 *New York World*, quoted in Zinn, *People's History*, 326.

17 *New York Times*, April 21, 1914, quoted in "The Ludlow Massacre," American Experience, PBS.org, www.pbs.org (accessed December 27, 2022).

18 Jones, *Autobiography of Mother Jones*, 192, 193.

19 "The Socialist Party's Platform," 1912, available online at www.laborhistorylinks .org (accessed December 27, 2022).

20 Eugene V. Debs, "Statement to the Court upon Being Convicted of Violating the Sedition Act," September 18, 1918, available online at www.marxists.org (accessed December 27, 2022); Debs, quoted in "Pacifism," Eugene V. Debs Foundation, available online at debsfoundation.org (accessed January 1, 2023).

21 Ralph Darlington, *Syndicalism and the Transition to Communism: An International Comparative Analysis* (Aldershot, UK: Ashgate, 2008), 114; Industrial Workers of the World, "Preamble to the IWW Constitution," www.iww .org (accessed December 27, 2022).

22 Quoted in Michael Miller Topp, *Those without a Country: The Political Culture of Italian American Syndicalists* (Minneapolis: University of Minnesota Press, 2001), 102. The witness was Margaret Sanger.

23 Industrial Workers of the World, *Little Red Songbook*, 19th ed. (Chicago: IWW, 1923), 22–23.

24 Quoted in William M. Adler, *The Man Who Never Died: The Life, Times, and Legacy of Joe Hill, American Labor Icon* (New York: Bloomsbury, 2011), 13.

25 Emma Goldman, *Anarchism and Other Essays*, 2nd ed. (New York: Mother Earth, 1911), 233, 238.

26 Ibid., 238.

27 Emma Goldman, "Essay in the *Firebrand*, New York, 18 July 1897," in *Emma Goldman: A Documentary History of the American Years*, vol. 1 *Made for America, 1890–1901*, ed. Candace Falk (Berkeley: University of California Press, 2003), 273.

28 Quoted in Bruce Bartlett, *Wrong on Race: The Democratic Party's Buried Past* (New York: Macmillan, 2008), 102.

29 Quoted in Nina Mjagkij, *Loyalty in Time of Trial: The African American Experience during World War I* (Lanham, MD: Rowman and Littlefield, 2011), 21.

3. WAR AND ITS DISSIDENTS

1 W. E. B. Du Bois, "Close Ranks," *Crisis* 16, no. 3 (1918): 111.

2 Sedition Act of 1918, Pub. L. No. 65–150, 40 Stat. 553 (1918).

3 Robert M. La Follette, "The People Do Not Want This War," April 4, 1917, in *We Who Dared to Say No to War: American Antiwar Writing from 1812 to Now*, ed. Murray Polner and Thomas E. Woods, Jr. (New York: Basic Books, 2008), 127, 128–129.

4 Robert M. La Follette, speech to the Senate, *Congressional Record*, 65th Cong., 1st sess., vol. 55, 7878–7888 (October 6, 1917).

5 Eugene V. Debs, "The Canton, Ohio Speech, Anti-War Speech," June 16, 1918, available online at www.marxists.org (accessed December 27, 2022).

6 Ibid.
7 Quoted in Ernest Freeberg, *Democracy's Prisoner: Eugene V. Debs, the Great War, and the Right to Dissent* (Cambridge: Harvard University Press, 2008), 99.
8 The full speech is in Scott Nearing, *The Debs Decision*, 2nd ed. (New York: Rand School of Social Science, 1919), 18, 24, 25. Also see Debs, "Address to the Jury (1918)," in *Protest Nation: Words That Inspired a Century of American Radicalism*, ed. Timothy Patrick McCarthy and John Campbell McMillian (New York: New Press, 2010), 30; and Freeberg, *Democracy's Prisoner*, 100.
9 Quoted in Freeberg, *Democracy's Prisoner*, 181.
10 Randolph Bourne, "War and the Intellectuals," *Seven Arts* 2 (June 1917): 136.
11 Randolph Bourne, "The State," in *The Radical Will: Selected Writings, 1911–1918*, ed. Olaf Hansen (New York: Urizen Books, 1977), 359. (The original manuscript is in the Randolph Silliman Bourne Papers, Rare Book & Manuscript Library, Columbia University Libraries, New York.) The full (unfinished) essay can also be found online at http://struggle.ws (accessed December 27, 2022).
12 Ibid., 356.
13 Ibid., 360–361.
14 Ibid., 364.
15 Ibid., 372.
16 Quoted in Ronald Schaffer, *America in the Great War* (New York: Oxford University Press, 1991), 16.
17 Quoted in Bill Kauffman, *Ain't My America: The Long, Noble History of Antiwar Conservatism and Middle-American Anti-Imperialism* (New York: Macmillan, 2008), 74.
18 Richard Halworth Rovere and Gene Brown, *Loyalty and Security in a Democratic State* (New York: Arno, 1979), 21.
19 The American Civil Liberties Union's "Statement of Purpose" is available on the ACLU website: www.aclu.org (accessed December 27, 2022).
20 Quoted in Jay Feldman, *Manufacturing Hysteria: A History of Scapegoating, Surveillance, and Secrecy in Modern America* (New York: Anchor Books, 2012), 135.
21 Quoted in Susan Tejada, *In Search of Sacco and Vanzetti: Double Lives, Troubled Times, and the Massachusetts Case That Shook the World* (Lebanon, NH: University Press of New England, 2012), 228.

4. CULTURE WARS IN THE JAZZ AGE

1 Available online at www.equalrightsamendment.org (accessed December 27, 2022). Congress eventually passed it in 1972, but it was never ratified.
2 Quoted in Vicki Cox, *Margaret Sanger* (New York: Infobase, 2009), 26.
3 Margaret Sanger, *Woman and the New Race* (New York: Brentano's, 1920), 192–193.
4 Ibid., 197, 232.
5 F. Scott Fitzgerald, *This Side of Paradise* (New York: Scribner, 1920), 304.

6 H. L. Mencken, *A Mencken Chrestomathy: His Own Selection of His Choicest Writing* (New York: Random House, 1949), 145.

7 Roger Butterfield, "Mr. Mencken Sounds Off," *Life*, August 5, 1946, 52.

8 Quoted in Kirby Goidel, *America's Failing Experiment: How We the People Have Become the Problem* (Lanham, MD: Rowman and Littlefield, 2013), 4.

9 H. L. Mencken, "Last Words," 1926, available online at https://cooperative -individualism.org (accessed January 1, 2023).

10 Marcus Garvey, *The Philosophy and Opinions of Marcus Garvey; or, Africa for the Africans*, comp. Amy Jacques Garvey, vol. 1 (New York: Universal, 1923), 24.

11 Marcus Garvey, "Address to the UNIA Supporters in Philadelphia, October 21, 1919," in *African American Political Thought, 1890–1930: Washington, Du Bois, Garvey, and Randolph*, ed. Cary D. Wintz (Armonk, NY: M. E. Sharpe, 1996), 203.

12 Claude McKay, "If We Must Die," in *Harlem Shadows: The Poems of Claude McKay* (New York: Harcourt, Brace, 1922), available online at http://history matters.gmu.edu (accessed December 27, 2022). Howard Zinn notes that Senator Henry Cabot Lodge was so alarmed at the sentiment expressed in McKay's poem that he had it printed in the *Congressional Record* (*People's History*, 444).

13 Langston Hughes, "The Negro Artist and the Racial Mountain," *Nation*, June 23, 1926.

14 *El Paso Herald*, April 20, 1923, 5.

15 One of the best analyses of the Ku Klux Klan is Glenn Feldman, *Politics, Society, and the Klan in Alabama, 1915–1949* (Tuscaloosa: University of Alabama Press, 1999). Feldman links the Reconstruction-era KKK with the 1920s KKK and beyond to the 1950s Klan in its xenophobia to anything considered "foreign"— racially, ethnically, religiously, *and morally*.

16 Quoted in Edward J. Larson, *Summer for the Gods: The Scopes Trial and America's Continuing Debate over Science and Religion* (New York: Basic Books, 2006), 71. For a comprehensive biography of Darrow, see John A. Farrell, *Clarence Darrow: Attorney for the Damned* (New York: Penguin Random House, 2012).

17 Quoted in Larson, *Summer for the Gods*, 39, 27.

18 Quoted in Diana Klebanow and Franklin L. Jonas, *People's Lawyers: Crusaders for Justice in American History* (Armonk, NY: M. E. Sharpe, 2003), 129.

5. DEPRESSION AND WAR

1 Quoted in Jean Edward Smith, *FDR* (New York: Random House, 2007), 284.

2 Ibid., 277.

3 Elizabeth Kirkpatrick Dilling, *The Red Network: A "Who's Who" and Handbook of Radicalism for Patriots* (Chicago: Elizabeth Dilling, 1934), 74, 75.

4 Franklin D. Roosevelt to Felix Frankfurter, February 9, 1937, in *Roosevelt and Frankfurter: Their Correspondence, 1928–1945*, ed. Max Freedman (Boston: Little, Brown, 1968), 382.

5 *Congressional Record*, 73rd Cong., 2nd sess., February 5, 1934.

6 Quoted in David M. Kennedy, *Freedom from Fear: The American People in Depression and War, 1929–1945* (New York: Oxford University Press, 1999), 278.

7 Quoted in Alan Brinkley, *Voices of Protest: Huey Long, Father Coughlin, and the Great Depression* (New York: Knopf, 1982), 108.

8 Charles E. Coughlin, "Address on the National Union for Social Justice," November 11, 1934, in *A Series of Lectures on Social Justice* (Royal Oak, MI: Radio League of the Little Flower, 1935), available online at http://web.mit.edu (accessed December 27, 2022).

9 Charles E. Coughlin, "National Radio Address," June 19, 1936, in ibid., available online at www.austincc.edu (accessed December 22, 2022).

10 Conrad Black, *Franklin Delano Roosevelt: Champion of Freedom* (New York: PublicAffairs, 2005), 386.

11 Emma Goldman, "The Individual, Society, and the State," in *Red Emma Speaks: Selected Writings and Speeches*, ed. Alix Kates Shulman (New York: Random House, 1972), 100.

12 Quoted in Black, Franklin Delano Roosevelt, 329.

13 Quoted in Kennedy, *Freedom from Fear*, 220.

14 Quoted in ibid.

15 Quoted in ibid., 222.

16 Brinkley, *Voices of Protest*, 160–161.

17 Woody Guthrie, *Pastures of Plenty: A Self Portrait*, ed. Dave Marsh and Harold Leventhal (New York: HarperCollins, 1990), 10. Also see Ronald D. Cohen, *Woody Guthrie: Writing America's Songs* (New York: Routledge, 2012), 25.

18 Quoted in Kennedy, *Freedom from Fear*, 433.

19 Charles A. Lindbergh, *Address by Charles Lindbergh: Delivered at an America First Committee Meeting in New York City on April 23, 1941* (New York: America First Committee, 1941), available online at www.charleslindbergh.com (accessed January 1, 2023). By this time, Lindbergh's speeches were becoming increasingly anti-Semitic.

20 Quoted in Ethan Fishman, "The Prudential FDR," in *FDR and the Modern Presidency: Leadership and Legacy*, ed. Mark J. Rozell and William D. Pederson (New York: Greenwood, 1997), 157.

21 Charles F. Wilson to President Franklin Delano Roosevelt, May 9, 1944, in *Taps for a Jim Crow Army: Letters from Black Soldiers in World War II*, ed. Phillip McGuire (Santa Barbara, CA: ABC-CLIO, 1983), 134, 135, 137.

22 Lloyd Brown, quoted in Leon F. Litwack, *How Free Is Free? The Long Death of Jim Crow* (Cambridge: Harvard University Press, 2009), 75.

23 Quoted in H. W. Brands, *Traitor to His Class: The Privileged Life and Radical Presidency of Franklin Delano Roosevelt* (New York: Doubleday, 2008), 657.

24 Quoted in Shirley Castelnuovo, *Soldiers of Conscience: Japanese American Military Resisters in World War II* (Westport, CT: Greenwood, 2008), 13.

25 Minoru Yasui, "Response to Executive Order 9066," available online at www.aclu
.org (accessed January 1, 2023).

26 Minoru Yasui to Yuka Yasui, November 30, 1942, in Yuka Yasui Fujikura's private
collection; used by permission.

27 Steve Cary, World War II conscientious objector, quoted in "In the Camps," *The
Good War and Those Who Refused to Fight It*, PBS.org, available at www.youtube
.com/watch?v=NmoP3kpc4LE (accessed January 1, 2023).

28 David Dellinger, "Why I Refused to Register in the October 1940 Draft and a
Little of What It Led To," in *A Few Small Candles: War Resisters of World War II
Tell Their Stories*, ed. Larry Gara and Lenna Mae Gara (Kent, OH: Kent State
University Press, 1999), 27.

29 Ibid., 34.

6. CONFORMITY AND DISSENT

1 Winston Churchill, speech at Westminster College, Fulton, Missouri, March 5,
1946, available online at www.fordham.edu (accessed December 27, 2022).

2 The high-profile Rosenberg espionage case, combined with the House Committee
on Un-American Activities and McCarthy hearings, created a tremendous
outpouring of paranoia in the country. And as paranoia increased, it had a
hampering effect on dissent because liberals and other left-of-center commentators were afraid to express legitimate criticism of American foreign policy for fear
of being labeled unpatriotic "pinkoes" or denounced as communists. The fear of
being ostracized and blacklisted inhibited healthy, robust political debate and
dissenting opinions. Well into the next decade everyone was, or at least proclaimed they were, vehemently anticommunist.

3 U.S. Congress, House, Committee on Un-American Activities, *Hearings Regarding
the Communist Infiltration of the Motion Picture Industry*, 80th Cong., 1st sess.,
October 29, 1947.

4 John Howard Lawson, "A Statement by John Howard Lawson," in *Thirty Years of
Treason: Excerpts from Hearings before the House Committee on Un-American
Activities, 1938–1968*, ed. Eric Bentley (New York: Viking, 1971), 161–165.

5 U.S. Congress, House, Committee on Un-American Activities, *Investigation of
Communist Activities, New York Area (Entertainment): Hearings*, 84th Cong., 1st
sess., August 18, 1955.

6 U.S. Congress, House, Committee on Un-American Activities, *Investigation of the
Unauthorized Use of U.S. Passports*, 84th Cong., 2nd sess., June 12, 1956.

7 Quoted in Anne Edwards, *Katharine Hepburn: A Remarkable Woman* (New York:
Macmillan, 2000), 345.

8 Margaret Chase Smith, "Declaration of Conscience" and "Statement of Seven
Senators," *Congressional Record*, 82nd Cong., 1st sess., June 1, 1950.

9 John Keats, *The Crack in the Picture Window* (Boston: Houghton Mifflin,
1957).

10 Quoted in Bill Morgan, *I Celebrate Myself: The Somewhat Private Life of Allen Ginsberg* (New York: Viking, 2006), 209.

11 Allen Ginsberg, *Howl and Other Poems* (San Francisco: City Lights Books, 1956), 9, 12, 17.

12 Ibid., 32, 31.

13 Allen Ginsberg, interviewed in the documentary film *The Source: The Story of the Beats and the Beat Generation*, dir. Chuck Workman (Beat/Calliope, 1999).

14 Jack Kerouac, *On the Road* (New York: Viking, 1957), 5–6.

15 Harry S. Truman, "Special Message to the Congress on Civil Rights," February 2, 1948, in *Public Papers of the Presidents of the United States, Harry S. Truman, 1948*, vol. 4 (Washington, DC: U.S. Government Printing Office, 1963), 122.

16 Brown v. Board of Education, 347 U.S. 483, 494, 495 (May 17, 1954).

7. CIVIL RIGHTS

1 "*Le Peuple*, the daily Belgian Socialist newspaper, calls the acquittal 'a judicial scandal in the United States.' *Le Drapeau Rouge* (the Red Flag) publishes: 'Killing a black person isn't a crime in the home of the Yankees: The white killers of young Emmett Till are acquitted!' In France, *L'Aurore* newspaper publishes: 'The Scandalous Acquittal in Sumner' and the daily newspaper *Le Figaro* adds: 'The Shame of the Sumner Jury.' . . . The French daily newspaper *Le Monde* runs an article: 'The Sumner Trial Marks, Perhaps, an Opening of Consciousness.' . . . In West Germany, the newspaper *Freies Volk* publishes: 'The Life of a Negro Isn't Worth a Whistle.'" American Experience documentary *The Murder of Emmett Till*, PBS, available online at www.pbs.org (accessed December 27, 2022).

2 Martin Luther King, Jr., "MIA Mass Meeting at Holt Street Baptist Church," speech in Montgomery, Alabama, December 5, 1955, in *The Papers of Martin Luther King, Jr.: Birth of a New Age, December 1955–December 1956*, ed. Clayborne Carson (Berkeley: University of California Press, 1997), 73.

3 The Student Nonviolent Coordinating Committee (SNCC) was an offshoot of SCLC, established as a separate entity of primarily young Black college students.

4 Quoted in Lynne Olson, *Freedom's Daughters: The Unsung Heroines of the Civil Rights Movement from 1830 to 1970* (New York: Simon and Schuster, 2001), 184.

5 Martin Luther King, Jr., "Acceptance Address for the Nobel Peace Prize," in *A Call to Conscience: The Landmark Speeches of Dr. Martin Luther King, Jr.*, ed. Clayborne Carson (New York: Grand Central, 2001), 105.

6 "White Ministers' Good Friday Statement, April 12, 1963," in *Blessed Are the Peacemakers: Martin Luther King, Jr., Eight White Religious Leaders, and the "Letter from Birmingham Jail,"* by S. Jonathan Bass (Baton Rouge: Louisiana State University Press, 2001), 235.

7 Martin Luther King, Jr., "Letter from Birmingham Jail," in *Why We Can't Wait* (New York: Mentor, 1964), 80–82.

8 Ibid., 82, 77, 88, 86, 87.

9   John F. Kennedy, "Address on Civil Rights," June 11, 1963, available online at https://millercenter.org (accessed January 1, 2023).

10 Martin Luther King, Jr., "I Have a Dream," in *A Testament of Hope: The Essential Writings and Speeches of Martin Luther King, Jr.*, ed. James M. Washington (San Francisco: HarperCollins, 1991), 219.

11 Malcolm X, "Message to the Grass Roots," November 10, 1963, in *Malcolm X Speaks: Selected Speeches and Statements*, ed. George Breitman (New York: Grove, 1965), 16.

12 Malcolm X, "Speech on 'Black Revolution,'" April 8, 1964, in *Two Speeches by Malcolm X* (New York: Merit, 1965), 5, 14.

13 Quoted in Robert A. Caro, *The Passage of Power: The Years of Lyndon Johnson* (New York: Knopf, 2012), 430.

14 Pub. L. 88–352, 78 Stat. 241, enacted July 2, 1964.

15 Fannie Lou Hamer, "Testimony before the Credentials Committee at the Democratic National Convention, Atlantic City, New Jersey, August 22, 1964," in *The Speeches of Fannie Lou Hamer: To Tell It Like It Is*, ed. Maegan Parker Brooks and Davis W. Houck (Jackson: University Press of Mississippi, 2011), 45.

16 Quoted in Robert Cohen, *Freedom's Orator: Mario Savio and the Radical Legacy of the 1960s* (New York: Oxford University Press, 2009), 327.

17 Quoted in Barbara Harris Combs, *From Selma to Montgomery and Freedom: The Long March to Freedom* (New York: Routledge, 2014), 43.

18 Lyndon B. Johnson, "Special Message to the Congress: The American Promise," March 15, 1965, in *Public Papers of the Presidents of the United States, Lyndon B. Johnson, 1965*, no. 1 (Washington, DC: U.S. Government Printing Office, 1965), 281–287; also available online at the LBJ Presidential Library, https://www.youtube.com/watch?v=5NvPhiuGZ6I (accessed January 1, 2023).

19 Petition to Alabama Governor George C. Wallace by Selma-to-Montgomery Marchers, March 25, 1965, available online at www.crmvet.org (accessed January 1, 2023).

20 Martin Luther King, Jr., "Address at the Conclusion of the Selma to Montgomery March," March 25, 1965, text and audio available online at https://www.youtube.com/watch?v=44RNoC5jLDc&t=5s (accessed January 1, 2023).

21 Stokely Carmichael, "Berkeley Speech," in *Contemporary American Voices: Significant Speeches in American History, 1945–Present*, ed. James R. Andrews and David Zarefsky (White Plains, NY: Longman, 1992), 106.

22 The Kerner Report, available online at www.archive.org (accessed December 27, 2022).

8. COUNTERCULTURE

1   Carl Oglesby, "Let Us Shape the Future," November 27, 1965, available online at the Students for a Democratic Society Document Library, www.sds-1960s.org (accessed January 1, 2023).

2 The Catholic peace movement was a bloc of dedicated Catholic pacifists influenced by Pope John XXIII's encyclical *Pacem in Terris*, in which he urged Catholics to work for world peace, as well as by the teachings of the pacifist social activists Dorothy Day (founder of the Catholic Worker Movement) and Trappist monk Thomas Merton.

3 Bob Dylan, "Blowin' in the Wind," *The Freewheelin' Bob Dylan*, Columbia Records, 1963.

4 Bob Dylan, "Masters of War," ibid.

5 The Beatles, "Nowhere Man," *Rubber Soul*, Parlophone, 1965; The Mothers of Invention, "Plastic People," *Absolutely Free*, Verve, 1967; Jefferson Airplane, "White Rabbit," *Surrealistic Pillow*, RCA Victor, 1967; Edwin Starr, "War," single, Gordy, 1970.

6 The impact of these artists' antiwar, antimainstream message cannot be overstated. Who can forget Jimi Hendrix's mesmerizing version of the national anthem at Woodstock? Or the Rolling Stones singing about "Street Fighting Man" or "Sympathy for the Devil"? Or the MC5 screaming "kick out the jams motherfuckers!"? Or Janis Joplin's version of Kris Kristofferson's cautionary observation that "freedom's just another word for nothing left to lose"?

7 Quoted in Peter Stafford, *Psychedelics* (Oakland, CA: Ronin, 2003), 63.

8 Lenny Bruce on *The Steve Allen Show*, April 9, 1959; the full performance is available online at https://www.youtube.com/watch?v=G3QgxmiBfNY (accessed January 1, 2023).

9 For a discerning analysis of Pop Art and Warhol's oeuvre, see Louis Menand, *The Free World: Art and Thought in the Cold War* (New York: Farrar, Straus and Giroux, 2021).

10 Quoted in "Corita Kent and the Language of Pop," San Antonio Museum of Art, www.samuseum.org (accessed January 1, 2023).

11 Martin Luther King, Jr., "Beyond Vietnam: A Time to Break the Silence," speech at Riverside Church, New York, April 4, 1967, available online at www.digitalhistory.uh.edu (accessed December 27, 2022).

12 Quoted in G. Calvin Mackenzie and Robert Weisbrot, *The Liberal Hour: Washington and the Politic of Change in the 1960s* (New York: Penguin, 2008), 343–344.

13 *Guardian*, October 18, 1969, quoted in Jeremy Varon, *Bringing the War Home: The Weather Underground, the Red Army Faction, and Revolutionary Violence in the Sixties and Seventies* (Berkeley: University of California Press, 2004), 84.

14 I took part in the London demonstration. It was a very moving vigil. Thousands of us marched around Grosvenor Square, and as each person passed in front of the U.S. embassy, we were handed a card with the name of a U.S. soldier killed in Vietnam. We stepped up to a microphone, read the soldier's name, and then placed the card in a coffin on the embassy steps. I was there for more than eight hours, and it was still going on when I left.

15 The burglars came forward more than forty years later. See Betty Medsger, *The Burglary: The Discovery of J. Edgar Hoover's Secret FBI* (New York: Knopf, 2014).

16 U.S. Congress, Senate, Committee on Foreign Relations, "Legislative Proposals Relating to the War in Southeast Asia," *Hearings before the Committee on Foreign Relations*, 92nd Cong., 1st sess., April–May 1971 (Washington, DC: Government Printing Office, 1971), 180, 181, 182.

9. MOBILIZATION AND BACKLASH

1 Betty Friedan, *The Feminine Mystique* (1963; repr., New York: Dell, 1970), 11.

2 National Organization for Women, "Statement of Purpose," 1966, www.now.org (accessed December 27, 2022).

3 Redstockings, "Manifesto," 1969, in *Dear Sisters: Dispatches from the Women's Liberation Movement*, ed. Rosalyn Baxandall and Linda Gordon (New York: Basic Books, 2000), 90.

4 Gloria Steinem, "'Women's Liberation' Aims to Free Men, Too," *Washington Post*, June 7, 1970.

5 Second wave feminism, however, was (rightly) criticized for focusing exclusively on the plight of middle-class white women and completely ignoring the unique struggles of women of color.

6 Indians Of All Tribes, "We Hold the Rock!," in *Alcatraz: Indian Land Forever*, ed. Troy R. Johnson (Los Angeles: UCLA American Indian Studies Center, 1995), 11.

7 The list of their demands is available online at www.aimovement.org (accessed January 1, 2023).

8 For a comprehensive account of the Attica uprising, see Heather Ann Thompson, *Blood in the Water: The Attica Prison Uprising of 1971 and Its Legacy* (New York: Pantheon, 2016).

9 Quoted in Donn Teal, *The Gay Militants* (New York: St. Martin's, 1971), 24, 25.

10 Quoted in ibid., 36, 37.

11 Quoted in "Pat Robertson Thinks the GOP Base Is Too Extreme? Hehehehe," *Daily Kos* (blog), October 24, 2011, www.dailykos.com (accessed January 1, 2023).

12 Among them are Manning Marable, *Race, Reform, and Rebellion: The Second Reconstruction in Black America* (Jackson: University Press of Mississippi, 1991); Mary Louise Frampton, Ian F. Haney López, and Jonathan Simon, eds., *After the War on Crime: Race, Democracy, and a New Reconstruction* (New York: NYU Press, 2008); David Garland, *The Culture of Control: Crime and Social Order in Contemporary Society* (Chicago: University of Chicago Press, 2002); Bruce Western, *Punishment and Inequality in America* (New York: Russell Sage Foundation, 2007); Todd Clear, *Imprisoning Communities: How Mass Incarceration Makes Disadvantaged Neighborhoods Worse* (New York: Oxford University Press, 2009); and Heather Ann Thompson, "Why Mass Incarceration

Matters: Rethinking Crisis, Decline, and Transformation in Postwar American History," *Journal of American History* 97, no. 3 (December 2010): 703–734. See also *Black Americans in Congress, 1870–2007*, History, Art, and Archives, U.S. House of Representatives (Washington, D.C.: U.S. Government Printing Office, 2008); and "The Civil Rights Movement and the Second Reconstruction, 1945–1968," History, Art, and Archives, U.S. House of Representatives, https://history.house.gov (accessed February 19, 2023).

10. DISSENT IN A NEW AGE

1 Ted Kaczynski, "Industrial Society and Its Future," available online at "The Unabomber Trial: The Manifesto," *Washington Post*, September 22, 1995, www.washingtonpost.com (accessed January 1, 2023).

2 Carl Rosebraugh, "Written Testimony Submitted on February 7, 2002 to the U.S. House Subcommittee on Forests and Forest Health for the February 12, 2002, Hearing on 'Ecoterrorism,'" in *The Earth Liberation Front, 1997–2002*, by Leslie James Pickering (Oakland, CA: PM, 2007), 134, 135.

3 Ralph Nader, "It's Time to End Corporate Welfare as We Know It," 1996, in *The Ralph Nader Reader* (New York: Seven Stories, 2000), 154, 158.

4 Ani Di Franco, "self evident," 2001, https://www.youtube.com/watch?v=gTY8sCzHTNc (accessed January 1, 2023).

5 Amnesty International, "Amnesty International's Concerns Regarding Post September 11 Detentions in the USA," March 14, 2002, www.amnesty.org (accessed January 1, 2023).

6 ACLU, "Freedom under Fire: Dissent in Post-9/11 America," May 8, 2013, www.aclu.org (accessed January 1, 2023).

7 The original CNN interview with Wolf Blitzer on September 8, 2002, is available online at http://transcripts.cnn.com (accessed January 1, 2023).

8 "Call to Conscience from Veterans to Active Duty Troops and Reservists," December 6, 2002, available online at https://wri-irg.org (accessed January 1, 2023).

9 David Wiggins, "Message to the Troops: Resist!" Strike the Root, posted March 10, 2003, www.strike-the-root.com (accessed January 1, 2023).

10 Immortal Technique, "The 4th Branch," *Revolutionary, Vol. 2* (Viper Records, 2003).

11 Steve Earle, "Rich Man's War," *The Revolution Starts Now* (Artemis Records, 2004).

12 See Jane Mayer, "Covert Operations: The Billionaire Brothers Who Are Waging a War against Obama," *New Yorker*, August 23, 2010, and Matt Taibbi, "The Truth about the Tea Party," *Rolling Stone*, September 28, 2010. Taibbi, in his report, was astonished that a Tea Party rally he attended in Kentucky was in "a hall full of elderly white people in Medicare-paid scooters, railing against government spending and imagining themselves revolutionaries. . . ."

13 "Declaration of the Occupation of New York City," September 29, 2011, available at the NYC General Assembly website, https://nyu-dss.github.io/occupy (accessed January 1, 2023).

11. DISSENT, LIES, AND INSURRECTION

1 As early as 1959 Columbia University sociologist C. Wright Mills argued that the "power elite" controlled the American economic and political machinery to such a complete degree that electoral politics was rendered largely meaningless. The interests of the working class would always be sacrificed to those of the ruling class. See C. Wright Mills, *The Power Elite* (New York: Oxford University Press, 1959).

2 If there had been sixteen Democrats vying for the nomination as was the case with the Republicans, Sanders might very well have wrested the nomination from the establishment candidate Clinton.

3 See the wealth of studies of the Republicans' "Southern Strategy," using states rights as a smokescreen to validate the "southern values," which was played so skillfully by Nixon and then Reagan. One such study is Glen Feldman, ed., *Painting Dixie Red: When, Where, Why, and How the South Became Republican* (Gainesville: University of Florida Press, 2011).

4 Richard Hofstadter, *Anti-Intellectualism in American Life* (New York, Vintage, 1964). Hofstadter's study provides the historical context of the development of the entrenched hostility and distrust of intellectualism and expertise that many Americans harbor.

5 The reaction began even during the campaign, with the rise of "birtherism"—the false accusation that Obama was not an American citizen.

6 Black Lives Matter, "Herstory," https://blacklivesmatter.com (accessed August 6, 2022).

7 Ibid.

8 Black Lives Matter, "About," https://blacklivesmatter.com (accessed August 6, 2022).

9 During Chauvin's trial, which resulted in his conviction for second- and third-degree murder, it was established that the actual time he knelt on Floyd's neck was nine minutes, twenty-nine seconds.

10 K. K. Rebecca Lai, Bill Marsh, Anjali Singhvi, "Here Are the 100 U.S. Cities Where Protesters Were Tear-Gassed," *New York Times*, June 18, 2020, www.nytimes.com (accessed August 6, 2022).

11 During the three months after the George Floyd killing there were "more than 10,600 demonstration events across the country. Over 10,100 of these—or nearly 95%—involve peaceful protesters. Fewer than 570—or approximately 5%—involve demonstrators engaging in violence." The Armed Conflict Location & Event Data Project (ACLED), "Demonstrations & Political Violence in America: New Data for Summer 2020," https://acleddata.com (accessed October 11, 2022).

12 Derrick Bryson Taylor, "George Floyd Protests: A Timeline," *New York Times*, November 5, 2021, www.nytimes.com (accessed October 11, 2022).

13 For a thorough analysis of political violence and peaceful BLM protests, see the ACLED report cited above.

14 Tarana Burke, "History & Inception," MeToo Website, https://metoomvmt.org (accessed August 7, 2022).

15 "Our Story: Not One More," March for Our Lives, https://marchforourlives.com (accessed August 7, 2022).

16 The *Washington Post*, "Did You Attend the March for Our Lives?," April 13, 2018, www.washingtonpost.com (accessed August 7, 2022).

17 Fridays For Future, "What We Do," https://fridaysforfuture.org, accessed August 11, 2022.

18 There's a vast literature by climate scientists, journalists, and activists about climate change and the devastating consequences of not addressing it. See the works of James Hansen, Sylvia Earle, Susan Solomon, Phil D. Jones, Peter Fiekowsky, and Elizabeth Kolbert, among others.

19 Margaret Osborne, "To Prevent Catastrophic Damage by 2100, Climate Experts Warn, 'It's Now or Never,'" *Smithsonian Magazine*, April 6, 2022, www.smithsonianmag.com (accessed August 11, 2022).

20 Cara Buckley, "These Groups Want Disruptive Climate Protests. Oil Heirs Are Funding Them," *New York Times*, August 10, 2022, www.nytimes.com (accessed August 12, 2022).

21 Lisa Friedman and Coral Davenport, "As Historic Climate Bill Heads to Biden's Desk, Young Activists Demand More," *New York Times*, August 12, 2022. www.nytimes.com (accessed August 13.2022).

22 The Southern Poverty Law Center has posted a map on its website of the distribution of 733 "hate groups" in the United States as of 2021. "See Hate in Your State," www.splcenter.org (accessed August 14, 2022).

23 "The 1619 Project," *New York Times Magazine*, www.nytimes.com (accessed September 4, 2022).

24 See Meerabelle Jesuthasan, "The 1619 Project Sparks Dialogue and Reflection in Schools Nationwide," The Pulitzer Center, December 20, 2019, https://pulitzercenter.org (accessed September 4, 2022).

25 Stephen Sawchuck, "What Is Critical Race Theory and Why Is It Under Attack?" *Education Week*, May 18, 2021, www.edweek.org (accessed September 4, 2022).

26 Paige Williams, "Class Warfare: School Boards Are Being Attacked by Partisan Saboteurs," *New Yorker*, November 7, 2022, 52–63.

27 Heather C. McGhee and Victor Ray, "For Making Citizens," Sunday Opinion Section, *New York Times*, September 4, 2022, 8.

28 "Members of Right-Wing Militias, Extremist Groups Are Latest Charged in Capitol Siege," NPR, www.npr.org (accessed August 15, 2022). The United States has had a long tradition of extremism flowing through the social fabric: the Know-Nothings, the anti-Masons, the persecution of the Mormons, the Klan, the routine practice of lynching, and the John Birch Society, as well as right-wing militias.

29 Quoted in John A. Farrell, *Ted Kennedy: A Life* (New York: Penguin Press, 2022), 509. Reich goes on to say, "Once unbottled, mass resentments can poison the very fabric, the moral integrity, of society—replacing ambition with envy, replacing tolerance with hate."

30 As *Atlantic* journalist Tom Nichols observed, their "minimal demand was the suspension of the Constitution (to say nothing of those who wanted to see the execution of senior elected officials of the United States Government. . . . The rioters at the Capitol wanted to nullify an election and hang the vice president of the United States. Sometimes, there is nothing left on the table to discuss." Tom Nichols, "Contain and Defeat," *Atlantic Daily*, September 12, 2022. www.theatlantic.com (accessed September 13, 2022). See also W. J. Hennigan and Vera Bergengruen, "For the Oath Keepers and Proud Boys, Jan. 6 Was Just the Start," *Time*, July 11, 2022. https://time.com (accessed October 9, 2022). The violent storming of the Capitol on January 6, 2021 does demonstrate a truism that historians have long noted: that what people *believe* to be true, or wish to be true, often has more of an impact on the unfolding of events than what actually *is* true.

BIBLIOGRAPHY

Adams, John, and Abigail Adams. *Adams Family Correspondence.* Edited by L. H. Butterfield. 9 vols. Cambridge: Harvard University Press, 1963.

Addams, Jane. *Twenty Years at Hull-House.* New York: Macmillan, 1910.

Adler, William M. *The Man Who Never Died: The Life, Times, and Legacy of Joe Hill, American Labor Icon.* New York: Bloomsbury, 2011.

American Civil Liberties Union. "Freedom under Fire: Dissent in Post-9/11 America." May 8, 2013. www.aclu.org (accessed January 1, 2023).

———. "Statement of Purpose." www.aclu.org (accessed December 27, 2022).

Amnesty International. "Amnesty International's Concerns Regarding Post September 11 Detentions in the USA." March 14, 2002. www.amnesty.org (accessed January 1, 2023).

Anthony, Susan B. "Is It a Crime for a U.S. Citizen to Vote?" January 16, 1873. In *The Selected Papers of Elizabeth Cady Stanton and Susan B. Anthony*, vol. 2, *Against an Aristocracy of Sex, 1866–1873*, edited by Ann D. Gordon, 554–583. New Brunswick: Rutgers University Press, 2000.

———. "Remarks by SBA in the Circuit Court of the United States for the Northern District of New York." June 19, 1873. In *The Selected Papers of Elizabeth Cady Stanton and Susan B. Anthony*, vol. 2, *Against an Aristocracy of Sex, 1866–1873*, edited by Ann D. Gordon, 612–615. New Brunswick: Rutgers University Press, 2000.

Armed Conflict Location & Event Data Project, The (ACLED). "Demonstrations & Political Violence in America: New Data for Summer 2020." https://acleddata.com (accessed October 11, 2022).

Asbury, Herbert. *Carry Nation.* New York: Knopf, 1929.

Bartlett, Bruce. *Wrong on Race: The Democratic Party's Buried Past.* New York: Macmillan, 2008.

Bass, S. Jonathan. *Blessed Are the Peacemakers: Martin Luther King, Jr., Eight White Religious Leaders, and the "Letter from Birmingham Jail."* Baton Rouge: Louisiana State University Press, 2001.

Beatles, The. "Nowhere Man," *Rubber Soul*, Parlophone, 1965.

Black Americans in Congress, 1870–2007. History, Art, and Archives, U.S. House of Representatives. Washington, DC: U.S. Government Printing Office, 2008.

Black, Conrad. *Franklin Delano Roosevelt: Champion of Freedom.* New York: PublicAffairs, 2005.

Black Lives Matter. https://blacklivesmatter.com (accessed August 6, 2022).

Blackmon, Douglas A. *Slavery by Another Name: The Re-enslavement of Black Americans from the Civil War to World War II*. New York: Random House, 2008.

Bourne, Randolph. "The State." In *The Radical Will: Selected Writings, 1911–1918*, edited by Olaf Hansen, 355–395. New York: Urizen Books, 1977.

———. "War and the Intellectuals." *Seven Arts* 2 (June 1917): 133–146.

Branch, Taylor. *Parting the Waters: America in the King Years, 1954–63*. New York: Simon and Schuster, 1988.

Brands, H. W. *Traitor to His Class: The Privileged Life and Radical Presidency of Franklin Delano Roosevelt*. New York: Doubleday, 2008.

Brinkley, Alan. *Voices of Protest: Huey Long, Father Coughlin, and the Great Depression*. New York: Knopf, 1982.

Bruce, Lenny. Performance on *The Steve Allen Show*. April 9, 1959. Available online at https://www.youtube.com/watch?v=G3QgxmiBfNY (accessed January 1, 2023).

Bryan, William Jennings. "Notification Speech." August 8, 1900. In *Life and Speeches of Hon. Wm. Jennings Bryan*, 390–411. Baltimore: R. H. Woodward, 1900.

Buckley, Cara. "These Groups Want Disruptive Climate Protests. Oil Heirs Are Funding Them." *New York Times*, August 10, 2022. www.nytimes.com (accessed August 12, 2022).

Burke, Tarana. "History & Inception." MeToo Website. https://metoomvmt.org (accessed August 7, 2022).

Butterfield, Roger. "Mr. Mencken Sounds Off." *Life*, August 5, 1946, 52.

"Call to Conscience from Veterans to Active Duty Troops and Reservists." December 6, 2002. Available online at https://wri-irg.org (accessed January 1, 2023).

Carmichael, Stokely. "Berkeley Speech." In *Contemporary American Voices: Significant Speeches in American History, 1945–Present*, edited by James R. Andrews and David Zarefsky, 100–107. White Plains, NY: Longman, 1992.

Caro, Robert A. *The Passage of Power: The Years of Lyndon Johnson*. New York: Knopf, 2012.

Castelnuovo, Shirley. *Soldiers of Conscience: Japanese American Military Resisters in World War II*. Westport, CT: Greenwood, 2008.

Churchill, Winston. Speech at Westminster College Fulton, Missouri, March 5, 1946. Available online at www.fordham.edu (accessed December 27, 2022).

"The Civil Rights Movement and the Second Reconstruction, 1945–1968." History, Art, and Archives: The United States House of Representatives. https://history.house.gov (accessed February 19, 2023).

Clear, Todd. *Imprisoning Communities: How Mass Incarceration Makes Disadvantaged Neighborhoods Worse*. New York: Oxford University Press, 2009.

Cochrane, Emily. "Congress Gives Final Approval to Make Lynching a Hate Crime." *New York Times*, March 7, 2022. www.nytimes.com (accessed October 14, 2022).

Cohen, Robert. *Freedom's Orator: Mario Savio and the Radical Legacy of the 1960s*. New York: Oxford University Press, 2009.

Cohen, Ronald D. *Woody Guthrie: Writing America's Songs*. New York: Routledge, 2012.

Combs, Barbara Harris. *From Selma to Montgomery and Freedom: The Long March to Freedom*. New York: Routledge, 2014.

Congress.Gov. H.R.55—Emmett Till Antilynching Act, www.congress.gov (accessed October 14, 2022).

Cooper, John Milton, Jr. *Pivotal Decades: The United States, 1900–1920*. New York: Norton, 1990.

Coughlin, Charles E. "Address on the National Union for Social Justice." November 11, 1934. In *A Series of Lectures on Social Justice*. Royal Oak, MI: Radio League of the Little Flower, 1935.

———. "National Radio Address." June 19, 1936. In *A Series of Lectures on Social Justice*. Royal Oak, MI: Radio League of the Little Flower, 1935.

Cox, Vicki. *Margaret Sanger*. New York: Infobase, 2009.

Darlington, Ralph. *Syndicalism and the Transition to Communism: An International Comparative Analysis*. Aldershot, UK: Ashgate, 2008.

Debs, Eugene V. "Address to the Jury (1918)." In *Protest Nation: Words That Inspired a Century of American Radicalism*, edited by Timothy Patrick McCarthy and John Campbell McMillian, 27–31. New York: New Press, 2010.

———. "The Canton, Ohio Speech, Anti-War Speech." June 16, 1918. Available online at www.marxists.org (accessed December 27, 2022).

———. "Pacifism." Eugene V. Debs Foundation. Available online at debsfoundation.org (accessed January 1, 2023).

———. "Statement to the Court upon Being Convicted of Violating the Sedition Act." September 18, 1918. Available online at www.marxists.org (accessed December 27, 2022).

"Declaration of the Occupation of New York City." September 29, 2011. Available at https://nyu-dss.github.io/occupy (accessed January 1, 2023).

Dellinger, David. "Why I Refused to Register in the October 1940 Draft and a Little of What It Led To." In *A Few Small Candles: War Resisters of World War II Tell Their Stories*, edited by Larry Gara and Lenna Mae Gara, 20–37. Kent, OH: Kent State University Press, 1999.

DiFranco, Ani. "self evident." 2001. Available at https://www.youtube.com/watch?v=gTY8sCzHTNc (accessed January 1, 2023).

Dilling, Elizabeth Kirkpatrick. *The Red Network: A "Who's Who" and Handbook of Radicalism for Patriots*. Chicago: Elizabeth Dilling, 1934.

Du Bois, W. E. B. "Close Ranks." *Crisis* 16, no. 3 (1918): 111.

Dunaway, David King. *How Can I Keep from Singing?: The Ballad of Pete Seeger*. New York: Villard Books, 2008.

Dylan, Bob. *Bringing It All Back Home*. Columbia Records, 1965.

———. *The Freewheelin' Bob Dylan*. Columbia Records, 1963.

———. *Highway 61 Revisited*. Columbia Records, 1965.

Earle, Steve. *The Revolution Starts Now*. Artemis Records, 2004.

Echols, Alice. *Daring to Be Bad: Radical Feminism in America, 1967–1975*. Minneapolis: University of Minnesota Press, 1989.

Edwards, Anne. *Katharine Hepburn: A Remarkable Woman*. New York: Macmillan, 2000.

Emerson, Ralph Waldo. *The Essay on Self-Reliance*. East Aurora, NY: Roycroft, 1908.

Falk, Candace, ed. *Emma Goldman: A Documentary History of the American Years*, vol. 1. *Made for America, 1890–1901*. Berkeley: University of California Press, 2003.

Farrell, John A. *Clarence Darrow: Attorney for the Damned*. New York: Penguin Random House, 2012.

———. *Ted Kennedy: A Life*. New York: Penguin Press, 2022.

Feldman, Glenn, ed. *The Disfranchisement Myth: Poor Whites and Suffrage Restriction in Alabama*. Athens: University of Georgia Press, 2004.

———. *Painting Dixie Red: When, Where, Why, and How the South Became Republican*. Gainesville: University of Florida Press, 2011.

———. *Politics, Society, and the Klan in Alabama, 1915–1949*. Tuscaloosa: University of Alabama Press, 1999.

Feldman, Jay. *Manufacturing Hysteria: A History of Scapegoating, Surveillance, and Secrecy in Modern America*. New York: Anchor Books, 2012.

Fishman, Ethan. "The Prudential FDR." In *FDR and the Modern Presidency: Leadership and Legacy*, edited by Mark J. Rozell and William D. Pederson, 147–166. Westport, CT: Greenwood, 1997.

Fitzgerald, F. Scott. *This Side of Paradise*. New York: Scribner, 1920.

Foner, Eric. *The Story of American Freedom*. New York: Norton, 1998.

Frampton, Mary Louise, Ian F. Haney López, and Jonathan Simon, eds. *After the War on Crime: Race, Democracy, and a New Reconstruction*. New York: New York University Press, 2008.

Freeberg, Ernest. *Democracy's Prisoner: Eugene V. Debs, the Great War, and the Right to Dissent*. Cambridge: Harvard University Press, 2008.

Fridays For Future. https://fridaysforfuture.org (accessed August 11, 2022).

Friedan, Betty. *The Feminine Mystique*. 1963. Reprint, New York: Dell, 1970.

Friedman, Lisa, and Coral Davenport. "As Historic Climate Bill Heads to Biden's Desk, Young Activists Demand More." *New York Times*, August 12, 2022. www.nytimes.com (accessed August 13, 2022).

Fuller, Margaret. *Woman in the Nineteenth Century*. New York: Greeley and McElrath, 1845.

Gara, Larry. "My War on War." In *A Few Small Candles: War Resisters of World War II Tell Their Stories*, edited by Larry Gara and Lenna Mae Gara, 78–97. Kent, OH: Kent State University Press, 1999.

Garland, David. *The Culture of Control: Crime and Social Order in Contemporary Society*. Chicago: University of Chicago Press, 2002.

Garvey, Marcus. "Address to the UNIA Supporters in Philadelphia, October 21, 1919." In *African American Political Thought, 1890–1930: Washington, Du Bois, Garvey, and Randolph*, edited by Cary D. Wintz, 199–207. Armonk, NY: M. E. Sharpe, 1996.

———. *The Philosophy and Opinions of Marcus Garvey; or, Africa for the Africans*. Compiled by Amy Jacques Garvey. Vol. 1. New York: Universal, 1923.

Ginsberg, Allen. *Howl and Other Poems*. San Francisco: City Lights Books, 1956.

Goidel, Kirby. *America's Failing Experiment: How We the People Have Become the Problem*. Lanham, MD: Rowman and Littlefield, 2013.

Goldman, Emma. *Anarchism and Other Essays*. 2nd ed. New York: Mother Earth, 1911.

———. "The Individual, Society, and the State." In *Red Emma Speaks: Selected Writings and Speeches*, edited by Alix Kates Shulman, 86–100. New York: Random House, 1972.

Good War and Those Who Refused to Fight It, The. Directed by Judith Ehrlich and Rick Tejada-Flores. Bull Frog Films / PBS / ITVS / Paradigm Productions, 2000. www.pbs.org (accessed September 24, 2014).

Goodwin, Doris Kearns. *No Ordinary Time: Franklin and Eleanor Roosevelt: The Home Front in World War II*. New York: Simon and Schuster, 1994.

Guthrie, Woody. *Bound for Glory*. New York: E. P. Dutton, 1943.

———. *Pastures of Plenty: A Self Portrait*. Edited by Dave Marsh and Harold Leventhal. New York: HarperCollins, 1990.

———. *The Woody Guthrie Songbook*. Edited by Harold Leventhal and Marjorie Guthrie. New York: Grosset and Dunlap, 1976.

Hajdu, David. *Positively Fourth Street: The Life and Times of Joan Baez, Bob Dylan, Mimi Baez Fariña, and Richard Fariña*. New York: Farrar, Straus, and Giroux, 2001.

Hamer, Fannie Lou. "Testimony before the Credentials Committee at the Democratic National Convention, Atlantic City, New Jersey, August 22, 1964." In *The Speeches of Fannie Lou Hamer: To Tell It Like It Is*, edited by Maegan Parker Brooks and Davis W. Houck, 42–45. Jackson: University Press of Mississippi, 2011.

Hamilton, Neil A. *American Social Leaders and Activists*. New York: Infobase, 2002.

Hennigan, W. J. and Vera Bergengruen. "For the Oath Keepers and Proud Boys, Jan. 6 Was Just the Start." *Time*, July 11, 2022. https://time.com (accessed October 9, 2022).

Hofstadter, Richard. *The Age of Reform: From Bryan to FDR*. New York: Knopf, 1955.

———. *Anti-Intellectualism in American Life*. New York: Vintage Press, 1964.

Hughes, Langston. "The Negro Artist and the Racial Mountain." *Nation*, June 23, 1926.

Immortal Technique. *Revolutionary, Vol. 2*. Viper Records, 2003.

Indians Of All Tribes. "We Hold the Rock!" In *Alcatraz, Indian Land Forever*, edited by Troy R. Johnson. Los Angeles: UCLA American Indian Studies Center, 1995.

Industrial Workers of the World. *Little Red Songbook*. 19th ed. Chicago: IWW, 1923.

———. "Preamble to the IWW Constitution." www.iww.org (accessed December 27, 2022).

Jefferson Airplane. *Surrealistic Pillow*. RCA Victor, 1967.

Jesuthasan, Meerabelle. "The 1619 Project Sparks Dialogue and Reflection in Schools Nationwide." The Pulitzer Center, December 20, 2019. https://pulitzercenter.org (accessed September 4, 2022).

Johnson, Lyndon B. "Special Message to the Congress: The American Promise." March 15, 1965. In *Public Papers of the Presidents of the United States, Lyndon B. Johnson, 1965*, no. 1. Washington, DC: U.S. Government Printing Office, 1965.

Jones, Mary. *The Autobiography of Mother Jones*. Edited by Mary Field Parton. Chicago: Charles H. Kerr, 1925.

Kaczynski, Ted. "Industrial Society and Its Future." Available online at "The Unabomber Trial: The Manifesto." *Washington Post*, September 22, 1995, www.washingtonpost.com (accessed January 1, 2023).

Keats, John. *The Crack in the Picture Window*. Boston: Houghton Mifflin, 1957.

Kennedy, David M. *Freedom from Fear: The American People in Depression and War, 1929–1945*. New York: Oxford University Press, 1999.

Kennedy, John F. "Address on Civil Rights." June 11, 1963. Available online at http://millercenter.org (accessed May 14, 2014).

Kerner Report, The. Available online at www.archive.org (accessed December 27, 2022).

Kerouac, Jack. *On the Road*. New York: Viking, 1957.

King, Martin Luther, Jr. "Acceptance Address for the Nobel Peace Prize." In *A Call to Conscience: The Landmark Speeches of Dr. Martin Luther King, Jr.*, edited by Clayborne Carson, 101–110. New York: Grand Central, 2001.

———. "Address at the Conclusion of the Selma to Montgomery March," March 25, 1965. Available online at https://www.youtube.com/watch?v=44RNoC5jLDc&t=5s (accessed January 1, 2023).

———. "Beyond Vietnam: A Time to Break the Silence." Speech at Riverside Church, New York, April 4, 1967. Available online at www.digitalhistory.uh.edu (accessed December 27, 2022).

———. "I Have a Dream." In *A Testament of Hope: The Essential Writings and Speeches of Martin Luther King, Jr.*, edited by James M. Washington, 217–220. San Francisco: HarperCollins, 1991.

———. "MIA Mass Meeting at Holt Street Baptist Church." Speech in Montgomery, Alabama, December 5, 1955. In *The Papers of Martin Luther King, Jr.: Birth of a New Age, December 1955–December 1956*, edited by Clayborne Carson, 71–79. Berkeley: University of California Press, 1997.

———. *Why We Can't Wait*. New York: Mentor, 1964.

Klebanow, Diana and Franklin L. Jonas. *People's Lawyers: Crusaders for Justice in American History*. Armonk, NY: M. E. Sharpe, 2003.

La Follette, Robert M. "The People Do Not Want This War." April 4, 1917. In *We Who Dared to Say No to War: American Antiwar Writing from 1812 to Now*, edited by Murray Polner and Thomas E. Woods, Jr., 123–132 New York: Basic Books, 2008.

———. Speech to the Senate, *Congressional Record*, 65th Cong., 1st sess., vol. 55, 7878–7888 (October 6, 1917).

Lai, K. K. Rebecca, Bill Marsh, Anjali Singhvi. "Here Are the 100 U.S. Cities Where Protesters Were Tear-Gassed." *New York Times*, June 18, 2020, www.nytimes.com (accessed August 6, 2022).

Larson, Edward J. *Summer for the Gods: The Scopes Trial and America's Continuing Debate over Science and Religion*. New York: Basic Books, 2006.

Lawson, John Howard. "A Statement by John Howard Lawson." In *Thirty Years of Treason: Excerpts from Hearings before the House Committee on Un-American Activities, 1938–1968*, edited by Eric Bentley, 153–165. New York: Viking, 1971.

Leary, Timothy. *The Psychedelic Experience: A Manual Based on the Tibetan Book of the Dead*. New York: Citadel, 1964.

Lepore, Jill. *The Whites of Their Eyes: The Tea Party's Revolution and the Battle over American History*. Princeton: Princeton University Press, 2010.

Lindbergh, Charles A. *Address by Charles Lindbergh: Delivered at an America First Committee Meeting in New York City on April 23, 1941*. New York: America First Committee, 1941. Available online at www.charleslindbergh.com (accessed January 1, 2023).

Logan, Rayford W., ed. *What the Negro Wants*. Chapel Hill: University of North Carolina Press, 1944.

"Ludlow Massacre, The." American Experience, PBS.org. www.pbs.org (accessed December 27, 2022).

Mackenzie, G. Calvin, and Robert Weisbrot. *The Liberal Hour: Washington and the Politic of Change in the 1960s*. New York: Penguin, 2008.

Marable, Manning. *Race, Reform, and Rebellion: The Second Reconstruction in Black America*. Jackson: University Press of Mississippi, 1991.

March for Our Lives. "Our Story: Not One More." https://marchforourlives.com (accessed August 7, 2022).

Mayer, Jane. "Covert Operations: The Billionaire Brothers Who Are Waging a War against Obama." *New Yorker*, August 23, 2010.

McCarthy, Timothy Patrick, and John Campbell McMillian, eds. *Protest Nation: Words That Inspired a Century of American Radicalism*. New York: New Press, 2010.

McGhee, Heather C. and Victor Ray. "For Making Citizens." Sunday Opinion Section. *New York Times*, September 4, 2022.

McGuire, Phillip, ed. *Taps for a Jim Crow Army: Letters from Black Soldiers in World War II*. Santa Barbara, CA: ABC-CLIO, 1983.

McKay, Claude. "If We Must Die." In *Harlem Shadows: The Poems of Claude McKay*, 53. New York: Harcourt, Brace, 1922.

Medsger, Betty. *The Burglary: The Discovery of J. Edgar Hoover's Secret FBI*. New York: Knopf, 2014.

"Members of Right-Wing Militias, Extremist Groups Are Latest Charged in Capitol Siege." National Public Radio, January 19, 2021. www.npr.org (accessed August 15, 2022).

Menand, Louis. *The Free World: Art and Thought in the Cold War*. New York: Farrar, Straus and Giroux, 2021.

Mencken, H. L. "Last Words." 1926. Available online at https://cooperative -individualism.org (accessed January 1, 2023).

———. *A Mencken Chrestomathy: His Own Selection of His Choicest Writing*. New York: Random House, 1949.

Mills, C. Wright., *The Power Elite*. New York: Oxford University Press, 1959.

Mjagkij, Nina. *Loyalty in Time of Trial: The African American Experience during World War I*. Lanham, MD: Rowman and Littlefield, 2011.

Morgan, Bill. *I Celebrate Myself: The Somewhat Private Life of Allen Ginsberg*. New York: Viking, 2006.

Mothers of Invention, The. *Absolutely Free*. Verve, 1967.

Murder of Emmett Till, The. Directed by Stanley Nelson. American Experience, PBS. 2003. Available online at www.pbs.org (accessed December 27, 2022).

Nader, Ralph. "It's Time to End Corporate Welfare as We Know It." 1996. In *The Ralph Nader Reader*, 154–158. New York: Seven Stories, 2000.

National Organization for Women. "Statement of Purpose." 1966. www.now.org (accessed October 5, 2014).

Nearing, Scott. *The Debs Decision*. 2nd ed. New York: Rand School of Social Science, 1919.

New York Times Magazine. "The 1619 Project." www.nytimes.com (accessed September 4, 2022).

"Niagara's Declaration of Principles, 1905." Yale MacMillan Center. Available online at https://glc.yale.edu (accessed February 14, 2023).

Nichols, Tom. "Contain and Defeat." *Atlantic Daily*, September 12, 2022. www .theatlantic.com (accessed September 13, 2022).

Oglesby, Carl. "Let Us Shape the Future." November 27, 1965. Available online at the Students for a Democratic Society Document Library, www.sds-1960s.org (accessed January 1, 2023).

Olson, Lynne. *Freedom's Daughters: The Unsung Heroines of the Civil Rights Movement from 1830 to 1970*. New York: Simon and Schuster, 2001.

Osborne, Margaret. "To Prevent Catastrophic Damage by 2100, Climate Experts Warn, 'It's Now or Never.'" *Smithsonian Magazine*, April 6, 2022, www.smithsonianmag .com (accessed August 11, 2022).

"Pat Robertson Thinks the GOP Base Is Too Extreme? Hehehehe." *Daily Kos* (blog), October 24, 2011. Available online at www.dailykos.com (accessed January 1, 2023).

Petition to Alabama Governor George C. Wallace by Selma-to-Montgomery March- ers. March 25, 1965. Available online at https://www.crmvet.org (accessed January 1, 2023).

Pickering, Leslie James. *The Earth Liberation Front, 1997–2002*. Oakland, CA: PM, 2007.

Redstockings. "Manifesto." 1969. In *Dear Sisters: Dispatches from the Women's Libera- tion Movement*, edited by Rosalyn Baxandall and Linda Gordon, 90–91. New York: Basic Books, 2000.

Rice, Condaleeza. Interview by Wolf Blitzer, September 8, 2002. CNN. Available online at http://transcripts.cnn.com (accessed January 1, 2023)

Riesman, David. *The Lonely Crowd*. New York: Doubleday, 1953.

Roosevelt, Franklin Delano, and Felix Frankfurter. *Roosevelt and Frankfurter: Their Correspondence, 1928–1945*. Edited by Max Freedman. Boston: Little, Brown, 1968.

Rosenberg, Chaim M. *Child Labor in America: A History*. Jefferson, NC: McFarland, 2013.

Rovere, Richard Halworth, and Gene Brown. *Loyalty and Security in a Democratic State*. New York: Arno, 1979.

Rutherfurd, Livingston. *John Peter Zenger, His Press, His Trial, and a Bibliography of Zenger Imprints*. New York: Dodd, Mead, 1904.

Ryan, Fr. John A. *Distributive Justice: The Right and Wrong of Our Present Distribution of Wealth*. New York: Macmillan, 1916.

Sanger, Margaret. *Woman and the New Race*. New York: Brentano's, 1920.

Sawchuck, Stephen. "What Is Critical Race Theory and Why Is It Under Attack?" *Education Week*, May 18, 2021. www.edweek.org (accessed September 4, 2022).

Schaffer, Ronald. *America in the Great War*. New York: Oxford University Press, 1991.

Schurz, Carl. "The Issue of Imperialism." January 4, 1899. In *Speeches, Correspondence, and Political Papers of Carl Schurz*, vol. 6, *January 1, 1899–April 8, 1906*, edited by Frederic Bancroft, 1–35. New York: Putnam, 1913.

Sedition Act of 1918. Pub. L. No. 65–150, 40 Stat. 553.

Sheldon, Charles. *In His Steps: "What Would Jesus Do?"* Chicago: Advance Publishing Company, 1898.

Smith, Jean Edward. *FDR*. New York: Random House, 2007.

Smith, Margaret Chase. "Declaration of Conscience" and "Statement of Seven Senators." *Congressional Record*, 82nd Cong., 1st sess., June 1, 1950.

"Socialist Party's Platform, The." 1912. Available online at www.laborhistorylinks.org (accessed December 27, 2022).

The Source: The Story of the Beats and the Beat Generation. Dir. Chuck Workman. Beat/ Calliope, 1999.

Southern Poverty Law Center, The. "See Hate in Your State." www.splcenter.org (accessed August 14, 2022).

Stafford, Peter. *Psychedelics*. Oakland, CA: Ronin, 2003.

Starr, Edwin. "War." Single. Gordy Records, 1970.

Steinem, Gloria. "'Women's Liberation' Aims to Free Men, Too." *Washington Post*, June 7, 1970.

Sunrise Movement. www.sunrisemovement.org (accessed August 12, 2022).

Taibbi, Matt. "The Truth about the Tea Party." *Rolling Stone*, September 28, 2010.

Taylor, Derrick Bryson. "George Floyd Protests: A Timeline." *New York Times*, November 5, 2021. www.nytimes.com (accessed October 11, 2022).

Teal, Donn. *The Gay Militants*. New York: St. Martin's, 1971.

Tejada, Susan. *In Search of Sacco and Vanzetti: Doubles Lives, Troubled Times, and the Massachusetts Case That Shook the World*. Lebanon, NH: University Press of New England, 2012.

Thompson, Heather Ann. *Blood in the Water: The Attica Prison Uprising of 1971 and its Legacy*. New York: Pantheon, 2016.

———. "Why Mass Incarceration Matters: Rethinking Crisis, Decline, and Transformation in Postwar American History." *Journal of American History* 97, no. 3 (December 2010): 703–734.

Thoreau, Henry David. *Walden*. New York: Thomas Y. Crowell, 1910.

———. *Walden; and Resistance to Civil Government*. 3rd ed. Edited by William Rossi. New York: Norton, 2008.

Topp, Michael Miller. *Those without a Country: The Political Culture of Italian American Syndicalists*. Minneapolis: University of Minnesota Press, 2001.

Truman, Harry S. "Special Message to the Congress on Civil Rights." February 2, 1948. In *Public Papers of the Presidents of the United States, Harry S. Truman, 1948*, vol. 4, 121–126. Washington, DC: U.S. Government Printing Office, 1963.

U.S. Congress, House, Committee on Un-American Activities. *Hearings Regarding the Communist Infiltration of the Motion Picture Industry*, 80th Cong., 1st sess., October 29, 1947.

U.S. Congress, Senate, Committee on Foreign Relations. "Legislative Proposals Relating to the War in Southeast Asia." *Hearings before the Committee on Foreign Relations*. 92nd Cong., 1st sess., April–May 1971. Washington, DC: Government Printing Office, 1971.

Varon, Jeremy. *Bringing the War Home: The Weather Underground, the Red Army Faction, and Revolutionary Violence in the Sixties and Seventies*. Berkeley: University of California Press, 2004.

Ward, Lester Frank. "Mind as a Social Factor." *Mind* 9, no. 36 (1884): 563–573.

Washington Post. "Did You Attend the March for Our Lives?" April 13, 2018, www .washingtonpost.com (accessed August 7, 2022).

Wells-Barnett, Ida B. "Lynch Law in America." 1900. Available online at www .digitalhistory.uh.edu (accessed December 27, 2022).

———. *Lynch Law in Georgia: A Six-Weeks' Record in the Center of Southern Civilization, as Faithfully Chronicled by the "Atlanta Journal" and the "Atlanta Constitution."* Chicago: Chicago Colored Citizens, 1899.

Western, Bruce. *Punishment and Inequality in America*. New York: Russell Sage Foundation, 2007.

Whyte, William H. *The Organization Man*. New York: Simon and Schuster, 1956.

Wiggins, David. "Message to the Troops: Resist!" October 11, 2002. Strike the Root, posted March 10, 2003. Available online at www.strike-the-root.com (accessed January 1, 2023).

Williams, Paige. "Class Warfare: School Boards Are Being Attacked by Partisan Saboteurs." *New Yorker*, November 7, 2022, 52–63.

Williams, Roger. *The Bloudy Tenent of Persecution*. 1644. Edited by Samuel L. Caldwell. Providence, RI: Narragansett Club, 1867.

Wintz, Cary D. *African American Political Thought, 1890–1930: Washington, Du Bois, Garvey, and Randolph*. Armonk, NY: M. E. Sharpe, 1996.

Woodward, C. Vann. *The Strange Career of Jim Crow*. New York: Oxford University Press, 1974.

X, Malcolm. "Message to the Grass Roots." November 10, 1963. In *Malcolm X Speaks: Selected Speeches and Statements*, edited by George Breitman, 3–17. New York: Grove, 1965.

———. "Speech on 'Black Revolution.'" April 8, 1964. In *Two Speeches by Malcolm X*, 7–21. New York: Merit, 1965.

Yasui, Minoru. "Response to Executive Order 9066." Available online at www.aclu.org (accessed January 1, 2023).

Young, Ralph. *Dissent: The History of an American Idea*. New York: New York University Press, 2015.

———. *Dissent in America: The Voices That Shaped a Nation*. New York: Pearson Longman, 2006.

Zinn, Howard. *A People's History of the United States: 1492–Present*. New York: HarperCollins, 2001.

INDEX

Page numbers in italics indicate Figures.

ABOUT THE AUTHOR

RALPH YOUNG is Professor of Instruction in History at Temple University. He has won several major teaching awards and is the author of *Dissent: The History of an American Idea*, *Make Art Not War: Political Protest Posters from the Twentieth Century* and *Dissent in America: The Voices That Shaped a Nation*. He is also the founder of weekly campus-wide teach-ins at Temple, in which students and faculty examine the historical context of controversial contemporary issues.